Perspectives on Experimental Social Psychology in India

By the Same Author

- Dialogue for Development: Festschrift dedicated to Professor **Jai B.P. Sinha** *jointly edited with* T.N. Sinha and A.K. Sinha
- Social Reality: Perspectives and Understanding

About the Editors

Janak Pandey, a Ph. D. of Kansas State University, currently ICSSR National Fellow and was the Former First Vice Chancellor, Central University Bihar. He also served as Vice Chancellor of Allahabad University and also as Director, Govind Balabh Pant Social Science Institute, Allahabad.

Perspectives on Experimental Social Psychology in India

Edited by
Janak Pandey

CONCEPT PUBLISHING COMPANY PVT. LTD.
NEW DELHI-110059

ISBN-13 : 978-81-7022-186-9

Edition 2026

Published and Printed by

Concept Publishing Company Pvt. Ltd.
A/15-16, Commercial Block, Mohan Garden
New Delhi-110059 (India)
T: 25351460, 25351794, *F*: 091-11-25357109
E: publishing@conceptpub.com, W: www.conceptpub.com
Editorial Office: H-13, Bali Nagar, New Delhi-110 015, India.

Cataloging in Publication Data--*Courtesy:* D.K. Agencies (P) Ltd. <docinfo@dkagencies.com>

Perspectives on experimental social psychology in India / edited by Janak Pandey.
pages cm
Reprint. Originally published: 1981.
Includes bibliographical references and index.
ISBN 9788170221869

1. Social psychology--India. I. Pandey, Janak, 1945- editor.

HM251.P47 2016 DDC 302.0954 23

PREFACE

THE INCEPTION of this book can be traced back to a series of formal and informal communications that took place among the contributors in the past several years. The basic dilemmas, issues, and obstacles involved in the use of experimental psychological approach in social psychology have been debated for a long time. Although, the discipline of social psychology has shown a major breakthrough with the use of experimental methods in the last thirty years, we recognize that for a variety of reasons, the field of social psychology and its experimental paradigm research is at important crossroads. Social scientists of a developing country like ours now realize that accumulation of knowledge should not only provide understanding but also provide solutions to complex social problems. Hence, there is a great need to continually discuss, deliberate, communicate and exchange the research ideas and results of ongoing research. This was the major impetus for organizing a workshop on 'Experimental Social Psychology.'

Through a variety of minor events, supplemented by several major efforts, we were able to persuade the Indian Council of Social Science Research to fund the workshop. It was held in the Department of Psychology, Allahabad University, from December 7 to 9, 1979. We are thankful to Professors A. K. Singh and Jai B. P. Sinha who helped us at the different stages of its planning. The book presents a collection of selected papers and discussion from the workshop. We are grateful to the contributors for revising their papers and incorporating comments received during the workshop and from the editor.

Several people and organizations contributed in organizing the workshop and completion of this book whose help is gratefully acknowledged. The facilities available under the University Grants Commission's Centre for the Psychological Study of Social Change and National Development at the Department of Psychology, Allahabad University helped enormously in the completion of this project. Professor D. Sinha, Chairman of the Department, always remained a source of encouragement and inspiration. He also agreed to present in the workshop a historical perspective of social psychology in India on a short notice. The presence of two senior psychologists, Professor S. M. Mohsin and Professor Rajnarain during the workshop was highly inspiring for the participants. Professors S. M. Mohsin, Rajnarain, D. Sinha, A. K. Singh, Jai B. P. Sinha, and S. Kanekar chaired different sessions of the workshop for which we are especially thankful to them. Besides, we are thankful to Shalini Bisht, K. D. Broota, A. K. Dalal, E. S. K. Ghosh, R. K. Naidu, K. C. Panda, Namita Pande, Rashmi Kumar, Girishwar Misra, Anand Prakash, Arvind K. Sinha, Yoganand Sinha, and Meera Verma, who participated as discussants and commentators for various papers.

Completion of a book like this requires several critical editorial decisions. My colleague Professor R. C. Tripathi was always helpful in such decisions and other editorial work. To prepare a publishable draft from a session entitled "Looking Ahead" recorded on tapes was an arduous task. However, with the help of Ms. Saroj Kakkar, it became possible to organize the material in its present form. I am also thankful to Ms. Vandana Misra and Mr. R. P. Singh, for their help in preparation of the manuscript for the press. Mr. M. A. Siddiqui painstakingly produced the typescript. Thanks are also due to Mr. Rajendra Kumar for his secretarial assistance.

Finally, we are obliged to our publishers.

JANAK PANDEY

Department of Psychology
Centre for the Psychological Study of
Social Change & National Development
Allahabad University
Allahabad-211002

June 1981

CONTENTS

SECTION THREE
CRITICAL ASSESSMENT

WORKSHOP PARTICIPANTS

K. D. Broota, Ph. D. (Delhi)
Reader and Head, Department of Psychology,
Delhi University, Delhi

Suresh Kanekar, Ph. D. (Iowa)
Reader, Department of Applied Psychology,
University of Bombay, Bombay-400029

Lila Krishnan, Ph. D. (Mc Master)
Assistant Professor, Department of Humanities and Social Sciences, Indian Institute of Technology,
Kanpur-208016

Sasi Misra, Ph. D. (U.C.L.A.)
Professor, Indian Institute of Management,
Vastrapur, Ahmedabad

S. M. Mohsin, Ph. D. (Edinburgh)
Retd. Professor, Department of Psychology,
Patna University, Patna

Rajnarain, Ph. D. (Columbia)
Retd. Professor, Department of Psychology,
Lucknow University, Lucknow

K. C. Panda, Ph. D. (Indiana)
Professor, Regional College of Education, Bhubaneswar

Janak Pandey, Ph. D. (Kansas State)
Professor, Department of Psychology,
Allahabad University, Allahabad-211002

Amar Kumar Singh, Ph. D. (London)
Professor and Head, Department of Psychology,
Ranchi University, Ranchi

Ramadhar Singh, Ph. D. (Purdue)
Professor, Indian Institute of Management,
Vastrapur, Ahmedabad

Durganand Sinha, M. Sc. (Cantab)
Professor and Head, Department of Psychology,
Allahabad University, Allahabad-211002

Jai B. P. Sinha, Ph. D. (Ohio State)
Professor, A. N. Sinha Institute of Social Studies, Patna-1

R. C. Tripathi, Ph. D. (Michigan)
Professor, Department of Psychology, Allahabad University,
Allahabad-211002

LIST OF CONTRIBUTORS

Suresh Kanekar
Reader, Department of Applied Psychology, University of Bombay, Bombay-400029

Lila Krishnan
Assistant Professor, Department of Humanities and Social Sciences, Indian Institute of Technology, Kanpur-208016

Sasi Misra
Professor, Indian Institute of Management, Vastrapur, Ahmedabad

Janak Pandey
Professor, Department of Psychology, Allahabad University, Allahabad-211002

Ramadhar Singh
Professor, Indian Institute of Management, Vastrapur, Ahmedabad

Amar Kumar Singh
Professor and Head, Department of Psychology, Ranchi University, Ranchi

Durganand Sinha
Professor and Head, Department of Psychology, Allahabad University, Allahabad-211002

Jai B. P. Sinha
Professor, A.N. Sinha Institute of Social Studies, Patna-1

R. C. Tripathi
Professor, Department of Psychology, Allahabad University, Allahabad-211002

LIST OF FIGURES

SECTION ONE

HISTORICAL PERSPECTIVE

ONE

Durganand Sinha

SOCIAL PSYCHOLOGY IN INDIA
A Historical Perspective

PROVIDING a historical perspective helps to impart a sense of continuity and identity not only to the individual but also to any scientific endeavour. Psychological research on social behaviour in India along modern scientific lines has gone on for over five decades. But there has been very little effort to trace in any systematic way the course of its development and the trends that are perceptible therein. In the present paper an effort has been made to indicate the beginnings of social psychology in India so that the present research activities can be viewed against that background. Since the Indian scholars have derived their inspiration from scholars working mainly in England and in universities in the United States, a quick glance at the beginnings of the subject in the West is also necessary to provide the necessary perspective.

The first textbook on the subject bearing the name of *Social Psychology* was published in U.S.A. by a sociologist E.A. Ross in the year 1908. In the same year, the famous psychologist William McDougall (1908) published his *Introduction to Social Psychology*. But those of us who had the privilege of going through the book—because in our days it was regarded as an important textbook while today the students rarely bother even to examine its cover—know that it was anything but "social" in the modern sense of the term. It mainly dealt with man's instincts, and was completely individualistic in orientation.

The next significant publication was in 1924 by F.H. Allport called *Social Psychology* where the subject seems to record its true scientific beginning, and a distinct psychological orientation to the analysis of social behaviour and interactions of man. Since then there has been a steady increase in the volume of work in this branch, and social psychology as far as it goes has never looked back. It is to be noted that since the boundaries dividing social psychology from other social sciences are not sharp, many of the early textbooks in the subject were written by sociologists with a distinct sociological orientation.

Scholars have tried to delve into the origins of social psychology and have asked whether it is an ancient discipline or a modern or an ultramodern one. Allport (1954) poses this question in his chapter entitled "The Historical Background of Modern Social Psychology" in Lindzey's *Handbook of Social Psychology*. He asks whether it is a new discipline, a product of the post-World War II era and like Minerva it was born full-grown. The question also implies as to who founded social psychology. One can at one's choice take any name of ancient or modern scholar and trace the roots of the subject. One can find the beginnings of the analysis of social behaviour in the dialogues of Plato, the discourses of Aristotle and, if one is not too fond of the ancient scholars, one can come to modern times to Hegel, to Hobbes, to the French sociologist Comte, Tarde or to Ross, or to McDougall. Or, if one is a little more psychologically oriented he would trace it to F.H. Allport. Personally I feel that it is a futile exercise to go on debating about who was the founding-father. In the realm of human endeavour, it is not always very pertinent to look for the founder. It is important to remember that the key problem of understanding man's social nature and behaviour is not only an ancient one but a persistent question which has agitated the academicians whether in the West or in the East, since the very dawn of human civilization. But unfortunately those of us who have been dazzled by the Western traditions and have received the training in that setting tend to feel that the roots of social psychology lie distinctly in the Western tradition and civilization.

It has been asserted that the intellectual soil of social psychology was provided by the Western civilization in its tradition of free enquiry, a philosophy and ethics of democracy, and in the orderly growth of science from physical to biological. Not only these features of the Western civilization were regarded as the nourishing sources for the growth of the subject, but what is more significant is that some have even gone to the length of asserting that its flowering is characteristically an American phenomenon. It is said that the pragmatic tradition that prevails in the United States has been most congenial to the growth of social psychology. This is something which is not quite accurate. What has happened is that the post-World War II upsurge in research which was largely American, and the sudden popularity and productivity of the subject made us disregard its multifarious roots in both Western and non-Western traditions. The enormous volume of research that is coming up on the conveyor-belt of the American mill generates in us the impression that it is an entirely Euro-American product, if not purely an American product. It is only recently that through the efforts of Henri Tajfel and his colleagues that European social psychologists are trying to establish their own identity and distinctness from the culture of American social psychology that seems to dominate the subject. My own feeling is that if we start searching for the roots, they are as firm and as favourable in our Indian tradition as they are in any other tradition—Western, American or European.

As far as the speculative side is concerned, curiosity into analysing and understanding man's social behaviour, which is the true root of any scientific endeavour, was present all over, and we need not bother too much about its original root. However, what we seem to have got from the West is the modern scientific tradition which we in the East lacked. The Indian endeavour was more speculative and intuitive. What we imported from the West is not social psychology as such but its new scientific tradition, a new method of enquiry into social behaviour and the nature of man. Therefore, what has been borrowed is not the discipline of social psychology, but only the scientific methodology which is Western.

Now let us look at the roots of social psychology in India. Only a few examples would suffice. There is a very enlightening discourse in the Upanisads on interpersonal attraction which is a favourite topic of modern social psychology. In *Brihadaranyak Upanisad*, the student asks the sage : what makes a person attracted towards his son, what draws him towards friends, towards this person or that person. It is obviously a problem of interpersonal attraction. The analysis goes on, and at the end what you may call the *Upanisadic* theory of interpersonal attraction is propounded in the famous saying that *atmanastu kamaya sarvam priyam bhavati*, i.e., it is because of your own self that everything else is liked or loved. This dictum can easily serve as a model for generating our research problems. You may call it the similarity or the identity theory of interpersonal attraction or by whatever name you like, but it is a good model to look into.

Let us take another favourite area of modern social psychology, namely, pro-social or helping behaviour or the problem of altruism in man. The question is as to why we do a good turn to others. For this, we have the concept of ever-expanding sheaths of human self or the ego. The ideal that is laid down by the ancient sages is that a good man expands his identification from himself to others and goes on expanding it and ultimately he encompasses the entire universe. It is an interesting conceptualization of our altruism. It may be speculative and intuitive but useful all the same.

If you want to know about human nature and behaviour of man in society, there is plenty of good social psychology in Kautilya's *Arthasastra*, and keen analysis of political behaviour in *Mahabharat*. In the latter one gets insightful discourses on the sources and sanctions of power which can be excellent supplements to our modern psychological knowledge about the bases of power. These are very valuable sources of knowledge giving excellent insight into man's nature and social behaviour.

Many social psychologists like Moscovici (1972) have emphasized the necessity of having a model of man for social psychological experiments. In this respect, the concept which seems very basic to our tradition visualises the closest relationship between man and society. Man's very existence and action have meaning only in the social context. The word 'only' has been emphasized because in the West, social psychology still appears to remain individualistic in its orientation and approach.

Despite the corrective influence of Kurt Lewin and his associates, the model of man underlying almost all experiments in social psychology in the West is "man in society" or "man and society". As far as the Indian tradition goes, the model is "man-society", i.e. a kind of symbiotic relationship between man and society where you cannot separate the one from the other. If one has to understand man's behaviour it has to be in terms of the social system in which he invariably operates, and there cannot be any individual or general psychology which is divorced from the social context. A relationship of absolute non-duality between man and society is emphasized. This kind of conceptualization of man is distinctly Indian. Since we are very much under the influence of American social psychology which to my mind is somewhat individualistic, this orientation should act as a corrective in our planning and conduct of experiments on social behaviour and in interpretation of their results.

Now, a glance at the empirical studies in social psychology would reveal the trends that the discipline has taken both in the West and in India, and indicate the gaps in our knowledge. In the West, the first so-called scientific and objective study in the area can be traced to the work of Triplett in 1897 when he studied human behaviour in bicycle racing and observed an increase in the maximum speed of the individual bicyclist by 20 per cent when he was observed by others. The results of A. Mayer's study in 1903 favoured group over solitary work. F.H. Allport and his associates in 1924 through a series o studies called the "alone-and-together" experiments demonstrated the incremental and levelling influences of the group factor. We have an entire set of researches by Moede (1920) which being in German are not easily accessible to most of us. In 1928, Godwin Watson tried to examine whether groups could think more efficiently than the individuals. All these studies demonstrated the 'group effects' in performance and by and large pointed to greater output in a group as compared to individual situation. What is more significant is that these researches laid the foundation for experiments in social psychology. One may differ with these early pioneers in the way groups were conceptualized or the group factor introduced, but it will have to be conceded that the possibilities of analysing changes produced in the behaviour of the individual when he is with other individuals were conclusively demonstrated. From here it did not take too long for actual face-to-face groups to become a focal interest in social psychological research.

This type of work with several variations and elaborations remained popular for many years in American social psychology. Investigators tried to isolate the conditions which produced "social increment" or its reverse. A variation of the experimental paradigm can be seen in the investigations utilizing, 'planted content' and 'planted subjects'. H.T. Moore's (1921) experiments on the relative effects of 'expert' and 'majority' opinions on moral and aesthetic judgements provide an excellent example of this technique.

Soon after the Revolution, the Russian psychologists also got interested in problems of collective versus individual behaviour, and they were not very far behind the American researchers. Bechterew and de Lange in 1924 using face-to-face group (as against just *reports* of performance of a group) analysed its effect in modifying previous individual judgements, and in the true Russian tradition emphasized the efficiency of collective over private thinking.

In 1935 we have the famous experiments of Sherif (1936) on the formation and effect of social norms on individual perception. These experiments are so well known and their impact on subsequent research has been so phenomenal that it is unnecessary to discuss them at any length. From Sherif's experiment, Asch's famous study on conformity was a natural step. But as Allport (1954) has pointed out "group influence upon the mental processes of the individual was no longer the sole focus of experimental interest". Lewin and his associates (Lewin, Lippitt, and White, 1939) introduced some useful concepts like social climate or group atmosphere and we have researches galore in what has come to be known as group dynamics, which ultimately led to the investigations into the social psychology of organizations. The work in the area has been so extensive and vigorous with important practical implications to functioning in any organized set-up that it has given birth to an entirely new branch called organizational psychology.

Apart from groups, social psychologists for a long time remained almost exclusively interested in the formation and measurement of social attitudes so much so that for years almost three-fourth of social psychology was concerned with attitudes (Bird, 1940). But with ever-increasing challenges of social problems, psychologists began to utilise their knowledge in meeting the new demands. Lewin's (1947) experiments on modifying food habits through group discussion shows how the problem of food shortage due to war was tried to be solved by a psychologist. Many simulation studies were also made. To give only one example, Bartlett (1932) developed the technique of serial reproduction to study and analyse the modifications undergone when information is transmitted from one person to another in our daily life. It was a unique method utilized by Allport and Postman (1948) for psychological analysis of rumours and gossips the results of which they published in their famous book, *Psychology of Rumour*. Morneo (1934) developed the sociometric technique which enabled not only the study of group structure but also helped to assess the personal attractions and rejections among members of a group. It has even been utilized to study the structure of villages.

The above gives a general idea of the nature of researches in social psychology in the West in the recent past. The World War II produced an all round upsurge of work in this field. Not only the area of activity got enormously diversified, but the quantum of researches multiplied many times. What has been happening in social psychology since the World War II is contemporary and I would omit it for the purpose of the present review which has been attempted mainly to provide a historical background.

Shifting now to the Indian scene, the first book on social psychology by Indian authors was almost contemporaneous with that of Flloyd Allport's. As one can see it listed in Lindzey's (1954) *Handbook of Social Psychology*, Prof. R.K. Mukherjee and Prof. N.N. Sengupta published their book entitled *Social Psychology* in 1928. Since it was brought out by an English publisher, it readily got accepted by the academic circle and came to be regarded as a standard textbook. However, its orientation was not strictly psychological and like many other textbooks of that time, it was more sociological. In any case, the publication of the book indicates that Indian scholars were not far behind their Western counterparts in this respect.

As for researches, one of the earliest experimental investigations in the field was by N.N. Sengupta and C.P.N. Singh (1926) on group effects on performance. The study was modelled after the experiments of F.H. Allport and his colleagues and was presented at the first meeting of the Psychology Section of the Indian Science Congress in January 1926 in Varanasi and subsequently appeared in the same year in the *Indian Journal of Psychology*. A few years later we have the analysis of 1934-earthquake rumours by Professor Jamuna Prasad (1935) which appeared in the *British Journal of Psychology* (1935), and, as we know, was one of the starting points of Festinger's famous theory of cognitive dissonance. His comparative analysis of many earthquake rumours appeared in the same journal fifteen years later (Prasad, 1950). I being a student of Professor Prasad followed his line and conducted a study of rumours and behaviour of people during a natural catastrophe that occurred in 1950. It came out in the *British Journal of Psychology* (Sinha, 1952), and was used by Festinger as an illustrative base for cognitive dissonance. I also conducted a study on group conformity through artificially created norm in an ambiguous perceptual situation—a study that was directly inspired by Sherif's famous experiments on social norms (Sinha, 1952) and was referred to in his revised edition of *Social Psychology*. Along with N.K. Sinha, I tried to relate perceptual judgement of "ambiguous", faces in pictures to valence (Sinha and Sinha, 1957) which in a way anticipated the later researches by Tagiuri and their colleagues on person perception (Tagiuri and Petrullo, 1958). Transformations in memory due to interpolated social factor like discussions with others (Sinha, 1953) and exposure to relevant pictorial material (Davis and Sinha, 1950) were studied by us along Bartlettean lines. Professor S.M. Mohsin in an excellent paper published in the *Journal of Abnormal and Social Psychology* (Mohsin, 1954) analysed the effects of individual and group frustrations on problem solving behaviour. Professor H.S. Asthana (1960) using anisekonic lenses experimented on perceptual distortions as affected by subject's positive and negative valence of the target objects. These studies have all been done in the best experimental tradition and have almost all appeared in standard foreign journals.

Adinarayan has done systematic studies in the area of prejudice and attitudes. His researches on colour prejudice is one of the earliest conducted by an Indian psychologist, and was published in the *British Journal of Psychology* (Adinarayan, 1941), and later on he elaborated it in the form of a monograph (Adinarayan, 1964). He also conducted sustained work on racial and communal attitudes (Adinarayan, 1953), cognitive background of prejudice (Adinarayan, 1957), student attitude towards religion, the spiritual and the supernatural (Adinarayan, 1962), and analysed caste from a psychological angle (Adinarayan, 1958). He also studied attitudes and adjustment problems of African students in India (Adinarayan, 1964) reminding one of the publication of Singh (1963) on Indian students in Britain.

Apart from his monograph *The Case for Colour* (1964), he published a socio-psychological analysis of *The Human Mind* (Adinarayan, 1950) emphasizing the aspect of values, and a textbook on *Social Psychology* (1965). Many of his studies have been published abroad and have received wide recognition in the West. It is, however, strange that psychologists in this country have largely remained ignorant of them reflecting thereby their characteristic indifference to the researches done by their Indian contemporaries.

There are many other interesting studies in the field conducted by Indian scholars. N.P. Mukherjee's study (Mukherjee, 1940) on ability differentials in work as related to group and isolation situations, which also appeared in the *British Journal of Psychology* (1940), is worth noting. Mukhopadhyay and Ram Govind Chatterjee (1961) made an experimental study of group problem solving processes in leader and leaderless discussion situations. In the same tradition we have the study of Mukhopadhyay and Majumdar (1960) on effects of group pressure on visual estimation of length with and without reference to actual values of the presented stimuli.

These studies starting from the one made by Sengupta and Singh (1926) represent the beginnings of the experimental social psychology in India and indicate that the Indian scholars had readily caught up the experimental tradition. Though a lot of their work was repetitive and somewhat sporadic in character, they showed that Indian scholars were utilizing their experimental skills in analysing and understanding social phenomena.

Since the mid-sixties, the researches in the area display a new vigour and as they constitute the contemporary and have not yet turned into what can be called 'history', only a passing reference to them is made. A noteworthy study which in a way "simulates" the real-life condition under laboratory setting is that of J.B.P. Sinha on the performance differentials of high and low need for achievement, subjects under limited and unlimited resource condition and with egoistic and altruistic orientation (Sinha, 1968). The finding that high *n-Ach* individuals under scarcity of resources tend to resort to "hoarding" and other kinds of highly competitive behaviour which is not in the interest of the group is not only interesting in itself but has obvious practical implications for a country which has scarcity of resources for development. Ramadhar Singh's numerous studies on interpersonal attraction display the neatness of experimentalist's work in analysing an important facet of social behaviour (Singh, 1975). Suresh Kanekar's experiments on attribution behaviour also give us examples of the neat operation of an experimentalist in analysing social behaviour (Kanekar, 1977). My own studies on motivation and level of aspiration of farmers as related to the extent of agro-economic development (Sinha, 1969) using quasi-experimental design fall in the category of field experiments. There are other Indian psychologists who are employing the sophistication of experimenter's techniques on socio-psychological problems. These are "contemporary" and a detailed review of such researches would be out of place here.

Before concluding it would be pertinent to look at the position of experimental social psychology in India against the general pattern of researches conducted in social psychology. The review of psychology in India published by the ICSSR (1972) takes into account the studies conducted up to 1969. A little less than 3000 studies and publications in psychology since the establishment of the first laboratory in psychology in India in 1915 have been reviewed. Ninety per cent of publications in each field date from 1950. This is true of all other area excepting experimental and social psychology where the figures are 70 and 77 per cent respectively. In other words, three-fourths of all researches up to 1969 in social psychology belong to the post-1950 era. It indicates phenomenal upsurge of interest in this branch of the subject during the post-Independence phase. Now, taking all the researches in psychology, the three branches of social, clinical and personality account for 50 per cent of the total. Of the total of 2981 publications in psychology, 402 or about 15 per cent belong to the area of social psychology. Dr. Rath, who prepared the chapter on social psychology, has reviewed no less than 597 studies. The figure indicates that researches in social psychology constitute one-fifth of all studies till 1969.

Now, looking at the ICSSR review, the bulk of the studies (almost fifty per cent) have been classified by Professor Rath (ICSSR, 1972) under the heading of 'cultural and social processes' and one-sixth of all the reported studies (i.e., 93 out of a total of 597) deal with attitudes, opinion plus prejudice and stereotypes. Scanning through the review, it is difficult to find reference to studies that can strictly be regarded as 'experimental social'. In fact, the expression "experimental social psychology" has not been used as a classificatory heading nor it finds a place in the review. There was neither any reference nor a separate heading for experimental social psychology. Most of the studies in the area dealt with attitudes, stereotypes and personality, demographic and personal variables as related to attitudes and prejudice. This does not mean that no work on experimental social psychology had been conducted by Indian scholars. As has already been indicated, a few significant experimental studies had been done and the review does refer to some studies which come under experimental social psychology. But they were stray and isolated efforts and the volume of work in the area was so small that it did not deserve a separate classificatory label.

Even if attitude and stereotypes happen to be the main area of concern, there is plenty of scope for experimental work. Through manipulation of variables and experimental treatment, changes in attitudes can be studied. Somehow the Indian researchers have avoided this line and confined themselves to non-experimental studies and haphazard surveys. What is worse is that these attitudes surveys which for long have remained favourite topic for doctoral students fetching them easy degrees in many institutions, have been ill-conceived, badly planned, and conducted without proper scientific procedure. The lack of care with which these surveys are designed, questionnaires and inventories constructed and utter disregard of proper sampling procedures have produced a brand of social psychology which is anything but scientific in the strict sense of the term. As a result, bulk of social psychology in the country has remained unscientific and non-experimental, and has degenerated into what has been sometimes designated in derogatory terms as "questionnaire psychology". However, it is a good sign that Indian social psychologists in increasing numbers are gradually turning to experimental studies, both in the laboratory and in the field, and are trying to understand and unravel the social reality by the application of sophisticated experimental techniques. It is hoped that Dr. Shib Mitra's editorial summarization of the situation as prevailing in social psychology till 1969 that "no big social problem has been tackled and experimental social psychology remains neglected" (Mitra, 1972) will not remain true of researches in the area of social psychology in India in years to come.

REFERENCES

Adinarayan, S.P. A research in colour prejudice. *British Journal of Psychology*, 1941, **31**, 217-229.

Adinarayan, S.P. *The Human Mind* London : Hutchinsons, 1950.

Adinarayan, S.P. Before and after Independence : A study of racial and communal attitudes in India. *British Journal of Psychology*, 1953, **44**, 108-115.

Adinarayan, S.P. A study of racial attitudes in India. *Journal of Social Psychology*, 1957, **45**, 211-216.

Adinarayan, S.P. The cognitive background to prejudice. *Psychological Studies*, 1957, **2**, 45-51.

Adinarayan, S P. Caste in India : A psychological approach. *Religion and Society*, 1958, **5**.

Adinarayan, S.P. *The Case for Colour*. Bombay : Asia Publishing House, 1964.

Adinarayan, S.P. *Social Psychology*. Bombay : Allied Publishers, 1965.

Adinarayan, S.P. & Rajamanickam, M. A study of student attitude towards religion, the spiritual and the supernatural. *Journal of Social Psychology*, 1962, 57, 1, 105-111.

Adinarayan, S.P. & Swaminathan, M. Attitudes and adjustment problems of African students in India. *Journal of Social Psychology*, 1964, **63**, 65-72.

Allport, F.H. *Social Psychology*. Boston : Houghton Mifflin, 1924.

Allport, G.W. The historical background of modern social psychology. In G. Lindzey (ed.) *Handbook of Social Psychology* : Vol. I, Cambridge, Mass. : Addison-Wesley, 1954, 3-56.

Allport, G.W. & Postman, L. *The Psychology of Rumour*. New York : Henry Holt, 1948.

Asthana, H.S. Perceptual distortion as a function of the valence of perceived object. *Journal of Social Psychology*, 1960, **62**, 119-125.

Bartlett, F.C. *Remembering*. Cambridge, Eng. : Cambridge University Press, 1932.

Bechterew, V.M., & Lange, M. de. Die erbgenisse des experiments auf dem gebiete der kollektiven reflexologie *Z. angrew. Psychol.*, 1924, **24**, 305-344.

Bird, C. *Social Psychology*. New York : Appleton Century, 1940.

Davis, D.R. & Sinha, D. The influences of an interpolated experience upon recall. *Quarterly Journal of Experimental Psychology*, 1950, **2**.

I.C.S.S.R. : *A Survey of Research in Psychology*. Bombay : Popular Prakashan, 1972.

Kanekar, S. Decision as function of attribution and attributor's position. *Journal of Social Psychology*, 1977, **102**, 117-123.

Lewin, K. Group decision and social change. In T. Newcomb & E. Hartley (eds.) *Readings in Social Psychology*. New York : Henry Halt, 1947, 330-344.

Lewin, K., Lippitt, R., & White, R. Patterns of aggressive behaviour in experimentally created social climates. *Journal of Social Psychology*, 1939, **10**, 271-299.

Lindzey, G. (ed.) *Handbook of Social Psychology* (2 vols.), Cambridge Addison-Wesley, 1954.

McDougall, W. *Introduction to Social Psychology*. London : Methuen, 1908.

Mitra, S.K. Psychological research in India. In *A Survey of Research in Psychology* (ICSSR Publication), Bombay : Popular Prakashan, 1972.

Moede, W. *Experimentelle massenpsychologie*, Leipzig: S. Hirzel, 1920.

Mohsin, S.M. Effect of frustration on problem solving behaviour. *Journal of Abnormal and Social Psychology*, 1954, 49, (1).

Moore, H.T. The comparative influence of majority and expert opinion. *American Journal of Psychology*, 1921, **32**, 16-20.

Moreno, J.L. *Who Shall Survive*? Washington D.C. : Nervous and Mental Diseases Publishing Company, 1934.

Moscovici, S. Society and theory in social psychology. In J. Israel & H. Tajfel (ed.). *The Context of Social Psychology: A Critical Assessment*. London: Academic Press, 1972.

Mukherjee, N.P. An investigation of ability in work in groups and in isolation. *British Journal of Psychology*, 1940, **30**.

Mukherjee, R., & Sengupta, N.N. *Introduction to Social Psychology*. London: Heath, 1928.

Mukhopadhyay, P.K., & Chatterjee, R.G. An experimental study on group problem solving process in leaderless discussion situation. *Indian Journal of Psychology*, 1961, **36**.

Mukhopadhyay, P.K., & Majumdar, R.K. A cooperative study of the effect of group pressure on visual estimations with and without reference to actual values of the presented stimuli. *Journal of Psychological Researches*, 1960, **4**.

Prasad, J. The psychology of rumour: A study relating to the great Indian earthquake of 1934. *British Journal of Psychology*, 1935, **26**, 1-15.

Prasad, J. A comparative study of rumours and reports in earthquakes. *British Journal of Psychology*, 1950, **41**, 129-144.

Ross, E.A. *Social Psychology*. New York: Macmillan, 1908.

Sengupta, N.N. & Singh, C.P.N. Mental work in isolation and in group. *Indian Journal of Psychology*, 1926, **1**, 106-110.

Sherif, M. *The Psychology of Social Norms*. New York: Harper, 1936.

Singh, A.K. *Indian Students in Britain: A Survey of their Adjustment and Attitudes*. Bombay: Asia Publishing House, 1963.

Singh, R. Information integration theory applied to expected job attractiveness and satisfaction. *Journal of Applied Psychology*, 1975, **60**, 621-623.

Sinha, D. Behaviour in a catastrophic situation: A psychological study of reports and rumours. *British Journal of Psychology*, 1952, **43**, 200-209(a).

Sinha, D. An experimental study of a social factor in perception. *Patna University Journal*, January-April, 1952(b).

Sinha, D. The influence of interpolated discussion upon recall. *Journal of Education and Psychology*, 1953, **11**.

Sinha, D *Indian Villages in Transition: A Motivational Analysis*. New Delhi: Associated Publishing House, 1969.

Sinha, D. & Sinha, N.K. Affective reaction and perceptual judgement. *Social Studies*, 1957, **2**.

Sinha, J.B.P. The *n*-achievement, *n*-cooperation under limited/unlimited resource conditions. *Journal of Experimental Social Psychology*, 1968, 4, 233-246.

Tagiuri, R., & Petrullo, L. *Person Perception and Interpersonal Behaviour*. Stanford: Stanford University Press, 1958.

Triplett, N. The dynamogenic factors in pace making and competition. *American Journal of Psychology*, 1897, 9, 507-533.

SECTION TWO

RESEARCH PROGRESS

TWO

Ramadhar Singh

PREDICTION OF PERFORMANCE FROM MOTIVATION AND ABILITY
An Appraisal of the Cultural Difference Hypothesis*

HOW DO PEOPLE integrate information about motivation and ability of a person when they predict his performance? Heider (1958) made the following suggestion:

> The personal constituents, namely, power (ability) and trying (effort) are related as multiplicative combination, since the effective personal force (performance) is zero if either of them is zero. For instance, if a person has the ability but does not try at all he will make no progress toward the goal (p. 83).

If Heider's proposal is correct, then prediction of performance from motivation and ability information would follow the multiplying rule:

$$\text{Performance} = \text{Motivation} \times \text{Ability} \quad \ldots (1)$$

Heider's rationale for the multiplying rule is much the same as in Hull's (1943) formulation, Reaction Potential=Drive×

*I am grateful to Norman H. Anderson, Ajit K. Dalal, John H. Harvey, Suresh Kanekar, Jai B.P. Sinha, and Prabha Srivastava for their comments on the first draft of this paper. Preparation of this chapter was supported by a research project, Prediction and postdiction in social judgments, from the Indian Institute of Management, Ahmedabad.

Habit. In both formulations, an energizing factor and a capability factor are required to produce an action. Furthermore, the dynamic energizing factor (Motivation, Drive) is assumed to act as an amplifier of the static capacity factor (Ability, Habit). The algebraic model that entails such an operation is the multiplying rule. Accordingly, motivation and ability are expected to multiply each other.

Anderson's (1974a, 1974b, 1976a, 1981) theory of information integration and functional measurement which has guided much of the research by the author shows that such a multiplying rule implies a linear fan pattern in the factorial plot of the Motivation × Ability data. This linear fan prediction of the multiplying model has been supported in the United States but not in India.

The central task of the present chapter is to provide an explanation for the discrepancy in results obtained with American and Indian students. The position taken here is that the integration rules underlying prediction of performance are culture-specific, and that American and Indian students differ in their cultural outlook on how motivation and ability determine performance. This chapter will attempt, therefore, to put several studies by the author and his associates together in such a fashion that an objective appraisal of the cultural-difference hypothesis would be possible.

AMERICAN STUDIES

Anderson and Butzin, 1974

In a study of college students, Anderson and Butzin presented information about motivation and ability of target persons, applicants to graduate school or athletes trying out for college track, and asked subjects to predict how the target persons would perform. Target persons were products of a 4×4 (Motivation × Ability) factorial design, and the two factors had low (LO), moderately low (LO—), moderately high (HI—), and high (HI) as levels.

Mean judgments of performance as a function of motivation and ability information are plotted in Figure 2.1, for applicants to graduate school in the left side and for athletes in the right side. The general shape of the curves for the two types of stimulus persons is essentially the same. The curves have a clear tendency to diverge toward right. This divergence is real, for the test of the interaction term was statistically significant and most of the variance, 75 per cent for applicants to graduate school and 81 per cent for athletes, concentrated in the Linear × Linear trend. The data shown in Figure 2.1 thus conform to the linear fan pattern rather well. Accordingly, Anderson and Butzin concluded that subjects multiplied motivation and ability information in prediction of performance.

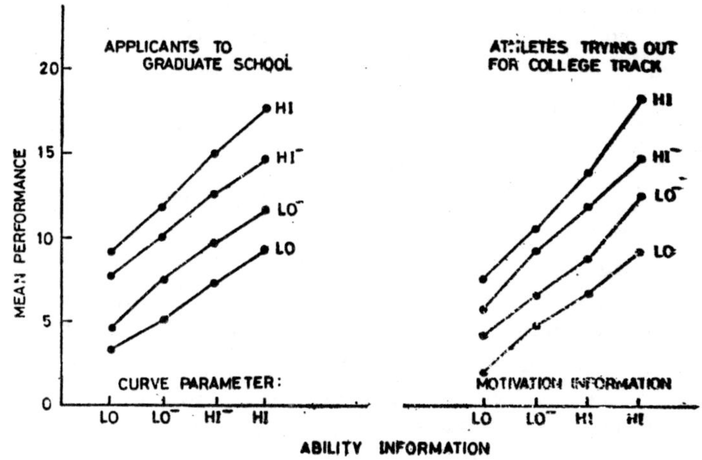

FIG. 2.1 *Mean judgments of performance from information about motivation and ability of applicants to graduate school (left side) and athletes try out for college track (right side). The curves are based on the data reported by Anderson and Butzin (1974).*

Graesser and Anderson, 1974

The possibility of a multiplying operation of an energizing factor and a capability factor was further checked by Graesser and Anderson. In two experiments, they presented information about generosity and annual income of sixteen stimulus persons constructed from a 4×4 design, and asked college students to predict size of gift each stimulus person would give to a family whose house had burnt down. As in the study by Anderson and Butzin (1974), Graesser and Anderson obtained linear fan pattern in the graphic plot of Generosity × Income data. Identical findings across the two conceptually similar judgmental tasks enabled them to provide a unifying, theoretical rationale for the multiplying rule :

> Both Gift size=Generosity × Income, and Performance= Motivation × Ability have the same psychological structure. In each case, an energizing factor or action tendency operates on a capability potential. These equations thus represent a judgmental analog of the behavioural equation used by Hull and others that Drive multiplies Habit strength. (pp. 696-697).

Kun, Parsons, and Ruble, 1974

In a developmental study, Kun and her associates studied attribution of performance on puzzles from effort and ability information about the stimulus children. They also obtained evidence for a linear fan pattern in the plot of Effort × Ability data. Judgments by the youngest children had a parallelism pattern, as if an adding-type rule was operative, whereas judgments by second graders and others had a linear fan pattern. Therefore, the authors suggested that a multiplying rule develops out of an adding rule around 8-9 years of age.

Comments

Results of the three studies just reviewed suggest that there is a considerable generality to the multiplying rule. The energizing and capability factors do operate in a multiplicative fashion to produce reaction as Heider (1958) and Hull (1943) hypothesized. Furthermore, there is a developmental progression in the integration rule: A multiplying-type rule evolves out of an adding-type rule.

If prediction of performance from motivation and ability follows a multiplying rule, then judgments of motivation from information about performance and ability, and judgments of ability from information about performance and motivation should follow a dividing rule :

$$\text{Motivation} = \text{Performance} \div \text{Ability} \qquad \ldots (2a)$$
$$\text{Ability} = \text{Performance} \div \text{Motivation} \qquad \ldots (2b)$$

This would happen if the subjects are mathematically consistent as Heider (1958) assumed. However, Anderson and Butzin (1974) obtained data supportive of a subtracting rule:

$$\text{Motivation} = \text{Performance} - \text{Ability} \qquad (3a)$$
$$\text{Ability} = \text{Performance} - \text{Motivation} \qquad (3b)$$

Anderson and Butzin concluded, therefore, that those judgments obeyed a simple cognitive algebra but that this cognitive algebra was not consistent mathematically.

At the Indian Institute of Technology, Kanpur, the author and his two doctoral students, Ajit K. Dalal and Meenakshi Gupta, thought that perhaps there is an alternative interpretation, one in which the subjects are mathematically consistent. The linear fan pattern is not restricted to the multiplying rule alone. This pattern can also be engendered by a conjunctive averaging rule with differential weighting (Anderson, 1974b). If lower value of motivation and/or ability had greater weight, then the averaging model would produce an approximate linear fan. This possibility was noted by Anderson and Butzin (1974) also, who said, "Since averaging process is pervasive in judgment, a conjunctive integration rule deserves consideration" (p. 602). However, neither they nor Kun et al., (1974) included a test to distinguish multiplying from conjunctive averaging. The author and his students, therefore, undertook experimental analyses of prediction of performance from motivation and ability information.

INDIAN STUDIES

Singh, Gupta, and Dalal, 1979

Singh and his associates tested the plausibility of the alternative interpretation as a conjunctive averaging rule in three experiments. The three experiments are described below in detail.

Experiment 1

Thirty-two engineering students were provided with information about interest in studies and intelligence of stimulus students, and were asked to predict how the stimulus students would perform at the Indian Institute of Technology, Kanpur. Sixteen stimulus students were prepared according to a 4×4 (Interest-in-Studies×IQ) factorial design; four stimulus students were described with respect to their IQ alone.

On the basis of the results reported in American studies, it was predicted that the judgments of sixteen persons described with respect to their interest in studies and IQ would yield a linear fan pattern, just as in the two sets of curves shown in Figure 2.1. Furthermore, the curve for judgments based on information about ability only would also form part of the linear fan. This would happen because the subjects would impute some value for the missing motivation information and multiply that with the given value of IQ. But if the conjunctive averaging rule would operate, then ability—only curve would cross over at least one of the four two-cue curve (Anderson, 1974b; Dalal and Singh, Note 1; Lampel and Anderson, 1968).

Figure 2.2 plots mean judgment of performance as a function of interests in studies (curve parameter) and IQ. The IQ levels are spaced on the horizontal axis according to the marginal means of the 4×4 factorial design. This spacing allows the linear fan pattern to appear. If the two pieces of information were integrated by multiplying rule, then the four solid curves would form a diverging fan of straight lines.

The pattern of the data in Figure 2.2 is quite contrary to the multiplying rule. There is not any evidence for divergence at all. Instead, the four solid curves exhibit neat parallelism. Perhaps subjects integrated the two given information by an adding or averaging rule.

A distinguishing test between the adding and averaging rule is provided by the dashed curve of Figure 2.2. This curve represents judgments based on IQ information alone, with interest in studies not specified. According to the adding rule, the dashed curve should be parallel to the solid curves. The averaging rule requires the dashed curve to have steeper slope

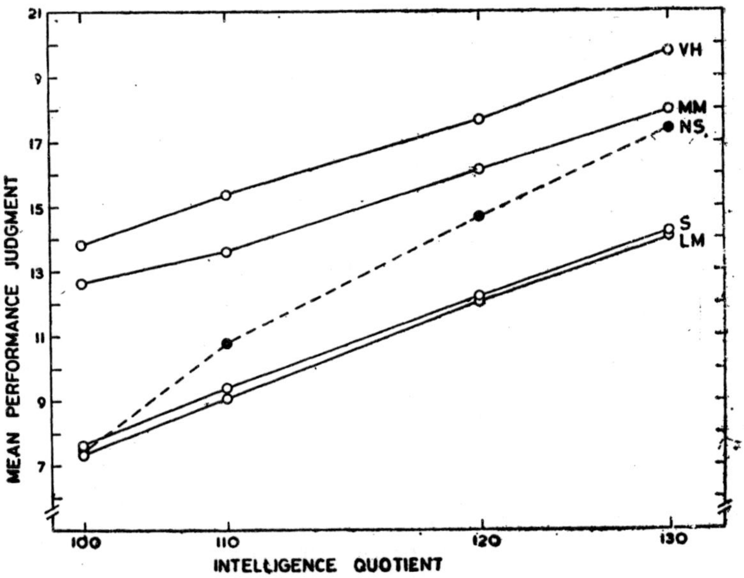

FIG. 2.2 *Mean judgment of performance as a function of interest in studies (curve parameter) and IQ (listed on the horizontal axis). Data from Singh, Gupta, & Dalal, 1979; Experiment 1, Figure 2.1. (VH=very high; MM=more than most; S=slight; LM=less than most; NS=interest in studies information not specified). Copyright 1979 by the American Psychological Association, Inc. Reproduced with permission.*

than the solid curves. This requirement of the averaging rule seems to have been satisfied in Figure 2.2.

To obtain statistical support for the averaging rule, the dashed curve data were considered as a fifth level of the Interest-in-Studies factor. The interaction term in this 5×4 (Interest-in-Studies $\times$ IQ) analysis of variance tests for nonparallelism in the set of all five curves in Figure 2.2. This interaction was highly significant, F (12, 372)=8.36, $p<.01$. Since the four solid curves are essentially parallel, F (9, 279)= 1.44, it appears that the dashed curve is reliably steeper than the solid curves. This test thus supports the averaging rule and rejects the alternative adding rule.

The principal finding of Experiment 1 is that the information about motivation and ability is integrated by a simple, equal-weight averaging rule. This result is contrary to the prediction; it disagrees with results from American subjects. One hypothesis is that this discrepancy in integration rules is a consequence of cultural differences in outlook on social motivation.

Before this hypothesis can be taken seriously, however, it is necessary to examine methodological differences between the present and previous experiments. Methodologically, this experiment was different from those of Anderson and Butzin (1974) in two notable ways. First, they asked their subjects to describe in writing how they integrated information about motivation and ability during the practice session. This was not done in the present experiment. This difference, however, does not seem to be serious at all. Kun et al., (1974) obtained the linear fan pattern with children of second grade even without following the Anderson and Butzin procedure. Second, and perhaps more important, the motivation factor was defined here as interest in studies, and the subjects may not have interpreted that in terms of motivation and trying. This possibility was checked in the next experiment by using more explicitly motivational information.

Experiment 2

This experiment was conducted chiefly as a reliability check on Experiment 1. However, there were three notable changes from Experiment 1. First, information about laboriousness was used as motivation factor to allow direct comparison of findings with those obtained in the United States. Second, the levels of the two factors, laboriousness and IQ, were drawn from a wider scale range to increase the opportunity for a linear fan pattern to appear. Finally, sufficient data were collected from each of the 12 engineering students to explore various integration rules at the individual level.

The upper left panel of Figure 2.3 plots mean judgment of performance as a function of laboriousness (curve parameter) and IQ (horizontal axis) of stimulus students. If the parallelism pattern of Figure 2.2 is indeed reliable, then the four solid

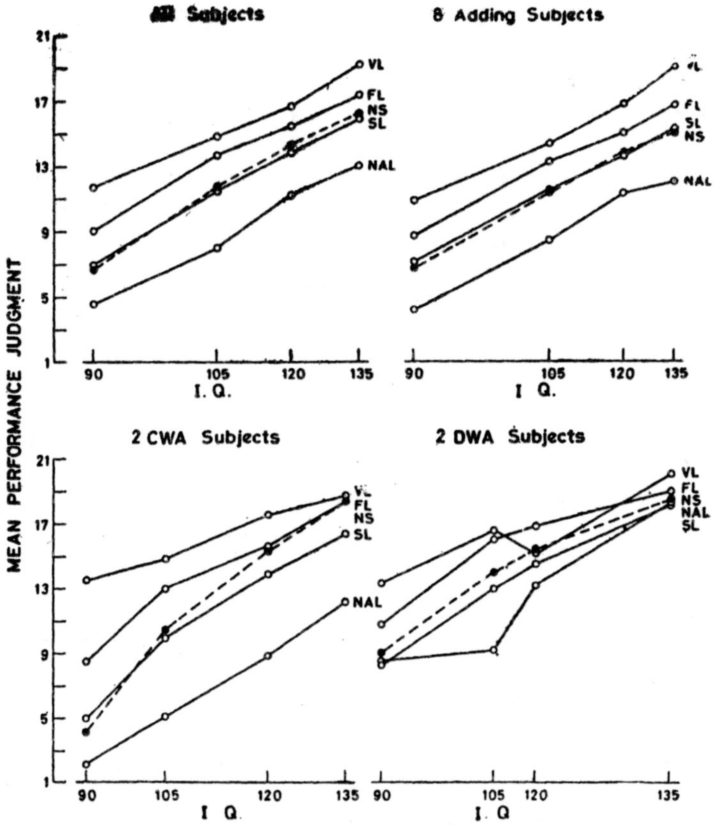

FIG. 2.3 *Mean judgment of performance as a function of laboriousness and IQ. (Levels of laboriousness are listed as curve parameters: NAL=not at all laborious; SL=slightly laborious; FL=fairly laborious; VL=very laborious; NS=laboriousness not specified. Classification of subjects into adding, constant-weight averaging (CWA), and differential-weight averaging (DWA) subgroups was based on results from single subject-analyses). Data from Singh, Gupta & Dalal, 1979; Experiment 2, Figure 2.2 Copyright 1979 by the American Psychological Association, Inc. Reproduced with permission.*

curves of Figure 2.3 should also be parallel. This seems to be true; the four curves are essentially parallel. Although the laboriousness × IQ interaction was statistically significant, $F(9, 99)=2.13$, $p<.05$, there is no sign of the linear fan pattern reported in the American studies. On the contrary, there is a slight tendency for the curves to converge to the right. Despite the change in the nature of the motivation cue, these results confirm those in Figure 2.2.

The dashed curve in the upper left panel of Figure 2.3 represents judgments based on IQ alone, with no information about laboriousness. This curve is nearly parallel to the solid curves, as though subjects added information about laboriousness and IQ. At face value, this result seems to argue for the adding rule and against the averaging rule. But the averaging rule can also account for it. If subjects inferred an implicit value of laboriousness when no information was given and they averaged that in with information given about IQ, then the corresponding dashed curve would be expected to be parallel to the solid curves.

In separate analyses for each subject, the subjects broke down into three subgroups. Mean judgments of performance for these three subgroups are shown in Figure 2.3. The upper right panel displays results for eight subjects, all of whom had non-significant interaction. Here parallelism is quite evident. Perhaps these subjects followed an adding or an averaging rule. The lower left panel has data from two subjects who apparently averaged, as shown by the crossover of the dashed and solid curves. The lower left panel shows data from two subjects who had a strong convergence tendency. However, the general shape of the curves is too irregular to be interpreted.

The most important information from these individual subject analyses is that not a single subject showed the linear fan pattern obtained in the American experiments. That supports the suggestion of Experiment 1 that Indian college students make prediction of performance in a rather different way from their American counterparts.

The findings of Experiments 1 and 2 converge to make a single point : Information about motivation and ability is added or averaged in making prediction of scholastic performance. The evidence leans toward the averaging rule, but the results of Experiment 2 require the supplementary assumption that subjects impute an implicit value for motivation when no information is given. This assumption is reasonable, since no performance is logically possible without some level of motivation. Nevertheless, more direct evidence was required.

We thought that direct evidence can be obtained by using three stimulus cues, for example, past performance, motivation, and ability. If the averaging model is correct, then the single-cue curves should be clearly steeper than the curves in the two-way factorial plots from the three-cue design. The reason is simple. When the single cue is given, any implicit inference about the absent motivation information will yield an effective two-cue response. But the averaging model implies that the slope of a curve based on two-cue will be greater than that based on three-cue. Accordingly, the crossover test remains valid even if the subjects do impute an implicit value to the missing dimension of information. The adding hypothesis, of course, still predicts parallelism in such a three-cue design.

Experiment 3

This experiment had 27 stimulus students prepared from a $3 \times 3 \times 3$ (Past Performance × Laboriousness × IQ) design and 9 stimulus students from a 3×3 (Laboriousness × IQ) design. In addition, there were nine single-cue stimulus persons, based on one of the three levels of each factor of the three-cue design. Twelve subjects predicted performance of all the stimulus students in their next examination.

If subjects use multiplying rule for information about motivation and ability, then performance judgments should conform to the compound averaging–multiplying rule :

$$\text{Performance} = \text{Past Performance} + \text{Motivation} \times \text{Ability} \quad \ldots (4)$$

In the three-factor design, therefore, two of the two-way plots, Past Performance × Motivation and Past Performance × Ability, should exhibit the parallelism pattern, and the third, Motivation × Ability, should exhibit linear fan pattern (Anderson &

Butzin, 1974). However, results from the previous two experiments suggested the three-term averaging model :

$$\text{Performance} = \text{Past Performance} + \text{Motivation} + \text{Ability} \quad \ldots (5)$$

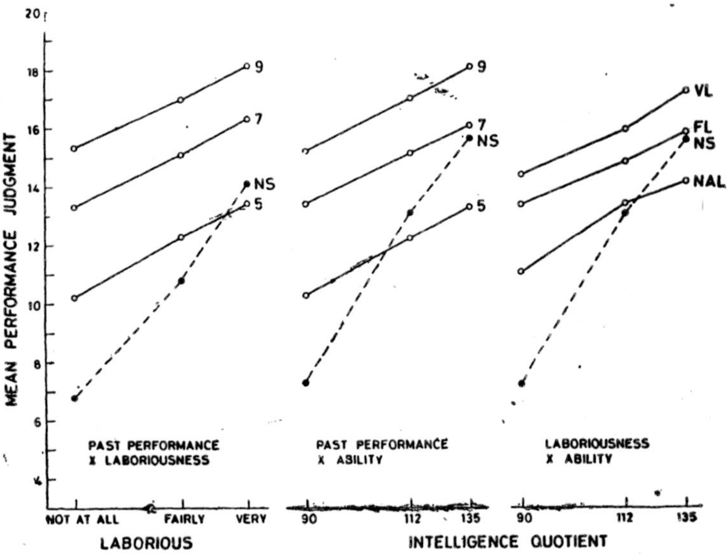

FIG. 2.4 *Two-way factorial graphs for Past Performance×Laboriousness, Past Performance×Ability, and Laboriousness×Ability effects on performance from the 3×3×3 (Past Performance×Laboriousness×Ability) design. (The dashed curve of each panel is based on just the single factor listed on the horizontal axis. Digits 5, 7, and 9 represent levels of past performance. NAL, FL, and VL represent not at all laborious, fairly laborious, and very laborious, respectively. NS=row information not specified). Data from Singh, Gupta, & Dalal, 1979; Experiment 3, Figure 2.3. Copyright 1979 by the American Psychological Association, Inc. Reprinted with permission.*

Each panel of Figure 2.4 shows one of the two-cue factorial graphs from the three-cue design. In each panel, the solid curves are nearly parallel. The right panel, which corresponds to the Laboriousness × Ability interaction, is marginally significant, F (4, 44)=2.46. However, the three solid curves indicate a slight convergence, as in Experiment 2, not the divergence required by the multiplying rule. The results shown in Figure 2.4 thus support the three-term averaging model.

A test between the adding and averaging rules is obtained by comparing the dashed curve with the solid curves in each panel of Figure 2.4. The dashed curve represents judgments based on just the single cue listed on the horizontal axis. In each panel, the dashed curve has much steeper slope and crosses over the lowest solid curve convincingly. This crossover interaction is evidence against the adding rule and for the averaging rule.

Results from two-cue design are shown in Figure 2.5. The solid curves are nearly parallel, but with a visible and barely significant tendency to converge to the right, F (4, 44)=2.85, $p<.05$. The dashed curve is again nearly parallel to but slightly steeper than the solid curves. These results are essentially the same as those in Experiment 2.

The two-cue data support the assumption of implicit inference about motivation information suggested by data of Experiment 2. The dashed curve in the centre and right panels of Figure 2.4 is the same as the dashed curve of Figure 2.5. The clear crossover of the dashed curve in Figure 2.4 supports the averaging rule. Hence, the failure to yield a clear crossover in Figure 2.5 would appear to reflect the presence of an inferred, implicit value for the missing motivation information.

Data of individual subject were also analyzed. Table 2.1 presents the F ratios for the four interactions for each of the twelve subjects in the main three-cue, 3×3×3 (Past Performance × Laboriousness × IQ) design.

As required by the three-term averaging rule, the two-way and three-way interactions are in general non-significant. Only five scattered interactions are statistically significant. Closer examination of the data disclosed that they reflected individual idiosyncrasies such as may be seen in the lower right panel of

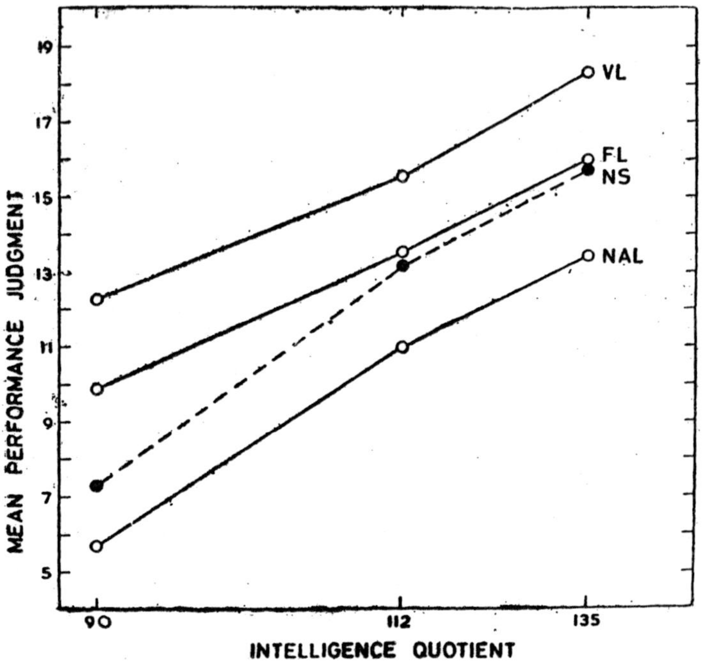

FIG. 2.5 *Mean judgment of performance as a function of laboriousness and IQ.* (*NAL*=not at all laborious; *FL* =fairly laborious; *VL*=very laborious; *NS*=*laboriousness information was not specified*). *Data from Singh, Gupta, & Dalal, 1979; Experiment 3, Two-cue design, Figure 2.4. Copyright 1979 by the American Psychological Association, Inc. Reproduced with permission.*

Figure 2.3. Almost all subjects showed the crossover interaction for the single-cue curves. Thus, the results showed the generality of the averaging rule at the level of the individual subject.

In single subject analyses of the two-cue Laboriousness × IQ data, 11 of the 12 subjects showed parallelism. Only 1 subject had a converging type of non-parallelism. It can thus be said that present two-cue results are indeed similar to those of Experiments 1 and 2.

Table 2.1 : F Ratios for Two-Way and Three-Way Interactions in Single-Subject Analyses (Experiment 3, Three-Cue Design)

Subject	AB F(4,52)	AC F(4,52)	BC F(4,52)	ABC F(8,52)
1	2.69*	.58	.94	.84
2	2.23	3.33*	1.28	1.79
3	1.64	.74	1.77	.98
4	.84	1.19	3.73*	1.41
5	1.72	1.14	1.22	.87
6	.78	1.15	.77	.53
7	.35	.59	.95	.93
8	2.75*	1.09	1.18	3.50*
9	.42	.16	.91	.75
10	.51	.23	1.29	.91
11	1.36	.51	1.73	.27
12	1.65	.76	1.32	.68

Note: A=Past Performance; B=Laboriousness; C=IQ.
*$p < .05$.
Data from Singh, Gupta & Dalal, 1979. Copyright 1979 by the American Psychological Association, Inc. Reproduced with permission.

Conclusion

The results of the present set of three experiments do not agree with the multiplying model suggested by Heider (1958) and supported by Anderson and Butzin (1974) with American adults and by Kun et al., (1974) with older American children. In the present experiments, prediction of performance from motivation and ability cues appears to have been governed by a process quite different from the multiplying. Strong evidence for parallelism pattern indicates that an equal-weight averaging could account for the data rather well. It seems reasonable to conclude, therefore, that prediction of scholastic performance from motivation and ability information obeys an averaging rule in India, and that integration rules underlying prediction of performance are culture-specific.

Gupta and Singh, 1981

A more thorough test of the cultural-difference hypothesis was made by Gupta and Singh. They patterned their experiment after Experiment 3 of Singh et al., (1979), and used twenty-four subjects from each of the five age groups of 6-7, 8-9, 10-11, 12-13-year-olds and adults (17-19-year-olds). This yielded not only greater generality of the averaging results but also direct comparison with Kun et al., (1974) on development of cognitive algebra. Results of this developmental study are presented in Figures 2.6-2.8.

Parallelism pattern

The upper part of Figure 2.6 shows the two-way graph for Past Performance × Motivation for each of the five age groups. The upward slope of the curves represents the effect of information about past performance, while the vertical separation of the curves represents the effect of information about motivation. The three curves are essentially parallel at all five age levels. Although the parallelism is not perfect, the overall picture is one of strong support for an adding-type rule for integration of information about past performance and motivation.

A quite similar picture emerges in the lower part of Figure 2.6 which plots the two-way graphs for Past Performance × Ability. Again the three curves for each age group are nearly parallel. This means that integration of information about past performance and ability also followed an adding-type rule.

Most important for cross-cultural comparison are the two-way graphs for Motivation × Ability. These are shown in Figure 2.7, for the three-cue design in the upper panel and for the two-cue design in the lower panel. The general shape of the curves from the two designs is exactly the same, and all ten graphs exhibit a prevailing pattern of near-parallelism. This pattern of near-parallelism supports an adding-type rule suggested by Singh et al., (1979) but rejects the multiplying rule

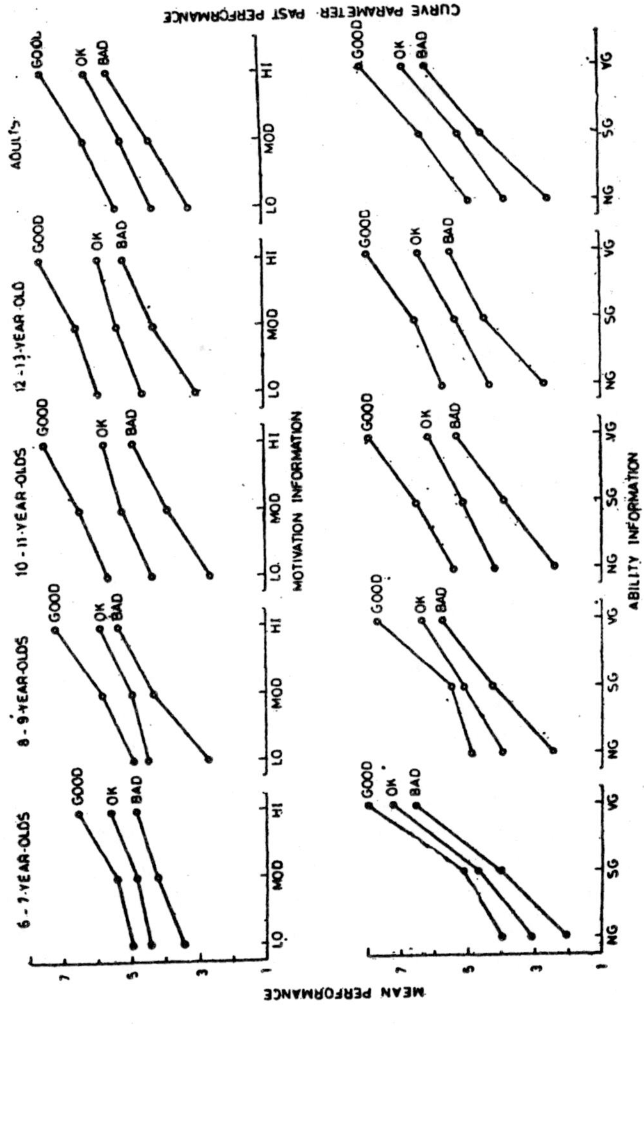

FIG. 2.6 : *Mean prediction of performance as a function of past performance and motivation (upper part) and past performance and ability (lower part) for each of the five age groups. Data from Gupta & Singh, 1981; Three-cue design, Figure 2.1. Copyright 1981 by the American Psychological Association, Inc.) Reproduced with permission.*

(Anderson and Butzin, 1974; Kun et al., 1974). Evidently, Indian students at all ages coordinate information pertaining to motivation and ability in a way quite different from that of their American counterparts.

A strict adding-type rule requires parallelism in the factorial graph, and hence a nonsignificant interaction term in the analysis of variance. In analyses of variance of the three-cue and two-cue design data, however, the interaction terms were generally significant for the graphs of Figures 2.6 and 2.7. Closer examination of the graphs for children of all the four age groups suggests that the deviations from parallelism reflect end effects in the response scale. There is a tendency for the lowest point to be too low and the highest point to be too high, as though children had a preference for the two end categories of the response scale. In any case, the fluctuations from parallelism are relatively small. Therefore, they do not seem to require any serious qualification on the adding-type rule.

Averaging versus adding

Both the adding and averaging rules can account for the parallelism pattern in Figures 2.6 and 2.7. Figure 2.8 presents distinguishing tests between adding and averaging rules for motivation and ability across the five ages. In each graph, the curve connected by circles is based on the single cue listed on the horizontal axis, namely, motivation in upper panel and ability in the lower panel. The other two curves are based on main effect of the very same cue from the two and three-cue designs.

The adding hypothesis requires the three curves in each graph to exhibit parallelism. The main reason is that the added information would have the same directional effect across the three levels of the factor listed on the horizontal axis. Figure 2.8 shows no sign of parallelism at all. Instead, all ten graphs exhibit crossovers. These crossovers are strong evidence against the adding rule.

The averaging rule predicts the crossover interaction that is present in all ten graphs of Figure 2.8. The two-cue curve crosses over the three-cue one clearly in eight cases. Similarly, the single-cue curve crosses over the two- and three-cue curves

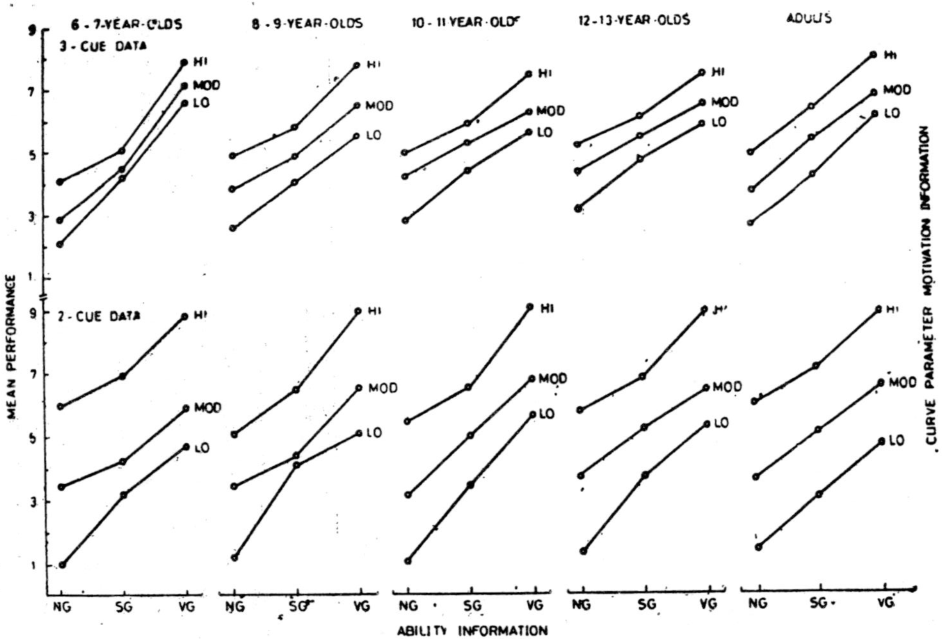

FIG. 2.7 : *Mean prediction of performance as a function of motivation and ability information for each of the five age groups. The upper and lower sets of curves are from the three-cue and two-cue designs, respectively. Data from Gupta and Singh, 1981; Figure 2.2. (Copyright 1981 by the American Psychology Association, Inc.) Reproduced with permission.*

in nine and ten cases, respectively. All statistical tests of cross-over interaction were statistically significant. Thus, it can be said that subjects averaged the three pieces of information in prediction of performance.

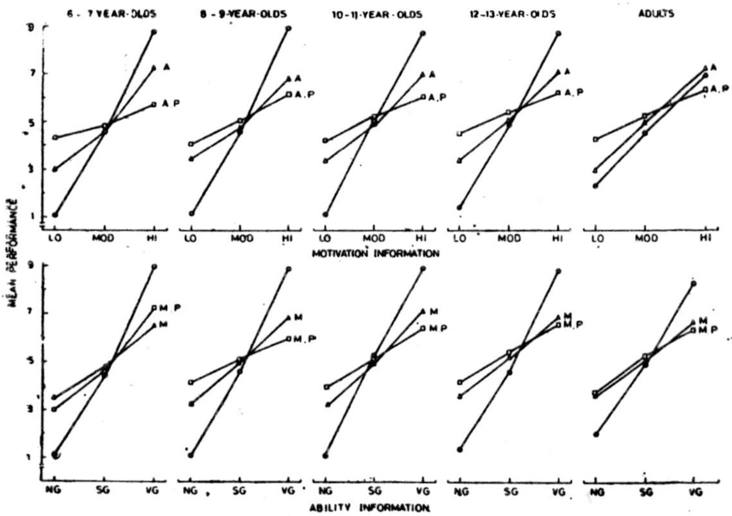

FIG. 2.8 *Distinguishing tests between alternative rules of information integration in prediction of performance at each of the five age levels. The upper sets of curves show how the subjects integrated information about ability (A), and Past Performance (P) with information about motivation (M). The lower sets of curves show how subject integrated information about motivation and past performance with ability information. The curves connected by circles, by triangles, and by squares are based on the main effect of the factor listed on the horizontal axis in single-, two-, and three-cue designs, respectively. Data from Gupta & Singh, 1981; Figure 2.3. (Copyright 1981 by the American Psychological Association, Inc.) Reproduced with permission).*

Information utilization

Developmental trends in capacity to utilize all three pieces of information were also examined. Only main effects from the individual subject analyses were considered (Anderson and Butzin, 1978). Most subjects of all ages except the youngest utilized all three pieces of information. In 6-7-year-old group, however, 5 subjects used just one cue, 5 used two cues, and the remaining 14 used all three cues.

Examination of the nature of cues used by the 6-7-year-old group disclosed an interesting information about the cultural difference hypothesis. The five children who used just one cue all used motivation, even though information about motivation appeared in the stimulus descriptions at different serial positions. Perhaps those children believed that motivation is all that is important for performance. Of the five subjects who used two cues, three utilized information about motivation and ability, and two utilized information about past performance and motivation. All these five children also used motivation information. In this way, all twenty four preoperational children considered motivation as a crucial determinant of performance. This indicates that belief in the power of trying to improve upon one's lot develops in Indian children at quite early age.

Conclusion

The primary finding of the research by Gupta and Singh is that prediction of performance from information about motivation and ability obeys an averaging rule. Not only adults but also preoperational children average relevant information when they predict performance. This result confirms the previous finding with adults (Singh et al., 1979), and extends the averaging process to children as young as six years of age. Therefore, prediction of performance by Indian students cannot be described as a multiplicative function of motivation and ability.

CULTURAL DIFFERENCE HYPOTHESIS

From the studies presented above, it is quite evident that prediction of performance from information about motivation and ability cannot be described by just one algebraic rule. In all studies of American students, judgments of future performance conformed rather well to the linear fan pattern which implies that Americans used a multiplying rule. On the contrary, all studies of Indian students obtained evidence for parallelism pattern which means that Indian subjects added or averaged information about motivation and ability. Distinguishing tests between adding and averaging rules further disclosed that the parallelism pattern was attributable to the equal weight averaging. Clearly, then, integration rules underlying prediction of performance are culture-specific: American students follow a multiplying rule; Indian students follow an equal-weight averaging rule.

Does the difference between the multiplying rule and the equal-weight averaging rule point to any important difference in cultural outlook between America and India ? For prediction of performance from information about motivation and ability, the following argument suggests at least one important social difference. According to the multiplying rule, effort or trying will be more effective with persons of high than low ability. Within a cultural system of attribution that obeys the multiplying rule, therefore, it will appear that persons of lower ability have less to gain by trying. In other words, persons with high ability can exercise more control over their performance than those with low ability. Given the achievement orientation of American culture, it is no surprise to see a multiplying rule emerge in the prediction of performance by American subjects, especially older school children and college students. From a social cultural view, however, the multiplying rule portrays an elitist orientation.

The equal-weight averaging rule, in contrast, implies that effort or trying will be equally effective with persons of low and high ability. Within the cultural system of attribution that obeys the equal-weight averaging rule, therefore, it will appear that a person of lower ability can gain as much by trying as a person of higher ability. The practice of keeping reserved seats in academic institutions and at work places for the down trodden people of Indian society clearly reflects this philosophy. From a social-cultural angle, therefore, the equal-weight averaging model for prediction of performance portrays a more egalitarian outlook. Perhaps students in India believe that each person, regardless of native ability, has equal opportunity to improve upon his or her lot. This egalitarian attitude is a healthy sign for progress in India, for Indian people have been described as high in dependency (Murphy, 1953 ; Pareek, 1968; Winter, 1969).

It should be emphasized that the equal-weight averaging rule for India and the multiplying rule for the United States rest on a very narrow cultural sample, namely, students. If the hypothesis of cultural-difference in social motivation has any merit, it would be expected to hold true with at least some subcultures within each country. Thus, some American subcultures would obey the multiplying rule just as the American subjects.

To the above, it may be added that the youngest children of the study by Kun et al., (1974) indeed obeyed the parallelism pattern just as the Indian subjects (Gupta and Singh, 1981; Singh et al., 1979). This additive rule for younger children was replaced by the multiplicative rule around 8-9 years of age. Maybe the multiplying orientation is stressed at home and school in the United States. If it is correct, then prediction of performance by American parents and school teachers would also be expected to obey the multiplying rule. On the contrary, Indian parents and school teachers would be expected to follow the equal-weight averaging rule.

According to Kun et al., (1974), the multiplying rule for older children and the adding rule for younger children reflect a difference in their cognitive capacity. But the present hypothesis of cultural difference in cognitive algebra suggests that two data patterns—parallelism and linear fan—denote different causal conceptions and social philosophy, and not necessarily the cognitive capacity. As a matter of fact, the parallelism pattern caused by the equal-weight averaging involves much more complex cognitive operations than the linear fan pattern produced by the multiplying rule.

The original hypothesis that the linear fan pattern obtained in American studies actually reflects a conjunctive-weight averaging process which led to the present line of inquiry by the author and his associates (Gupta and Singh, 1981; Singh et al., 1979) is still open. Accordingly, more extended studies of the cognitive algebra of performance attribution are needed. In future work, it would be useful to describe motivation and ability of the stimulus persons by at least two separate cues. This would require a four-factor design ($Motivation_1 \times Motivation_2 \times Ability_1 \times Ability_2$) which, together with the six two-cue sub-designs, should provide powerful distinguishing tests between multiplying and conjunctive-weight averaging rule.

It should be added that the adult subjects of the study by Singh et al., (1979) and by Gupta and Singh (1981) Note 2; were around 17-19 years of age. It is possible that multiplying-type causal conception develops in Indians at some later age. This possibility can be checked by extending age range and by using subjects from various sections of Indian society.

It deserves emphasis that diagnosis of real integration rule for information about motivation and ability has important educational and social implications. People who follow the multiplying rule and the equal-weight averaging rule may be expected to behave quite differently with persons varying in ability. For example, parents who obey the multiplying rule may spend more time with their high than low intelligent child. Similarly, teachers would be expected to encourage or help a high intelligent student more than a low intelligent student. At work places also, bosses may give more work facilities to a person high than low in work potential. A natural consequence of these practices would be that the "good" would become "better" and the "bad" would become "worse". On the contrary, people who obey the equal-weight averaging rule may provide persons of low and high ability with equal opportunities and facilities be it home, school, or work places. This may result in an egalitarian society which people ultimately aspire for. In this way, cognitive algebra may be useful in social planning and administration.

ALTERNATIVE HYPOTHESES

Can the difference between Indian and American results be explained in ways other than the cultural-difference hypothesis proposed above ? At least three other hypotheses may be suggested. First, perhaps subjects did not understand the instructions or tasks. Second, Indian subjects may lack the ability to use a multiplying rule. Finally, they may have simplified the experimental task as did American subjects in postdiction of motivation and ability (Anderson and Butzin, 1974). Let us examine the plausibility of these three alternative hypotheses.

Misunderstanding of instructions or task

In studies of information integration, experimenters usually take great pains to ensure understanding of the experimental task. Singh et al., (1979), therefore, gave a good deal of practice on the task, and also required the subjects to read the entire set of descriptions before beginning their actual judgments. In the study of Gupta and Singh (1981), the experimenter asked subjects to recall information about each stimulus student before rating. She also removed misunderstanding of task by giving detailed instructions and demonstration. Although subjects rated the stimuli thrice, the first replication was considered as additional practice and only the data from the second and third replications were analyzed. Moreover, the single subject analyses showed that most of the children took account of all pieces of information in a sensible way. Misunderstanding of the task thus seems most unlikely.

Inability to use multiplying rule

If Indian subjects lack the ability to use the multiplying rule in social perception, then evidence for multiplying-type rule should not be obtained at all. However, judgments of gift size from information about generosity and income of the donors, shown in Figure 2.9, exhibit linear fan shape. This experiment parallels that of Graesser and Anderson (1974) on Gift Size=Generosity ×Income, and exactly similar results are obtained.

The linear fan pattern in prediction of gift size shown in Figure 2.9 is highly reliable, for it invariably appeared in a series of six experiments performed by the author (Singh, Note 3) on subjects from the same population as in experiments by Singh et al., (1979). These experiments employed simple two-factor design similar to that of Graesser and Anderson as well as complex designs with one to four factors. Nevertheless, all experiments yielded clear linear fan pattern. Distinguishing

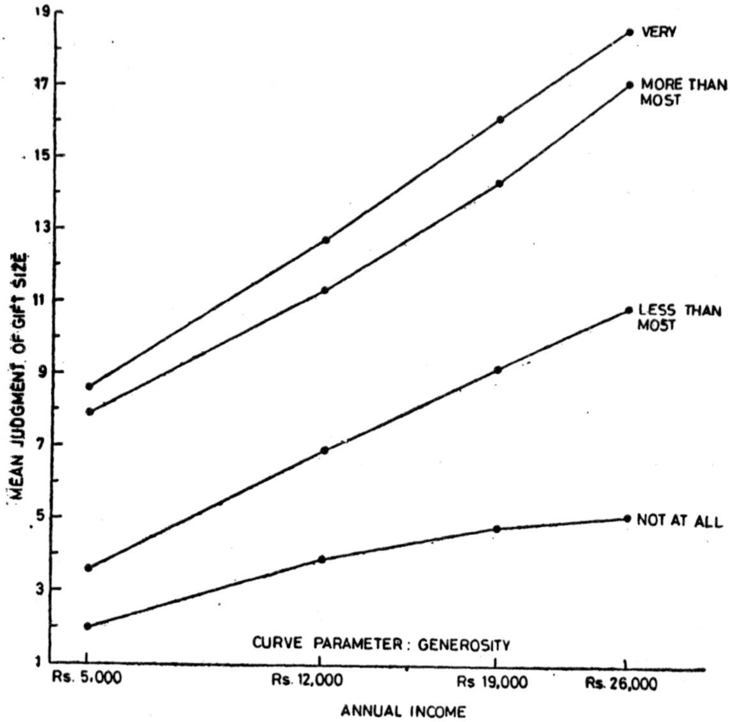

FIG. 2.9 *Mean judgments of gift size from information about generosity and income of the donors. The diverging linear fan supports the multiplying rule. Data from Singh, Note 2. (Copyright 1980 Ramadhar Singh.)*

tests further indicated that subjects indeed obeyed the multiplying rule. This clearly shows that Indian subjects are able to use the same integration rule as the Americans.

Evidence for multiplying process in attribution of gift size has an important methodological value. Singh et al., (1979) and Gupta and Singh (1981) employed single-, two-, and three-cue stimulus persons, but all the American investigators (Anderson and Butzin, 1974; Graesser and Anderson, 1974; Kun et al., 1974) employed only two-cue stimulus persons. One may thus argue that differences between American and Indian results arose out of the differences in stimulus presentation. Results from the gift size experiments help reject this possibility, for linear fan pattern was invariably obtained in experiments employing single-, two-, three-, and four-cue stimulus persons.

Another evidence against the hypothesis of lack of ability in Indians to use multiplying rule comes from another series of five experiments by the author (Singh, Note 4). Subjects received information about salary and competence of stimulus engineers and estimated how much influence those engineers exercised in getting their present job. Results from one experiment are shown in Figure 2.10 for purpose of illustration. The five salary curves show a nice convergence to the right, as though a dividing model, Influence=Salary÷Competence, was operative.

Singh, Palaniswamy, and Pradhan (1981) provide still another evidence against the lack of ability in Indians to employ multiplying rule. They constructed descriptions of hypothetical bus systems according to a Fare×Frequency of Service×Comfort factorial design and asked actual bus users to indicate how much they would like to travel in those buses. Factorial plots of liking ratings exhibited linear fan shape as required by the multiplying rule.

Results from these series of experiments on prediction and postdiction processes convincingly establish that Indian college students are able to use the multiplying and dividing rules whenever they are demanded by the experimental tasks. The hypothesis that Indian students lack ability to employ the multiplying rule is, therefore, not tenable.

Task simplification

When subjects are given complex tasks which may require multiplying or ratio rule, they sometimes tend to simplify them by adopting an adding-type rule. Anderson and Butzin (1974) suggested that task-simplification strategy may perhaps account for the mathematical inconsistency between prediction of performance and postdiction of motivation and ability. This tendency was suggested by Shanteau and Anderson (1972) as well as by Farkas and Anderson (1979) who failed to receive support for their multiplying and ratio models. As indicated earlier, it is possible that Indian students also simplified the multiplying task by adopting the adding-type integration strategy.

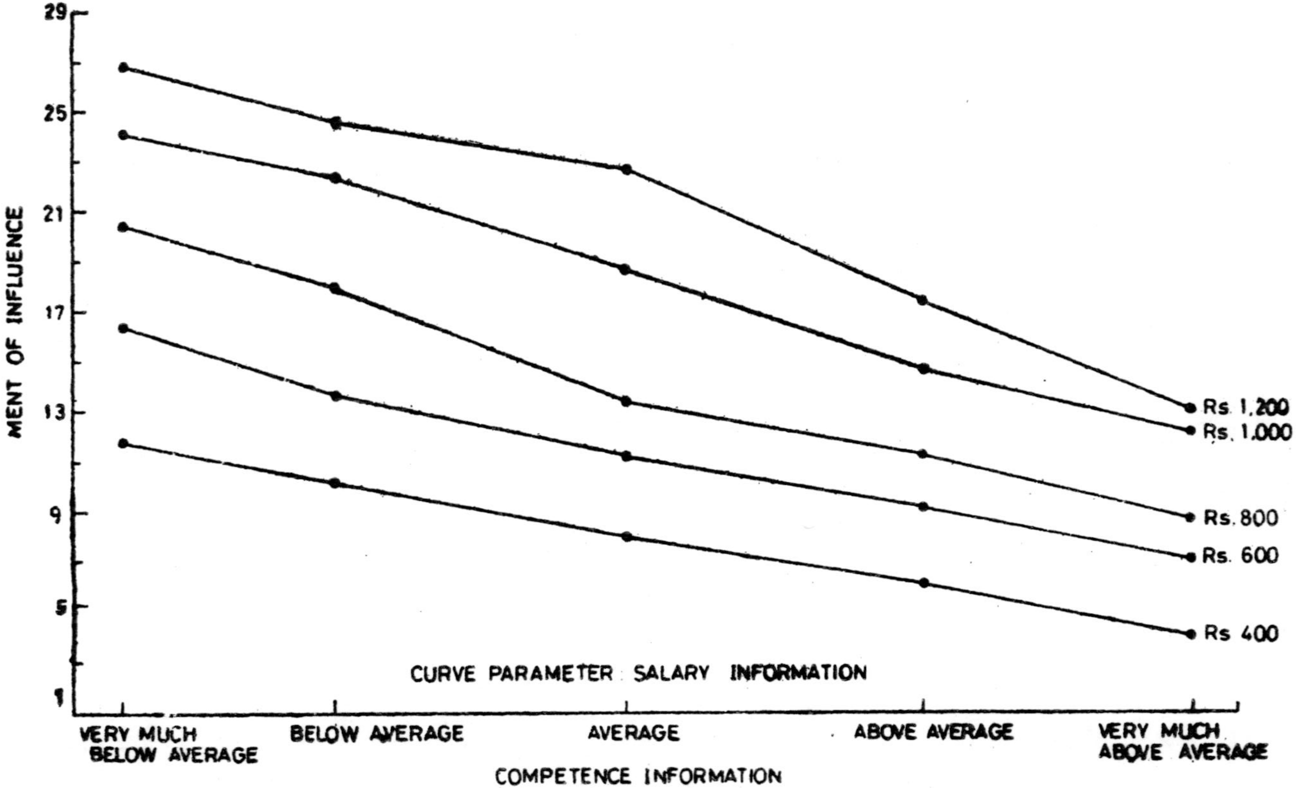

FIG. 2.10 : *Mean judgments of influence as a function of salary and competence information. The dividing rule predicts a fan of lines converging to the right. Data from Singh, Note 3. (Copyright 1980 Ramadhar Singh).*

The possibility of task simplification can also be rejected on the basis of the multiplying-type and dividing-type results yielded with Indian subjects (Singh, Note 3, Note 4; Singh et al., 1981). Furthermore, task simplification would be expected to yield an adding rule, and not the more complex averaging rule which has received support in experiments by Singh et al., (1979) and by Gupta and Singh (1981). It should also be mentioned that the author and his associates obtained strong evidence for the averaging rule in two other developmental studies of Indian children (Singh, Sidana, and Saluja, 1978a; Singh, Sidana, and Srivastava, 1978). There was no evidence for adding rule at all.

Task simplification does not appear to be the usual mode of information integration by Indian subjects. Two recent experiments on reward allocation have clearly revealed that subjects followed very complex process in distribution of reward. They first calculated equity ratios (Anderson, 1976b), using adding, dividing, and multiplying rules, and then averaged the equity ratios to decide fair reward for claimants. This happened in distribution of monetary reward (Singh, Note 5), and non-monetary rewards such as work facilities and praise time (Singh, Note 6). Although the allocation task was perhaps the most difficult and the equity integration model (Farkas and Anderson, 1979) was the most complex to follow, the subjects obeyed the equity integration model rather well. In fact, results from Indian subjects were much clearer than those from American subjects reported by Farkas and Anderson. The task simplification hypothesis would expect the subjects to follow a simple subtractive model instead of the more complex equity integration model. But this did not happen. Accordingly, the task simplification hypothesis cannot provide a parsimonious explanation for the equal-weight averaging process in prediction of performance.

Conclusion

From the preceding discussion, it is quite clear that the equal-weight averaging rule for prediction of performance by Indian subjects does not seem to be attributable to the subjects inappropriate understanding of the experimental task, their attempt to simplify it, or their inability to use the same integration rule as the Americans. It can, therefore, be concluded that the discrepancy between American and Indian results reflects a genuine difference in cultural outlook on how motivation and ability produce performance.

CONCLUDING COMMENTS

The research presented in this chapter indicates that prediction of performance from motivation and ability information obeys an averaging rule in India, and that the differences between Indians and Americans in this attributional task reflect true cultural differences. American students follow multiplying rule envisaged in most current behavioural theories of motivation, such as those of Hull and Tolman (see Anderson 1974b, p. 29), whereas Indian students obey an averaging rule consistent with the egalitarian philosophy and practices in India. Cognitive algebra employed in the two cultures thus directly bear upon the causal conceptions prevalent among the student populations of the two countries.

Cultural differences in social perception and cognition are no doubt difficult to study. The same physical stimuli may have different meanings in different cultures. Even if equal-interval scales for responses can be obtained, the number may not be comparable because the zero point and unit of such scales are always arbitrary, as with the Celsius and Fahrenheit scales. However, if cultures are compared with respect to psychological processes represented in integration rules, as illustrated here, many of these problems are automatically rendered insignificant.

An important advantage with the integration rules, it should be emphasized, is that they deal with patterns of responses, not the numerical value of single responses. This aspect is vital for crosscultural research. No a priori knowledge of value of stimuli or origin and unit of personal reference scales (Upshaw, 1969) is required. Groups as well as individuals are thus readily comparable with respect to the pattern in their judgments of stimuli constructed from factorial design. Search for integration rule also permits comparison of groups along the criteria of information utilization and information processing as already shown in work of the author and his associates. The author thus hopes that the present chapter will draw attention of Indian psychologists to the potential power that information integration approach (Dalal Singh, Nothe 2; Singh, Note 7) provides for experimental research in applied developmental, organizational and social psychology.

NOTES

1. A.K. Dalal, & R. Singh. An integration theoretical analysis of expected job attractiveness and satisfaction. Paper presented at the 67th session of the Indian Science Congress Association, Calcutta, 1980.
2. A.K. Dalal, & R. Singh. Serial position curve for integration of information about jobs. Working Paper. Ahmedabad : Indian Institute of Management, 1981.
3. R. Singh, Experiments on attribution of gift size. Unpublished data. Ahmedabad : Indian Institute of Management, 1981.
4. R. Singh, Consistency in social judgments of success in getting job, salary, influence, and competence. Unpublished data. Ahmedabad : Indian Institute of Management, 1981.
5. R. Singh, An information integration analysis of reward allocation. Paper presented at the 68th session of the Indian Science Congress Association, Varanasi, 1981.
6. R. Singh, Equity integration model applied to distribution of money, work facilities, praise time, and encouragement time. Working Paper. Ahmedabad : Indian Institute of Management, 1981.
7. R. Singh, Children's judgements of personal happiness. Research project sponsored by N.C.E.R.T. (1978-80). Ahmedabad : Indian Institute of Management, in progress.

REFERENCES

Anderson, N.H. Information integration theory : A brief theory. In D.H. Krantz, R.C. Atkinson, R.D. Luce, & P. Suppes (eds.), *Contemporary Developments in Mathematical Psychology* (Vol. 2). San Francisco : Freeman, 1974 a.

Anderson, N.H. Cognitive algebra : Integration theory applied to social attribution. In L. Berkowitz (ed.), *Advances in Experimental Social Psychology* (Vol. 7). New York : Academic Press, 1974 b.

Anderson, N.H. How functional measurement can yield validated interval scales of mental quantities. *Journal of Applied Psychology*, 1976 a, 61, 677-692.

Anderson, N.H. Equity judgments as information integration. *Journal of Personality and Social Psychology*, 1976 b, 33, 291-299.

Anderson, N.H. *Foundations of Information Integration Theory* (Vol. 1). New York : Academic Press, 1981, in press.

Anderson, N.H., & Butzin, C.A. Performance=Motivation×Ability : An integration-theoretical analysis. *Journal of Personality and Social Psychology*, 1974, 30, 598-604.

Anderson, N.H., & Butzin, C.A. Integration theory applied to children's judgments of equity. *Development Psychology*, 1978, 14, 593-606.

Farkas, A., & Anderson, N.H. Multidimensional inputs in equity theory. *Journal of Personality and Social Psychology*, 1979, **7**, 879-896.

Graesser, C.C., & Anderson, N.H. Cognitive algebra of the equation : Gift Size=Generosity×Income. *Journal of Experimental Psychology*, 1971, **103**, 692-699.

Gupta, M., & Singh, R. An integration-theoretical analysis of cultural and developmental differences in attribution of performance. *Developmental Psychology*, 1981, **17**, in press.

Heider, F. *The Psychology of Interpersonal Relations*. New York : Wiley, 1958.

Hull, C.L. *Principles of Behavior*. New York : Appleton Century-Crafts, 1943.

Kun, A., Parsons, J.E., & Ruble, D.N. Development of integration processes using ability and effort information to predict outcome. *Developmental Psychology*, 1974, **10**, 721-732.

Lampel, A.K., & Anderson, N.H. Combining visual and verbal information in an impression formation task. *Journal of Personality and Social Psychology*, 1968, **9**, 1-6.

Murphy, L.B. Roots of tolerance and tension in Indian child development. In G. Murphy (ed.), *In the Minds of Men*. New York : Basic Books, 1953.

Pareek, U. A motivational paradigm of development. *Journal of Social Issues*, 1968, **2**, 115-124.

Shanteau, J.C., & Anderson, N.H. Integration theory applied to the value of information. *Journal of Experimental Psychology*, 1972, **92**, 266-275.

Singh, R. Information integration theory applied to expected job attractiveness and satisfaction. *Journal of Applied Psychology*, 1975, **60**, 621-623.

Singh, R. Disciplinary judgments as information integration. *Journal of Social Psychology*, 1978, **104**, 197-206.

Singh, R., Bohra, K.A., & Dalal, A.K. Favourableness of leadership situations studied with information integration theory. *European Journal of Social Psychology*, 1979, **9**, 253-264.

Singh, R., Gupta, M., & Dalal, A.K. Cultural difference in attribution of performance: An integration-theoretical analysis. *Journal of Personality and Social Psychology*, 1979, **37**, 1342-1351.

Singh, R., Palaniswamy, S.P., & Pradhan, Y.P. An information integration theory analysis of attractiveness of bus systems. In N.K. Jaiswal (ed.), *Scientific Management of Transportation Systems*. Amsterdam: North-Holland, 1981.

Singh, R., Sidana, U.R., & Saluja, S.K. Playgroup attractiveness studied with information integration theory. *Journal of Experimental Child Psychology*, 1978a, **25**, 429-436.

Singh, R., Sidana, U.R., & Saluja, S.K. Integration theory applied to judgments of personal happiness by children. *Journal of Social Psychology*, 1978b, **105**, 27-31.

Singh, R., Sidana, U.R., & Srivastava, P. Averaging processes in children's judgments of happiness. *Journal of Social Psychology*, 1978, **104**, 123-132.

Upshaw, H.S. The personal reference scale: An approach to social judgment. In L. Berkowitz (ed.), *Advances in Experimental Social Psychology*, (Vol. 4). New York: Academic Press, 1969.

Winter, S.K. Case studies. In D.C. McClelland and D.G. Winter (eds.), *Motivation Economic Achievement*. New York: Basic Books, 1969.

THREE

Suresh Kanekar

ATTRIBUTION AND BEHAVIOUR

ATTRIBUTION seems to be the name of the research game in experimental social psychology in the decade of the seventies, as was dissonance in the sixties, and conformity, albeit less blatantly, in the fifties. Attribution theory and research were ushered in by the pioneer papers of Jones and Davis (1965) and Kelley (1967), although some seminal ideas regarding attribution can be found in the earlier writings of Heider (1944, 1946, 1958, cf. Harvey, Ickes, and Kidd, 1976, 1978). The predominant concern has been with attribution as an inference from behaviour, so that attribution is the effect or dependent variable while behaviour is the cause or independent variable. To a lesser extent, attribution has also been investigated as the cause or independent variable with behaviour as the effect or dependent variable. A third group of investigations appears to be concerned with attribution as an intervening variable. For the sake of precision, it should be noted that the distinction between attribution and behaviour is an ad hoc distinction under which behaviour refers to behaviour which excludes attribution. Attribution is of course part of the attributor's behaviour and the distinction is a matter of convenience rather than principle.

ATTRIBUTION AS AN INDEPENDENT VARIABLE

Attribution as a determinant of behaviour may be either direct or indirect. One can speak of direct attribution when the attributee receives a communication from the attributor, which describes a behavioural disposition on the part of the attributee, and the dependent measure involves the testing of the same behavioural disposition. Thus the attributee may be told that he is honest and then the dependent variable would be a measure of his honesty. One may speak of indirect attribution, on the other hand, when there is only a suggestion or implication, but no explicit communication, about the particular behavioural disposition involved in the dependent measure.

Direct attribution

There are apparently only five reports in the literature, which are concerned with behaviour as a function of direct attribution. Rosenbaum and his collaborators have been the pioneers of research on direct attribution, although they used the term "external commitment" (as distinguished from self-commitment cf. Deutsch and Gerard, 1955) for what is designated here as direct attribution. Rosenbaum and Zimmerman (1959) found that attribution of an attitude which was congruent with the subject's previously recorded attitude resulted in less change after exposure to a persuasive counter-communication as compared to the no attribution control condition. But, contrary to their expectations, attribution of an attitude which was incongruent with the previously recorded attitude did not facilitate change toward the persuasive counter-communication (which was in line with the incongruent attribution) as compared to the control condition. Rosenbaum and Franc (1960) were more successful and could report changes in the originally recorded attitude of the subject in increasing order as a result of congruent attribution, no attribution, and incongruent attribution. They argue that the ineffectiveness of incongruent attribution in the earlier study was probably due to the greater emotional involvement of the subjects in the attitudinal issue.

Munson and Kiesler (1974) also found that an incongruent direct attribution was able to bring about a change in the direction of the attribution. But the most dramatic demonstration of the effectiveness of direct attribution has been given by Miller, Brickman, and Bolen (1975) in two field experiments. In the first experiment, repeated attributions of neatness and tidiness to fifth-graders were successful in making them more neat and tidy in the classroom situation. In the second, repeated attributions of either the ability or the motivation to do well in mathematics had a significantly beneficial effect on the performance of second-graders in mathematics. What is even more crucial is the finding that in both experiments direct attribution was more effective than direct persuasion. Miller et al., suggest that persuasion is less effective because it implies negative attribution (a person should be what he is not), while attribution is more effective because it disguises persuasive intent.

None of the above four studies was designed specifically to identify the conditions which would either facilitate or inhibit the effectiveness of a direct attribution. This problem was the primary concern of Kanekar (1977). If attribution is effective because it disguises persuasive intent, a variation on the dimension of persuasive intent should result in differential effectiveness of the attribution. When an attributor does not know that the attributee is listening to him, the attribution cannot possibly have any persuasive intent (cf. Walster and Festinger, 1962). Thus an overheard attribution would be a pure *tact* in Skinnerian terminology (Bem, 1965, 1967, 1972; Skinner, 1953, 1957), while a *regular* attribution, with the attributor deliberately delivering the attribution to the attributee, would partake of the nature of *mand* to some extent, since there is obviously a possibility of persuasive intent in the latter situation.

Kanekar (1977) designed his experiment specifically to test the hypothesis that an overheard direct attribution should be more effective than a regular direct attribution because the overheard attributor would be seen as having no persuasive intent or ulterior motive and consequently as more trustworthy or credible than the regular attributor. The experiment was presented to the subjects (undergraduate male students at the University of Iowa) as a study of interpersonal judgment during which the attributor (a graduate student in clinical psychology) and the attributee (the subject) were to receive shocks, the intensity of which was to be determined by the receiver. The attributor predicted that the attributee would take either 70 volts (high attribution) or 30 volts (low attribution) of shock. The attributor also announced that he himself would take either 70 volts (high attributor's position) or 30 volts (low attributor's position) of shock. The attribution was either overheard (high attributor's trustworthiness) or regular (low attributor's trustworthiness). Thus the experiment had a 2×2 ×2 factorial design and the dependent measure was the voltage of shock that the attributee chose to receive. Such a measure would be called a behaviouroid measure in the terminology of Aronson and Carlsmith (1968), unlike the behavioural measure of Miller et al., (1975) and the paper-and-pencil measures of Rosenbaum and Zimmerman (1959), Rosenbaum and Franc (1960), and Munson and Kiesler (1974). (This distinction also should not be taken too seriously, like the distinction between attribution and behaviour. Strictly speaking, all the three measures are behavioural measures; the distinction probably serves to emphasize the differential commitment, cogency, or dependability that seems to be involved in the three kinds of measure).

Kanekar (1977) found that the attributees chose a higher voltage of shock in the high attribution condition than in the low attribution condition and also a higher voltage of shock in the high attributor's position condition than in the low attributor's position condition. The attributor's trustworthiness manipulation did not yield any effects at all. The particular experimental situation was contrived for several reasons. It was thought that subjects would not know what a voltage would mean in terms of the pain they could expect from the shock and so attribution as well as attributor's position were likely to be effective in this ambiguous situation. The attributor's position was communicated to the subject with the hope that this may strengthen the trustworthiness manipulation, since the attributor could intend to influence the attributee's decision so that it would compare favourably with his own. The attributor's expertise was established in order to make the attribution effective. But it appears that while the expertise of the attributor was successfully established as one may infer from the effectiveness of attribution, the trustworthiness manipulation was not successful, possibly precisely because of the success in establishing the expertise of the attributor. It is possible that while expertise was necessary to make the attribution effective, it was irrelevant to the effectiveness of the attributor's position. One could also wonder as to whether the overheard versus regular manipulation is effective only for persuasive communications under certain conditions (Walster and Festinger, 1962) and not for attributions, especially those from expert attributors. An orthogonal manipulation of expertise and trustworthiness with respect to both persuasion and attribution may yield interesting results (cf. Aronson and Golden, 1962).

It appears from the available evidence that direct attribution, in the absence of countervailing conditions, can bring about a change in the attributee's behaviour in the direction of the attribution. If you tell Johnny that he is a good boy, he is likely to behave like one, while if you suggest to him that he stutters, he could become a confirmed stutterer, as stuttering has been found to involve diagnosogenic factors (Johnson, 1959, 1961). Cooley (1902) refers to the reflected or looking-glass self to indicate how a person may accept or appropriate an idea about himself which comes from somebody else (cf. Mead, 1934). Direct attribution is perhaps the basic and common process that is involved in suggestion, hypnosis, and self-fulfilling prophecies (cf. Jones, 1977). An attribution apparently affects the response hierarchy of a person in such a manner as to increase the probability of the attribution relevant response at the cost of the alternative responses that are part of the hierarchy (Rosenbaum and Franc, 1960).

Indirect attribution

Indirect attribution refers to the situation wherein attribution is made with respect to one behavioural characteristic and the dependent measure involves a different behavioural characteristic. Previously Kanekar (1977) had included implied or inferred attribution and misattribution under the rubric of indirect attribution, but now it seems more appropriate to classify such cases under attribution as an intervening variable and to limit the category of indirect attribution to cases of explicit attribution as affecting behaviour which is not precisely the same as is covered by the attribution. There are not too many investigations of this genre available in the research literature.

The best example of indirect attribution is the study of Aronson and Mettee (1968) who gave their female subjects a false feedback as to the results of a personality test so as to induce either high or low self-esteem apart from the control condition. The subjects in the high self-esteem condition were given a generally positive appraisal ("generosity, good nature, and zest for living . . . . intellectually very mature"), while those in the low self-esteem condition were given a generally negative report ("very selfish person who clings to material things as a source of personal gratification and as an emotional crutch"). Since the dependent measure involved honesty, the appraisal did not at all make any reference to honesty, or moral behaviour, or "goodness" of conduct. The subjects were then given opportunities to be dishonest during a game of cards under conditions which appeared to make the detection of cheating impossible. More subjects from the low self-esteem condition cheated than from the high self-esteem condition. Thus cheating behaviour was affected by attributions which did not involve the mention of such behaviour (cf. Aronson and Carlsmith, 1962; Bramel, 1962; Wilson, 1965).

While direct attribution enhances the probability of the attribution-relevant response, such enhancing effect obviously can be generalized to a similar or related response. This apparently is the crucial aspect in indirect attribution. Generalization from maturity or generosity to honesty or from selfishness to dishonesty is naturally to be expected given the general nature of the social learning of ethical and cultural norms.

ATTRIBUTION AS AN INTERVENING VARIABLE

A series of fascinating studies began with the trail-blazing paper of Schachter and Singer (1962), in all of which conditions were so contrived as to induce a self-attribution which was generally nonveridical. In these studies, there is no explicit communication to the subject, which could be construed as an attribution, whether direct or indirect. The attributor and attributee are within the same skin, to use Bem's (1967) phrase, and the attribution is quite often inferred from the overt behaviour of the subject. The overt behaviour may itself be an overt self-attribution or it may be some other behaviour which is presumably mediated by self-attribution. In the former case, the studies could perhaps come under the category of attribution as a dependent variable, but for the present it may be convenient to classify all studies in which the attributor and attributee are one and the same person under attribution as an intervening variable and to use the categories of attribution as an independent and a dependent variable for situations in which the attributor and the attributee are in different skins.

Schachter and Singer (1962) found that subjects who were physiologically aroused with an injection of epinephrine tended to behave euphorically or angrily and rate themselves accordingly, depending upon the euphoric or angry behaviour of a confederate. Thus the self-attribution of euphoria or anger was determined by both physiological and environmental cues. Nisbett and Schachter (1966) gave their subjects a placebo before shocking them and half of them were told that the side effects of the pill would cause arousal symptoms such as palpitation, tremor, etc. These subjects thus could attribute shock-induced arousal symptoms to the pill and consequently were able to tolerate more intense shocks than the other subjects who could not make such an attribution. The actual greater tolerance of shocks by the experimental group of subjects was perhaps mediated by a self-attribution of greater ability to tolerate shocks which was a consequence of the misattribution of arousal symptoms to the pill (cf. Schachter, 1964; Schachter and Wheeler, 1962; Singer, 1963).

Valins (1966) gave a false heart-rate feedback to his male subjects while they were looking at slides of seminude females. Those slides to which the subjects thought they had responded with change in heart rate were liked by them more than those to which there was no such response. In a later study, Valins (1967) found that the above effect was more marked for emotional subjects than for unemotional subjects, consistent with his hypothesis that emotional and unemotional individuals differ with respect to the utilization of information concerning their internal reactions. Valins and Ray (1967) manipulated the false heart-rate feedback in such a way that the experimental subjects were led to believe that while electric shocks brought about a change in their heart rate, pictures of snakes did not. These experimental subjects later showed less fear and more approach behaviour when confronted with a live snake, as compared to control subjects (cf. Woll and McFall, 1979).

Davison and Valins (1969) tested the shock tolerance of their subjects three times. Before the second test, the subjects ingested a drug (really a placebo) and they were led to think that their tolerance had increased through the surreptitious halving of the shock intensities (so that the subject thought he was taking twice the shock he actually was receiving). After the second session, half of the subjects were told that they had actually received a placebo, whereas the other half continued to believe that they had received a real drug. The subjects who believed their increased tolerance in the second session was not due to the pill showed greater tolerance of shock in the third session than those who attributed their greater shock tolerance of the second session to the pill which was not supposed to be effective during the third session. Davison and Valins argued that behaviour changes which are believed to be brought about by oneself will be maintained to a greater degree than behaviour changes which are attributable to external forces or agents. In other words, as their data showed, self-attributed behaviour change is more likely to persist than drug-attributed change.

Ross, Rodin, and Zimbardo (1969) created a situation wherein subjects wrongly attributed their fear symptoms to noise and consequently showed less fear of shock as compared to subjects who did not make such a misattribution. Storms and Nisbett (1970) gave placebo pills to insomniac subjects who were advised to take them a few minutes before going to bed. Some were told that the pills would cause arousal and others were told that they would reduce arousal. As was predicted, arousal subjects got to sleep more quickly than they had on nights without pills, presumably because they attributed their arousal to the pills rather than to their emotions and consequently were less emotional. Similarly, relaxation subjects got to sleep less quickly than on other nights, presumably because they attributed unusual intensity to their emotions given that their arousal was high in spite of taking an arousal-reducing pill. These effects were precisely the opposite of the usual placebo or suggestion effects and Nisbett and Storms argue that the usual placebo effects are likely to be obtained with people who are naive with respect to their symptoms as well as drugs. For people who are familiar with their symptoms and the use of drugs, the opposite effects are more likely (cf. Kellog and Baron, 1975).

Rosenthal and Jacobson (1966, 1968) gave false information to classroom teachers about some randomly selected students in their classes to the effect that these students showed unusual potential for intellectual gains. Eight months later these experimental children showed significantly greater gains in IQ than the control subjects. Unlike in the study of Miller et al., (1975) who attributed high ability in mathematics to children who consequently improved their performance in mathematics, Rosenthal and Jacobson did not administer any attributions directly to the children. Apparently the teachers behaved differently with the children who were supposed to have a potential for intellectual gains as compared to other children and this differential behaviour might have induced self-attributions of intellectual ability which probably were responsible for the actual gains on the IQ test. The implication of this study is that the poor school performance of black and other underprivileged children in American schools is probably due to the fact that teachers expect them to perform poorly rather than due to inherent intellectual deficiencies. There is some controversy about the findings of Rosenthal and Jacobson (eg., Eysenck, 1973; Snow, 1969), but if the findings are dependably replicable, they have very serious implications for educational policy as well as for the unresolved issue of the influence of heredity on intellectual performance.

One of the most fascinating recent developments in experimental social psychology is the self-perception theory of Daryl J. Bem (1967, 1972). According to Bem's thesis, self-perception or an individual's ability to respond differentially to his own behaviour and its controlling variables is a product of social interaction. Skinner (1953, 1957) has discussed the limited resources available to the verbal community for training its members to "know themselves" and the fallibility of this training. For example, when the child is to be trained to describe its pain, the verbal community must teach him the correct response at the critical time when the private stimuli are impinging upon him. But the community does not have direct access to these private stimuli which have to be inferred on the basis of observable stimuli or responses. This analysis, according to Bem (1967), suggests that many of the self-descriptive statements that appear to be exclusively under the discriminative control of private stimuli may actually be partially controlled by the same accompanying public events as can be used by the verbal community to infer the individual's inner states. Thus just as an observer makes an inference about a person's feelings or attitudes on observing his behaviour and the circumstances of the behaviour, the person himself may infer his own inner states after observing his own behaviour and the conditions under which it has taken place.

Bem has shown that when a person has been trained to tell the truth under one light and to tell a lie under another light, later the person is more likely to believe himself when he sees himself talking under the truth light rather than the lie light (Bem, 1965, 1966). Bandler, Madaras, and Bem (1968) found that subjects reported shocks as more painful when they saw themselves escape the shocks rather than endure them, although the shocks were of the same intensity in the escaping and enduring conditions. Bem's self-perception analysis has given a devastating theoretical blow to the cognitive dissonance camp. With the help of what Bem calls interpersonal replications, Bem (1965, 1967) has shown that self-perception theory can account very well for the results of dissonance studies. The famous one-dollar and twenty-dollar experiment of Festinger and Carlsmith (1959) was, for example, subjected to an interpersonal replication in which subjects were asked to estimate Festinger and Carlsmith's subjects' attitudes after knowing about the latter's behaviour. The accurate estimations supported Bem's argument that, like an external observer, a person often estimates his own attitude as an inference from his own behaviour. One trusts oneself more if one thinks one is tacting rather than manding and one is more likely to see oneself as manding under high payment rather than under low payment. Bem has successfully extended his self-perception analysis to several other important findings of the dissonance research programme (Bem, 1972; cf. Greenwald, 1975).

ATTRIBUTION AS A DEPENDENT VARIABLE

By far the bulk of the attribution literature comes under this heading and in fact attribution theory is almost entirely concerned with attributions as consequences of behaviours (Jones, 1978, 1979; Jones and Davis, 1965; Jones, Kanouse, Kelley, Nisbett, Valins, and Weiner, 1972; Kelley, 1967, 1972, 1973; Ross, 1977, 1978; Weiner, 1974). Social psychologists have apparently progressed from crude person perception through impression formation to a systematic and sophisticated attributional approach. As Ross (1977) puts it, attribution theory deals with the attempts of ordinary people to understand the causes and implications of the events they witness. It focuses on two closely related tasks which a social observer faces. The first task is causal judgment: the observer tries to identify the cause or causes to which an event or outcome may be attributed. The second task is social inference: the observer of an event makes inferences about the attributes of relevant entities which may be either the dispositions of actors or the properties of situations to which these actors have responded. Recently a third task has also begun to receive some attention and this involves the prediction of outcomes and behaviour.

In investigating causal judgments, researchers have tried to study the factors which lead the observer to attribute an event to "internal" dispositions of the actor (e.g., motives, traits, or abilities) or to aspects of the "external" situation (e.g., group pressures, nature of the task, other environmental factors). As regards the second attribution task, i.e., the formation of social inferences, the research is concerned with how and why a subject determines that a particular behaviour reflects a personal disposition of the actor rather than some other factors. The third type of attribution task, i.e., the prediction of behaviour, would involve the prediction of future behaviour on the basis of present behaviour or the estimation of how typical or characteristic a particular behaviour would be in the relevant social group. As Ross (1977) points out, these three attribution tasks are obviously and intimately related and together they form an important basis for speculation about future events. All the three tasks can shed considerable light on the assumptions, strategies, and failures of the intuitive psychologist.

Against this backdrop of general attribution theory, the focus will now be shifted to two specific areas of programmatic research concerned with attribution of personality traits to an aggressor and his victim and with attribution of responsibility to a rape victim.

Aggression, retaliation, and attribution

Aggression is a phenomenon that has been studied in great depth by psychologists and other social scientists. There has not been a corresponding amount of investigation about the victims of aggression or about retaliation to aggression. The author and his colleagues have recently completed a series of studies which were concerned with the perception of an aggressor and his victim in relation to retaliation by the victim and other variables. The research has been long on data and short on theory, since it was primarily aimed at the investigation of norms or stereotypes regarding aggression and retaliation. In all the studies, subjects (undergraduate or graduate students in the city of Bombay) read a passage which described an incident of aggression and its consequence. The situation was artificial, simple, and aseptic one which avoided contamination with extraneous factors and facilitated the manipulation of the experimental variables. After reading the passage, subjects rated the aggressor or the victim on four seven-point rating scales representing intelligence, morality, adjustment, and likability, these dimensions were selected as being the most relevant and readily comprehensible to the layman.

When a victim of physical aggression does not retaliate in like manner, he could be perceived either as a coward who is afraid of counter-retaliation or as an idealist who is against aggression as well as retaliation as a matter of principle. Gandhi preached non-violence of the strong, which came out of conviction and moral courage, as against 'non-violence' of the weak, which arose out of fear. The latter was not non-violence in the real sense of the term and could be even considered as ethically inferior to violence from a retaliator.

.If the victim of aggression is weak, his choices of action are in practice more restricted than if he is strong. A strong victim can choose between retaliation and non-retaliation, while a weak victim has to consider the possibility of further aggression on the part of the aggressor. The perceiver's reconstruction of the action alternatives available to the actor (Jones and Davis, 1965) should lead to more favourable attributions to the non-retaliating victim when he is strong than when he is weak. A non-retaliating strong victim should be evaluated more positively than a retaliating strong victim because nobility is likely to be attributed to the former, while a non-retaliating weak victim should be evaluated less positively than a retaliating weak victim because cowardice is likely to be attributed to the non-retaliating weak victim.

Kanekar and Kolsawalla (1977a) tested the above hypothesis using the following passage for the manipulation of the relevant variables :

> Ramesh is a tall and strong (short and weak) young man. Sudhir is a young man of average height and build. Romesh and Sudhir, one day, were arguing in a restaurant over a political issue. In the heat of the argument, Sudhir lost his temper and slapped Ramesh on the face. Ramesh *slapped Sudhir in return* (did not say or do anything for a while) and then walked out of the restaurant.

The above passage, without italics and the words in parentheses, was used for the retaliating strong victim condition and by appropriate substitutions of the words in parentheses for the italicized words, the retaliating weak victim, the non-retaliating strong victim, and the non-retaliating weak victim conditions were obtained. On all the four dimensions, the non-retaliating victim was evaluated more positively than the retaliating victim, and the hypothesis as regards non-retaliation being perceived differentially in relation to the strength of the non-retaliator was not supported by the data.

Kanekar and Ahluwalia (1977), using the above situation, asked their subjects to rate the aggressor rather than the victim. Female subjects rated the aggressor lower on morality with a non-retaliating victim than with a retaliating victim and male subjects rated the aggressor lower on adjustment with a weak victim than with a strong victim. The results suggest that the evaluation of an aggressor by males is more affected by the victim's strength and less affected by the victim's retaliation as compared to females.

According to attribution theory, the more atypical a behaviour is, the more informative it is about the person or the more "correspondent" the inference is about the person (Jones and Davis, 1965; cf. Jones, 1978, 1979; Kelley, 1967, 1972, 1973). As stated in Kelley's (1972) augmentation principle, "If for a given effect, both a plausible inhibitory cause and a plausible facilitative cause are present the role of the facilitative cause in producing the effect will be judged greater than if it alone were present as a plausible cause for the effect" (p. 12). Engaging in atypical behaviour involves overcoming inhibitory causes, thus suggesting the presence of a strong disposition as a strong facilitative cause (Jones and Davis, 1965). Research on human aggression has generally shown that not only are males more aggressive than females but that females are less often the targets of aggression than are males (Frodi, Macaulay, and Thome, 1977; Maccoby and Jacklin, 1975). Since males and females are not similar in their aggressive behaviour, it is not surprising that social norms or stereotypes attribute aggressiveness to males and not to females (e.g., Stoppard and Kalin, 1978). A man hitting a woman displays atypical behaviour which probably involves the overcoming of some inhibition and consequently such a man may be considered more aggressive than a man who hits another man. A woman who elicits aggression from a man is also likely to receive more negative attributions than a male victim, because of the atypicality of her experience. She might have been really nasty to elicit such atypical aggression. A dog biting a man may not tell us much about either dog or man. But a man biting a dog may be more revealing about both animals because of the atypicality of the incident. Several studies have demonstrated the importance of behaviour typicality as a determinant of person perception (Jones and Harris, 1967; Jones, Worchel, Goethals, and Grumet, 1971; Lay, Burron, and Jackson, 1973; Mathes and Fiorito, 1978).

Kanekar, Nanji, Kolsawalla, and Mukerji (1981) studied the perception of an aggressor and a victim of aggression with reference to retaliation to aggression and sex differences. The nonretaliating victim received more positive ratings than the retaliating victim on all the four dimensions. Aggression against a female was perceived somewhat more negatively than aggression against a male. The female victim of male aggression as well as the male victim of female aggression tended to receive derogatory attributions. The fact that the female victim of a male aggressor was perceived more negatively than the male victim of a male aggressor appears to be especially significant for the atypicality hypothesis, since one would ordinarily expect a female victim to receive more sympathy than a male victim when the aggressor is a male because she is relatively less able to defend herself or to retaliate (cf. Schiff, Blackburn, Cohen, Furman, Jackson, Lapidos, Rotkin, and Thayer, 1980).

Kanekar, Duarte, and Kolsawalla (in press) studied the perception of a male agressor and a male victim of aggression with respect to age differences (24 vs. 46 years old) as well as retaliation. The non-retaliating victim received more positive ratings than the retaliating victim on all the four dimensions. The victim, especially if he was younger, was more positively evaluated when his aggressor was younger rather than older. The aggressor was more negatively evaluated with a non-retaliating rather than retaliating victim and the younger aggressor was evaluated more positively with a younger rather than older victim.

Kanekar, Mazumdar, Bulsara, and Kolsawalla (1979) found that the aggressor tended to be more positively evaluated when the victim was his superior rather than his subordinate, although this was not true of all conditions or of all dimensions. Perhaps more courage or idealism seems to be involved in aggression against a superior than against a subordinate. They also found as usual that the non-retaliating victim was rated more positively than the retaliating victim on all the four dimensions. Kanekar, Bulsara, Duarte, and Kolsawalla (1981) varied the aggressor-victim relationship as either friendly or unfriendly. The non-retaliating victim received more favourable ratings than the retaliating victim, especially from female subjects or within a friendly relationship. The unfriendly aggressor tended to receive less favourable ratings than the friendly aggressor, especially from male subjects. These findings suggest that aggression against a friend is perceived as less reprehensible and more justifiable than aggression against a disliked person. An intent to cause harm or injury is more likely to be assumed in the latter case than in the former. Consequently retaliation against a friendly aggressor may appear to be less justified than retaliation against an unfriendly aggressor.

Kanekar, Mazumdar, and Kolsawalla (1981) described the aggressor and the victim, both young men, as either physically attractive or unattractive. The non-retaliating victim received more positive ratings than the retaliating victim, especially from female subjects or with an attractive aggressor. While attractiveness tended to elicit positive evaluations for the victim, this was not generally true of the aggressor.

In the last study of this programme, Kanekar, Mazumdar, Pinto, Bulsara, and Kolsawalla (1981) varied the socio-economic status of the aggressor and his victim. Retaliation on the part of the victim had three levels : physical retaliation, verbal retaliation, and non-retaliation. On all of the four dimensions, the non-retaliator was rated more positively than both the physical and verbal retaliators. The verbal retaliator was evaluated more positively than the physical retaliator, though not on all dimensions. Surprisingly, the victim of low status was evaluated more positively than the victim of high status, while there was no such effect of status on the ratings of the aggressor.

The most dependable and significant finding of the research on the perception of an aggressor and his victim is that the non-retaliating victim was evaluated much more positively than the retaliating victim. Apparently, people do not always consider physical retaliation as the proper response to physical aggression (cf. Brown and Tedeschi, 1976). Non-violence or non-retaliation is considered noble and this finding may be of considerable importance for interpersonal, intergroup, and even international relations. People often behave as they think they are expected to behave, as has been cogently shown by the studies on direct attribution. One crucial consideration in this context is that while people tend to behave in accordance with what is attributed to or expected of them, there may be either individualistic or pluralistic ignorance about social norms and expectations (cf. Cantril, 1958; Schanck, 1932). Thus it is possible that people or nations often retaliate against verbal or physical aggression because such retaliation is considered socially desirable or de rigueur. One puts a premium on the saving of face. Even at the present stage of human civilization, the wielding of the big stick and gunboat diplomacy are salient features of international affairs. Well publicized social sanction for non-retaliation (as well as non-aggression) may prevent escalation of hostilities between nations as well as persons (cf. Blumenthal, Chadiha, Cole, and Jayaratne, 1975; Feshbach, 1971; Lincoln and Levinger, 1972; Pelton, 1975).

The results of the above studies seem to be broadly consistent with attribution theory according to which atypical behaviour is more informative about a person than is typical behaviour. In fact, polarization of attributions could probably be used as a criterion for determining the typicality of the behaviours on which the attributions are based.

Attribution of responsibility

Research on attribution of responsibility got under way with Walster's (1966) finding that the same behaviour was attributed greater responsibility when the consequences were severe rather than trivial (cf. Walster, 1967). Attribution of responsibility has been investigated in different situations with emphasis on accidents and crimes (cf. Brewer, 1977; Bulman and Wortman, 1977; Fishbein and Ajzen, 1973). In the recent years there seems to have been a sort of convergence on the issue of attributing responsibility to a rape victim for her own rape. The author and his colleagues have conducted a series of studies in this area with undergraduate and graduate students of the University of Bombay as their subjects.

More than any other crime, a rape is likely to raise the question of the responsibility of the victim for the crime that is committed against her. Even now there are people who believe that a woman just cannot be 'raped' without her consent. Some of these people, if pressed hard, may fall back on the concept of unconscious consent which of course puts the matter safely beyond the pale of independent empirical confirmation, since the very fact of rape can be circularly cited as evidence of the unconscious desire to be raped.

The present author got involved in this research area when his disbelief was provoked by the reasoning and results of Jones and Aronson (1973). According to Lerner (1977; Lerner and Miller, 1978), people tend to believe in a just world where one gets what one deserves and one deserves what one gets. If something (pleasant or unpleasant) happens to a person, he is likely to be perceived as deserving it either because his character merits the (good or bad) outcome or because his behaviour is responsible for the outcome. Jones and Aronson (1973) extended this reasoning to argue that if a person's character cannot be perceived as meriting an evil outcome, the person (i.e., his behaviour) is more likely to be blamed or held responsible for his misfortune. They made "the rather startling prediction that if a disaster befalls an individual, more fault is attributed to that victim if he is a respectable person than if he is less respectable" (p. 415). Their results supported their reasoning by showing that if the victim of a rape was described as a married woman or a virgin (more respectable victim), she was held more at fault or responsible for her own rape than if she was described as a divorcee (less respectable victim).

Jones and Aronson's reasoning implies that a person's character and his behaviour are perceived by people to be independent of each other. To test their hypothesis in the Indian situation, Kanekar and Kolsawalla (1977b) used in their case reports five levels of respectibility, viz., an unmarried virgin, a married woman, a widow, a divorcee, and a prostitute, as verified by a separate investigation (Kanekar and Kolsawalla, in press). Kanekar and Kolsawalla (1977b) found the difference in fault or responsibility attributed to the rape victim with respect to her respectability to be roughly in the direction opposite to Jones and Aronson's findings, *but the* effect of respectability was not even marginally significant. Also while Jones and Aronson found no sex differences in the attribution of responsibility to the rape victim, Kanekar and Kolsawalla (1977b) found their male subjects attributing greater responsibility to the victim than the female subjects.

The differences in the above two studies do not appear to be due to cultural differences. Most, though not all, studies in North America suggest that males tend to attribute greater responsibility to the rape victim than do females (Calhoun, Selby, Cann, and Keller, 1978; Calhoun, Selby, and Warring, 1976; Cann, Calhoun, and Selby, 1979; Feild, 1978; Selby, Calhoun, and Brock, 1977; Seligman, Brickman, and Koulack, 1977; cf. Gold, Landerman, and Bullock, 1977; Jones and Aronson, 1973; Krulewitz and Nash, 1979; Krulewitz and Payne, 1978; Paulsen, 1979). This is what one would expect, the crime being one that can be committed only by males against females. As regards respectability, Smith, Keating, Hester, and Mitchell (1976) varied the rape victim to be either a topless/bottomless dancer, a social worker, or a Catholic nun, and she was either acquainted or unacquainted with her assailant. They found that in the acquainted condition the dancer was attributed the greatest and the nun the least amount of responsibility. Jones and Aronson's (1973) findings regarding respectability and responsibility are apparently difficult to replicate (Kahn, Gilbert, Latta, Deutsch, Hagen, Hill, McGaughey, Ryen, and Wilson, 1977; Paulsen, 1979).

Sexual provocativeness of the rape victim is an obvious variable which would be expected to be directly related to the victim's responsibility for her own rape. But this variable has not been much used in attribution studies, possibly because of its transparent importance (Scroggs, 1976). Kanekar and Kolsawalla (1980) described the rape victim as either married or divorced, either very good-looking or not at all good-looking, and either dressed or not dressed in a sexually provocative manner. Male subjects held the rape victim more responsible than did female subjects and the provocative victim was held more responsible than the unprovocative victim. The differences between male subjects and female subjects were significant only for marginal or intermediate cases where respectability and provocativeness were not consistent in giving a completely positive or negative picture of the victim. Female subjects held the provocative divorced victim more responsible for her rape than the provocative married victim. Physical attractiveness of the victim did not at all affect the attributions of responsibility.

More recently, Kanekar and Kolsawalla (1981) varied the rapist's respectability (married vs. divorced) along with the victim's respectability and provocativeness. While provocativeness of the victim showed the expected main effect, there was also an interaction among subject's sex, victim's respectability, and victim's provocativeness. Female subjects held the unprovocative divorced victim more responsible for her rape than the unprovocative married victim. Also, there was no main effect of subject's sex in this study as there was in the previous two investigations (Kanekar and Kolsawalla, 1977b, 1980). Respectability of the rapist had no effect at all on the attributions of respectability to the rape victim (cf. Barnett and Feild, 1978; Landy and Aronson, 1969). Kanekar, Kolsawalla, and D'Souza (in press, study I) varied the rapist's and victim's status (upper middle class vs. lower working class) along with victim's provocativeness. While the provocative victim was held more responsible for the rape than the unprovocative victim, this effect of provocativeness was significant only with male subjects judging a low-status victim and with female subjects judging a high-status victim.

In the matter of attributing responsibility to the rape victim, it is perhaps useful to make an explicit distinction between causal responsibility and moral responsibility. This distinction does not have to be limited to the incident of rape. For example, a blind man may be causally, but not morally, responsible for his falling into a ditch, whereas an inebriated man would be held morally responsible for doing the same. It appears that moral responsibility implies causal responsibility but not the other way around, because causal responsibility is necessary but not sufficient for establishing moral responsibility. A physically attractive woman is perhaps more likely to be raped than an unattractive woman; so also is a woman walking in a bikini on a lonely road as compared to a fully dressed woman. In the former case one is dealing with causal responsibility and in the latter case with moral responsibility. It should be noted that the distinction is firmly within the attributional perspective and as such is a psychological, rather than a logical, distinction.

Calhoun, Selby, Cann, and Keller (1978) found that the more attractive victim of a rape was perceived as playing a somewhat greater role in her own rape than the less attractive victim. This perceived role was defined by a combination of measures on three items which required judgment of the extent to which her behaviour precipitated the assault, the extent to which she is "the kind of person who gets herself into these types of situations", and the extent to which the victim's appearance contributed to the likelihood of her being raped. Separate scores on these three items were not reported. While these items do not appear to limit themselves purely to causal responsibility, they together do seem to be loaded in that direction since none of the items refers to blame or fault in an explicit manner. This argument receives support from the fact that the physically attractive victim was accorded a higher degree of social acceptance (as measured by six other items) than the unattractive victim, even though the former was attributed a greater role in her own rape than the latter.

Seligman, Brickman, and Koulack (1977) have reported results that seem to be relevant to the proposed distinction between causal and moral responsibility. They also used photographs to manipulate the physical attractiveness of the rape victim, as did Calhoun et al., (1978). Seligman et al., (1977) found that the more attractive victim was perceived to be "more likely to be raped" than the less attractive victim. With respect to another item which was concerned with how much the victim was "to blame for the incident", there was no significant difference related to attractiveness. A third item brought out the fact that the unattractive victim must have "somehow provoked the rape" more than the attractive victim. Seligman et al., (1977) argue that a physically unattractive victim, being a less likely victim, is attributed greater responsibility for the crime in the sense of having provoked it. They explain the absence of any differences on the measure of blame in relation to attractiveness with the argument that blame refers to general causality and the provoke measure refers to specific actions on the part of the victim. What is even more intriguing is their earlier statement that in their study "the terms responsibility, provoke, and blame have been assumed to refer to the *causes* of a crime's occurrence rather than to the *moral* or legal aspects involved" (p. 560, italics added).

What is crucial is of course whether the subject's perceptions and attributions are indifferent to the distinction between causal and moral responsibility. It is argued here that blame involves moral responsibility and consequently no differences were found on this variable by Seligman et al., between the attractive and unattractive victims of rape. The provoke measure, which incidentally appears to be essentially similar to the first item of Calhoun et al., (1978), perhaps lies somewhere between the other two items with respect to moral responsibility as perceived by the subjects. The theory of "just world" as stated by Lerner (1977; Lerner and Miller, 1978) requires the 'blaming' of victims for their misfortunes so that the perceiver can continue to believe in justice. The blaming apparently implies attribution of moral responsibility. This is not recognised by Seligman et al., although they interpret their results in the light of the "just world" theory. Since attractiveness 'explains' the rape of the attractive victim but not of the unattractive victim, provocation is inferred to 'explain' ('justify'?) the rape of the unattractive victim (cf. Seligman, Paschall, and Takata, 1974).

Kanekar, Kolsawalla, and D'Souza (in press) used a subtle measure to operationalize the causal responsibility of the rape victim. The subjects read a case report of a rape and then were asked to indicate the likelihood of a rape in the given circumstances, assuming that they had all the relevant information except for the occurrence of the rape itself. This item replaced the item used in all the previous studies which required subjects to indicate how much they considered the crime to be the victim's fault. While fault was assumed to represent moral responsibility, variations on the likelihood measure as related to the variations in the description of the rape victim were assumed to represent differential attributions of causal responsibility to the rape victim, who was varied on marital status, physical attractiveness, and sexual provocativeness. Greater likelihood of rape was indicated with a provocative, rather than unprovocative, victim and female subjects indicated greater likelihood of rape than did male subjects in the case of a physically unattractive victim.

The findings of the five studies (Kanekar and Kolsawalla, 1977b, 1980, 1981; Kanekar, Kolsawalla, and D'Souza, in press) suggest some tentative generalizations. Provocativeness of the rape victim affects both victim's attributed fault and perceived likelihood of rape. Victim's marital status affects her fault but not the likelihood of her rape, while victim's attractiveness affects the likelihood of her rape but not her fault. Also while male subjects tend to attribute greater fault to the victim then female subjects at least in some conditions, female subjects indicate greater likelihood of rape than male subjects at least for an unattractive victim.

While the above findings are not precisely consistent with expectations, they do appear to suggest the heuristic usefulness of a theoretical distinction between causal and moral responsibility as represented by the likelihood and fault measures in the rape situation. Krulewitz and Payne (1978) found that female subjects attributed more "responsibility" to the rape victim than did male subjects. On the other hand, female subjects considered the rape victim as more "moral" and more "respectable" than did male subjects. There was no significant difference between male and female subjects in "blame" attributed to the victim. Krulewitz and Nash (1979) have also found their female subjects attributing greater "responsibility" to the rape victim than their male subjects and again there was no significant difference between male and female subjects in "blame" attributed to the victim. On the measure of victim's "fault" there was no main effect of subject's sex. Krulewitz and Nash (1979) suggest that *blame* and *fault* are concepts that imply moral wrongdoing and as such are pejorative in connotation. By comparison, responsibility may imply causal involvement without specifying "motive" (p. 571, original italics). The "responsibility" measured by Krulewitz and her colleagues is apparently construed by them as causal responsibility and thus is roughly like the likelihood measure of the previously reported study.

The findings of Kanekar, Kolsawalla, and D'Souza (in press), apart from their relevance to a distinction between causal and moral responsibility, also suggest the greater use of defensive attribution (e.g. Chaikin and Darley, 1973) on the part of female subjects as compared to male subjects. In Study I, the high-status victim was closer to the subjects in social status than the low-status victim. Male subjects apparently tended to condone provocativeness of the victim when she was similar to them in social status and so was more likely to elicit sympathy or consideration than a low-status victim. For female subjects, the rape of a low-status victim is less likely to be threatening than that of a victim who is similar to them in social status. The low status of the victim by itself may be an explanation of the event, but provocativeness becomes salient and weighty as a contributory factor in the rape of a high-status victim, thereby minimizing the subjective probability of the attributor herself being similarly victimized. In Study II, female subjects, who would be more likely to consider themselves as attractive rather than unattractive, were probably minimizing the subjective probability of finding themselves in a similar plight by indicating a high likelihood of rape in the case of an unattractive victim (cf. Seligman et al., 1977).

While female subjects tend to disassociate themselves from the possibility of their own becoming rape victims, male subjects tend to have more sympathy for the rapist than female subjects, as is often shown by the punishment recommended to the rapist as well as the fault attributed to the victim (e. g., Kanekar and Kolsawalla, 1980). But while men are more likely than women to hold rape victims morally responsible for their own rape, this apparently does not hold when the issue is of causal responsibility. The differences in the perceptions of men and women of the rape situation have obvious practical implications for the legal and social treatment of the rapist and his victim (cf. Sealy and Wain, 1980).

CONCLUDING REMARKS

A selective survey of attribution theory and research, along with a half-hearted attempt to provide the same with a systematic perspective was presented in the previous sections. Unfortunately there has been an overwhelming emphasis on attribution as a consequence of behaviour to the relative neglect of attribution as a determinant of behaviour. Bem (1968, 1972) seems to be more confident about behaviour determining attribution rather than the reverse relationship. But there seems to be sufficient evidence available by now which clearly shows that attributions can bring about significant changes in behaviour (e.g., Miller et al., 1975). While the theoretical issues are rather complex and not very easily amenable to a satisfactory resolution which would account for all the findings, one may venture to make the somewhat oversimplified suggestion that attributions and behaviours probably form a chain of events such that, depending upon what part of the chain is examined, one may find attribution either as a cause of behaviour or its consequence. What is apparently needed for significant theoretical advances as well as practical applications is more research on attribution as an independent and an intervening variable.

REFERENCES

Aronson, E., & Carlsmith, J.M. Performance expectancy as a determinant of actual performance. *Journal of Abnormal and Social Psychology*, 1962, **65**, 178-182.

Aronson, E., & Carlsmith, J.M. Experimentation in social psychology. In G. Lindzey & E. Aronson (eds.), *The Handbook of Social Psychology*, (2nd ed., Vol. 2). Reading, Massachusetts: Addison-Wesley, 1968.

Aronson, E., & Golden, B.W. The effect of relevant and irrelevant aspects of communicator credibility on opinion change. *Journal of Personality*, 1962, **30**, 135-146.

Aronson, E., & Mettee, D.R. Dishonest behaviour as a function of differential levels of induced self-esteem. *Journal of Personality and Social Psychology*, 1968, **9**, 121-127.

Bandler, R.J., Jr., Madaras, G.R., & Bem, D.J. Self-observation as a source of pain perception. *Journal of Personality and Social Psychology*, 1968, **9**, 205-209.

Barnett, N.J., & Feild, H.S. Character of the defendant and length of sentence in rape and burglary crimes. *Journal of Social Psychology*, 1978, **104**, 271-277.

Bem, D.J. An experimental analysis of self-persuasion. *Journal of Experimental Social Psychology*, 1965, **1**, 199-218.

Bem, D.J. Inducing belief in false confessions. *Journal of Personality and Social Psychology*, 1966, **3**, 707-710.

Bem, D.J. Self-perception: An alternative interpretation of cognitive dissonance phenomena. *Psychological Review*, 1967, **74**, 183-200.

Bem, D.J. Attitudes as self-descriptions: Another look at the attitude-behaviour link. In A.G. Greenwald, T.C. Brock, & T.M. Ostrom (eds.), *Psychological Foundations of Attitudes*, New York: Academic Press, 1968.

Bem, D.J. Self-perception theory. In L. Berkowitz (ed.), *Advances in Experimental Social Psychology* (Vol. 6). New York : Academic Press, 1972.

Blumenthal, M.D., Chadiha, L.B., Cole, G.A., & Jayaratne, T.E. *More about Justifying Violence: Methodological Studies of Attitudes and Behaviour*. Ann Arbor, Michigan: Institute for Social Research, 1975.

Bramel, D. A dissonance theory approach to defensive projection. *Journal of Abnormal and Social Psychology*, 1962, **64**, 121-129.

Brewer, M.B. An information-processing approach to attribution of responsibility. *Journal of Experimental Social Psychology*, 1977, **13**, 58-69.

Brown, R.C., Jr., & Tedeschi, J.T. Determinants of perceived aggression. *Journal of Social Psychology*, 1976, **100**, 77-87.

Bulman, R.J., & Wortman, C.B. Attributions of blame and coping in the "real world" : Severe accident victims react to their lot. *Journal of Personality and Social Psychology*, 1977, **35**, 351-363.

Calhoun, L.G., Selby, J.W., Cann, A., & Keller, G.T. The effects of victim physical attractiveness and sex of respondent on social reactions to victims of rape. *British Journal of Social and Clinical Psychology*, 1978, **17**, 191-192.

Calhoun, L.G., Selby, J.W., & Warring, L.J. Social perception of the victim's causal role in rape: An exploratory examination of four factors. *Human Relations*, 1976, **29**, 517-526.

Cann, A., Calhoun, L.G., & Selby, J.W. Attributing responsibility to the victim of rape: Influence of information regarding past sexual experience. *Human Relations*, 1979, **32**, 57-67.

Cantril, H. *The Politics of Despair*. New York : Basic Books, 1958.

Chaikin, A.L., & Darley, J.M. Victim or perpetrator? Defensive attribution of responsibility and the need for order and justice. *Journal of Personality and Social Psychology*, 1973, **25**, 268-275.

Cooley, C.H. *Human Nature and the Social Order*. New York : Charles Scribner's Sons, 1902.

Davison, G.C., & Valins, S. Maintenance of self-attributed and drug-attributed behaviour change. *Journal of Personality and Social Psychology*, 1969, **11**, 25-33.

Deutsch, M., & Gerard, H.B. A study of normative and informational social influences upon individual judgment. *Journal of Abnormal and Social Psychology*, 1955, **51**, 629-636.

Eysenck, H.J. *The Inequality of Man.* London: Temple Smith, 1973.

Feild, H.S. Attitudes towards rape: A comparative analysis of police, rapists, crisis counsellors, and citizens. *Journal of Personality and Social Psychology*, 1978, **36**, 156-179.

Feshbach, S. Dynamics and morality of violence and aggression: Some psychological considerations. *American Psychologist*, 1971, **26**, 281-292.

Festinger, L., & Carlsmith J.M. Cognitive consequences of forced compliance. *Journal of Abnormal and Social Psychology*, 1959, **58**, 203-210.

Fishbein, M. & Ajzen, I. Attribution of responsibility: A theoretical note. *Journal of Experimental Social Psychology*, 1973, **9**, 148-153.

Frodi, A., Macaulay, J., & Thome, P.R. Are women always less aggressive than men? A review of the experimental literature. *Psychological Bulletin*, 1977, **84**, 634-660.

Gold, A.R., Landerman, P.G., & Bullock, K.W. Reactions to victims of crime: Sympathy, defensive attribution, and the just world. *Social Behavior and Personality*, 1977, **5**, 295-304.

Greenwald, A.G. On the inconclusiveness of "crucial" cognitive tests of dissonance versus self perception theories. *Journal of Experimental Social Psychology*, 1975, **11**, 490-499.

Harvey, J.H., Ickes, W.J., & Kidd, R.F. (eds.), *New Directions in Attribution Research* (2 Vols). Hillsdale, New Jersey: Lawrence Erlbaum Associates, 1976, 1978.

Heider, F. Social perception and phenomenal causality. *Psychological Review*, 1944, **51**, 358-374.

Heider, F. Attitudes and cognitive organization. *Journal of Psychology*, 1946, **21**, 107-112.

Heider, F. *The Psychology of Interpersonal Relations.* New York: Wiley, 1958.

Johnson, W. *The Onset of Stuttering: Research Findings and Implications.* Minneapolis : University of Minnesota Press, 1959.

Johnson, W. *Stuttering and What You Can Do About It.* Minneapolis: University of Minnesota Press, 1961.

Jones, C., & Aronson, E. Attribution of fault to a rape victim as a function of respectability of the victim. *Journal of Personality and Social Psychology*, 1973, **26**, 415-419.

Jones, E.E. Update of "From acts to dispositions : The attribution processs in person perception." In L. Berkowitz (ed.), *Cognitive Theories in Social Psychology.* New York: Academic Press, 1978.

Jones, E.E. The rocky road from acts to dispositions. *American Psychologist*, 1979, **34**, 107-117.

Jones, E.E., & Davis, K.E. From acts to dispositions : The attribution process in person perception. In L. Berkowitz (ed.), *Advances in*

Experimental Social Psychology (Vol. 2). New York: Academic Press, 1965.

Jones, E.E., & Harris, V.A. The attribution of attitudes. *Journal of Experimental Social Psychology*, 1967, **3**, 1-24.

Jones, E.E., Kanouse, D.E., Kelley, H.H., Nisbett, R.E., Valins S., & Weiner, B. *Attribution: Perceiving the Causes of Behaviour*. Morristown, New Jersey : General Learning Press, 1972.

Jones, E.E., Worchel, S., Goethals, G.R., & Grumet, J.F. Prior expectancy and behavioural extremity as determinants of attitude attribution. *Journal of Experimental Social Psychology*, 1971, **7**, 59-80.

Jones, R.A. *Self-fulfilling Prophecies ; Social, Psychological, and Physiological Effects of Expectancies*. Hillsdale, New Jersey: Lawrence Erlbaum Associates, 1977.

Kahn, A., Gilbert, I.A., Latta, R.M., Deutsch, C., Hagen, R., Hill, M., McGaughey, T., Ryen, A.N., & Wilson, D.W. Attribution of fault to a rape victim as a function of respectability of the victim: A failure to replicate or extend. *Representative Research in Social Psychology*, 1977, **8**, 98-107.

Kanekar, S. Decision as a function of attribution and attributor's position. *Journal of Social Psychology*, 1977, **102**, 117-123.

Kanekar, S., & Ahluwalia, R.B. Perception of an aggressor as a function of the victim's strength and retaliation. *European Journal of Social Psychology*, 1977, **7**, 505-507.

Kanekar, S., Bulsara, R.M., Duarte, N.T., & Kolsawalla, M.B. Perception of an aggressor and his victim as a function of friendship and retaliation. *Journal of Social Psychology*, 1981, in press.

Kanekar, S., Duarte, N.T., & Kolsawalla, M.B. Perception of an aggressor and his victim in relation to age and retaliation. *Human Relations*, in press.

Kanekar, S., & Kolsawalla, M.B. The nobility of nonviolence: Person perception as a function of retaliation to aggression. *Journal of Social Psychology*, 1977, **102**, 159-160. (a).

Kanekar, S., and Kolsawalla, M.B. Responsibility in relation to respectability. *Journal of Social Psychology*, 1977, **102**, 183-188. (b).

Kanekar, S., and Kolsawalla, M.B. Responsibility of a rape victim in relation to her respectability, attractiveness, and provocativeness. *Journal of Social Psychology*, 1980, **112**, 153-154.

Kanekar, S., & Kolsawalla, M.B. Factors affecting responsibility attributed to a rape victim. *Journal of Social Psychology*, 1981, in press.

Kanekar, S., & Kolsawalla, M.B. Sex and respectability: The double standard, Indian style. *Indian Journal of Behaviour*, in press.

Kanekar, S., Kolsawalla, M.B., and D' Souza, A. Attribution of responsibility to a victim of rape. *British Journal of Social Psychology*, in press.

Kanekar, S., Mazumdar, D., Bulsara, R.M., & Kolsawalla, M.B. Perception of an aggressor and his victim as a function of their relationship and retaliation. *Psychological Reports*, 1979, **44**, 609-610.

Kanekar, S., Mazumdar, D., & Kolsawalla, M.B. Perception of an aggressor and his victim as a function of physical attractiveness and retaliation. *Journal of Social Psychology*, 1981, in press.

Kanekar, S., Mazumdar, D., Pinto, N.J.P., Bulsara, R.M., & Kolsawalla, M.B. Aggression, retaliation, and socioeconomic status. *Journal of Social Psychology*, 1981, in press.

Kanekar, S., Nanji, V.J., Kolsawalla, M.B., & Mukerji, G.S. Perception of an aggressor and a victim of aggression as a function of sex and retaliation. *Journal of Social Psychology*, 1981, in press.

Kelley, H.H. Attribution theory in social psychology. In D. Levine (ed.), *Nebraska Symposium on Motivation, 1967*. Lincoln : University of Nebraska Press, 1967.

Kelley, H.H. Attribution in social interaction. In E.E. Jones, D.E. Kanouse, H.H. Kelley, R.E. Nisbett, S. Valins, & B. Weiner (eds.), *Attribution : Perceiving the Causes of Behavior*. Morristown, New Jersey : General Learning Press, 1972.

Kelley, H.H. The processes of causal attribution. *American Psychologist*, 1973, **28**, 107-128.

Kellog, R., & Baron, R.S. Attribution theory, insomnia, and the reverse placebo effect: A reversal of Storms and Nisbett's findings. *Journal of Personality and Social Psychology*, 1975, **32**, 231-236.

Krulewitz, J.K., & Nash, J.E. Effects of rape victim resistance, assault outcome, and sex of observer on attributions about rape. *Journal of Personality*, 1979, **47**, 557-574.

Krulewitz, J.E., & Payne, E.J. Attributions about rape : Effects of rapist force, observer sex and sex role attitudes. *Journal of Applied Social Psychology*, 1978, **8**, 291-305.

Landy, D., & Aronson, E. The influence of the character of the criminal and his victim on the decisions of simulated jurors. *Journal of Experimental Social Psychology*, 1969, **5**, 141-152.

Lay, C.H., Burron, B.F., & Jackson, D.N. Base rates and informational value in impression formation. *Journal of Personality and Social Psychology*, 1973, **28**, 390-395.

Lerner, M.J. The justice motive : Some hypotheses as to its origins and forms. *Journal of Personality*, 1977, **45**, 1-52.

Lerner, M.J., & Miller, D.T. Just world research and the attribution process : Looking back and ahead. *Psychological Bulletin*, 1978, **85**, 1030-1051.

Lincoln, A., & Levinger, G. Observer's evaluations of the victim and the attacker in an aggressive incident. *Journal of Personality and Social Psychology*, 1972. **22**, 202-210.

Maccoby, E.E., & Jacklin, C.N. *The Psychology of Sex Differences*. Stanford, California: Stanford University Press, 1975.

Mathes, E.W., & Fiorito, F.R. The informativeness of atypical behaviour with respect to person perception. *Journal of Social Psychology*, 1978, **104**, 279-286.

Mead, G.H. *Mind, Self and Society*. Chicago: University of Chicago Press, 1934.

Miller, R.L., Brickman, P., & Bolen, D. Attribution versus persuasion as a means for modifying behaviour. *Journal of Personality and Social Psychology*, 1975, **31**, 430-441.

Munson, P., & Kiesler, C.A. The role of attributions by others in the acceptance of persuasive communications. *Journal of Personality*, 1974, **42**, 453-466.

Nisbett, R.E., & Schachter, S. Cognitive manipulation of pain. *Journal of Experimental Social Psychology*, 1966, **2**, 227-236.

Paulsen, K. Attribution of fault to a rape victim as a function of locus of control. *Journal of Social Psychology*, 1979, **107**, 131-132.

Pelton, L.H. *The Psychology of Non-violence*. Elmsford, New York: Pergamon Press, 1975.

Rosenbaum, M.E., & Franc, D.E. Opinion change as a function of external commitment and amount of discrepancy from the opinion of another. *Journal of Abnormal and Social Psychology*, 1960, **61**, 15-20.

Rosenbaum, M.E. & Zimmerman, I.M. The effect of external commitment on response to an attempt to change opinions. *Public Opinion Quarterly*, 1959, **23**, 247-254.

Rosenthal, R., & Jacobson, L. Teachers' expectancies : Determinants of pupils' IQ gains. *Psychological Reports*, 1966, **19**, 115-118.

Rosenthal, R., & Jacobson, L. *Pygmalion in the Classroom: Teacher Expectation and Pupils' Intellectual Development*. New York: Holt, Rinehart and Winston, 1968.

Ross, L. The intuitive psychologist and his shortcomings : Distortions in the attribution process. In L. Berkowitz (ed.), *Advances in Experimental Social Psychology* (Vol. 10). New York: Academic Press, 1977.

Ross, L. Some afterthoughts on the intuitive psychologist. In L. Berkowitz (ed.), *Cognitive Theories in Social Psychology*. New York: Academic Press, 1978.

Ross, L., Rodin, J., & Zimbardo, P.G. Toward an attribution therapy: The reduction of fear through induced cognitive-emotional misattribution. *Journal of Personality and Social Psychology*, 1969, **12**, 279-288.

Schachter, S. The interaction of cognitive and physiological determinants of emotional state. In L. Berkowitz (ed.), *Advances in Experimental Social Psychology* (Vol. 1). New York : Academic Press, 1964.

Schachter, S., & Singer, J.E. Cognitive, social, and physiological determinants of emotional state. *Psychological Review*, 1962, **69**, 379-399.

Schachter, S., & Wheeler, L. Epinephrine, chlorpromazine, and amusement. *Journal of Abnormal and Social Psychology*, 1962, **65**, 121-128.

Schanck, R.L. A study of a community and its groups and institutions conceived of as behaviours of individuals. *Psychological Monographs*, 1932, **43**, No. 2.

Schiff, W., Blackburn, H., Cohen, F., Furman, G., Jackson, A., Lapidos, E., Rotkin, H., & Thayer, S. Does sex make a difference? Gender, age, and stimulus realism in perception and evaluation of aggression. *American Journal of Psychology*, 1980, **93**, 53-78.

Scroggs, J.R. Penalties for rape as a function of victim provocativeness, damage, and resistance. *Journal of Applied Social Psychology*, 1976, **6**, 360-368.

Sealy, A.P., & Wain, C.M. Person perception and jurors' decisions. *British Journal of Social and Clinical Psychology*, 1980, **19**, 7-16.

Selby, J.W., Calhoun, L.G., & Brock, T.A. Sex differences in the social perception of rape victims. *Personality and Social Psychology Bulletin*, 1977, **3**, 412-415.

Seligman, C., Brickman, J., & Koulack, D. Rape and physical attractiveness: Assigning responsibility to victims. *Journal of Personality*, 1977, **45**, 554-563.

Seligman, C., Paschall, N., & Takata, G. Effects of physical attractiveness on attribution of responsibility. *Canadian Journal of Behavioural Science*, 1974, **3**, 290-296.

Singer, J.E. Sympathetic activation, drugs, and fear. *Journal of Comparative and Physiological Psychology*, 1963, **56**, 612-615.

Skinner, B.F. *Science and Human Behaviour*. New York: Macmillan, 1953.

Skinner, B.F. *Verbal Behaviour*. New York : Appleton-Century-Crofts, 1957.

Smith, R.E., Keating, J.P., Hester, R.K., & Mitchell, H.E. Role and justice considerations in the attribution of responsibility to a rape victim. *Journal of Research in Personality*, 1976, **10**, 346-357.

Snow, R.E. Unfinished Pygmalion (Review of *Pygmalion in the Classroom : Teacher's Expectation and Pupils' Intellectual Development* by R. Rosenthal & L. Jacobson). *Contemporary Psychology*, 1969, **14**, 197-199.

Stoppard, J.M., & Kalin, R. Can gender stereotypes and sex-role conceptions be distinguished? *British Journal of Social and Clinical Psychology*, 1978, **17**, 211-217.

Storms, M.D., & Nisbett, R.E. Insomnia and the attribution process. *Journal of Personality and Social Psychology*, 1970, **16**, 319-328.

Valins, S. Cognitive effects of false heart-rate feedback. *Journal of Personality and Social Psychology*, 1966, **4**, 400-408.

Valins, S. Emotionality and information concerning internal reactions. *Journal of Personality and Social Psychology*, 1967, **6**, 458-463.

Valins. S., & Ray, A.A. Effects of cognitive desensitization on avoidance behaviour. *Journal of Personality and Social Psychology*, 1967, **7**, 345-350.

Walster, E. Assignment of responsibility for an accident. *Journal of Personality and Social Psychology*, 1966, **3**, 73 79.

Walster, E. "Second guessing" important events. *Human Relations*, 1967, **20**, 239-250.

Walster, W., & Festinger, L. The effectiveness of overheard persuasive communication. *Journal of Abnormal and Social Psychology*, 1962, **65**, 395-402.

Weiner, B. *Achievement Motivation and Attribution Theory*. Morristown, New Jersey : General Learning Press, 1974.

Wilson, D.T. Ability evaluation, postdecision, dissonance, and co-worker attractiveness. *Journal of Personality and Social Psychology*, 1965, **1**, 486-489.

Woll, S.B., & McFall, M.E. The effects of false feedback on attributed arousal and rated attractiveness in female subjects. *Journal of Personality*, 1979, **47**, 214-229.

FOUR

Lila Krishnan

THEORY AND RESEARCH ON REACTIONS TO AID
A Review*

One of the virtues that have been highly commended and valued by the human race is 'altruism'. Stemming from the Latin 'alter' or 'other', altruism refers to a concern for others in contrast to selfishness or self-concern. While altruism would thus seem to be a topic of interest to moralists and philosophers, because of the obvious practical implications of altruistic and non-altruistic behaviour, social scientists have become interested in the origin, development and determinants of such behaviour. This growing concern with 'prosocial behaviour' which is described as the "antithesis of aggressive behaviour" (Wispe, 1972, p.3) represents a noticeable change from the concern with anti-social behaviour which was prevalent until fairly recently.

A typical prosocial exchange includes both giving and acceptance of help, but the two are not treated as equal in social desirability. 'Giving' is generally considered a positive form of social, moral or religious behaviour. In Hindu philosophy and religion, for example, charity of any sort is considered good, but frequently there are prescriptions regarding the object of 'giving'. The concept of 'dana' implies a duty to be charitable, especially on specific occasions. Some students of Hindu culture (e.g. McClelland, 1973) have commented on the explicit stress on 'giving' as a recurrent theme in Hindu life,

*The author is thankful for suggestions and comments to Guy Begin, Jeffrey D. Fisher, Janak Pandey and to B.N. Patnaik.

and have observed that 'giving' in this culture is supposed to be a primary way of attaining merit in the present life as well as in the life to come. However, parallel to this esteem for giving is a corresponding devaluation of acceptance of help. Kuppuswamy (1978) explains this point quoting Swami Vivekananda:

> The mind of the men who receive gifts is acted on by the mind of the giver, so the receiver is likely to become degenerate. Receiving gifts is prone to destroy the independence of mind and encourages slavishness. Therefore accept no gifts (Raja-Yoga, p. 223).

Such a wealth of research pertinent to helping has accumulated in recent years that it would not be easy to condense it into a brief review and yet do justice to it. This is clear from the reviews of Krebs (1970), Macaulay and Berkowitz (1970), Gergen (1974), Bar-Tal (1976) and Lau and Blake (1976) on the giving of help. But there is relatively less research on the recipient's reactions to aid, and this aspect of helping needs to be dealt with in greater detail. Therefore, in the present paper, the primary focus will be on reactions to aid. But since receiving aid assumes the giving of aid, the major features of research on the latter will be very briefly described, and this will be followed by a somewhat detailed review of research on recipient reactions. In the context of this review, a few of the present author's experiments will also be described. The major theoretical explanations of recipient reactions will be discussed. A comment will be made on the implications for a cross-cultural comparison of recipient reactions, considering the Indian context as an example. Finally, suggestions will be presented regarding the direction that future research on reactions to aid should take.

A glance at the research on the giving of help indicates that the paradigm typically followed is that a person requests help under various controlled conditions, the potential donor of help is placed in a position of helping, and the frequency and/or amount of help given is recorded. A very large number of experimental studies adopting this paradigm have been conducted in the past two decades or so, the results of which have helped in the identification of four broad classes of determinants of helping, namely, donor characteristics, recipient characteristics, resource characteristics, and situational or context characteristics (Gergen, 1974; Bar-Tal, 1976). Donor characteristics such as the donor's age (Midlarsky and Bryan, 1967; Staub, 1970; Lowe and Ritchey, 1973), sex of the donor (Schopler and Bateson, 1965; Schopler, 1967; Latané, 1970; Gaertner and Bickman, 1971; Wispé and Freshley, 1971; Moss and Page, 1972); race of the donor (Gaertner and Bickman, 1971; Wispé and Freshley, 1971), personal characteristics such as internal locus of control (Gore and Rotter, 1963), social responsibility (Harris, 1957; Berkowitz and Daniels, 1964), cooperativeness (Sawyer, 1966), high empathy (Liebhart, 1972) extroversion and warm-heartedness (Smith and Nelson, 1975) have been found to influence helping.

Similarly, recipient characteristics such as the recipient's age (Tipton and Browning, 1972), sex (Latané, 1970; Emswiller, Deaux and Willits, 1971; Pomazal and Clore, 1973; Clark, 1974), race (Gaertner and Bickman, 1971; Thayer, 1973), physical attributes of the recipient such as obesity (Tipton and Browning, 1972) and dress (Graf and Riddell, 1972; Morgan, 1973), perceived actual similarity of the recipient to the donor (Baron, 1971; Sole, Marton and Hornstein, 1975) have also been found to be determinants of helping.

With respect to resource characteristics, the cost of helping (Schopler and Bateson, 1965; Latané and Darley, 1970; Schaps, 1972; Gross, Wallston and Piliavin, 1975) has been identified as a prominent factor affecting helping. It may be understood that the cost of helping would also affect the magnitude of help given. Situational determinants of the giving of help include a wide variety of factors, such as a direct request or absence of a direct request (Latané, 1970; Gaertner and Bickman, 1971), arousal of psychological reactance (Horowitz, 1968; Jones, 1970), labelling of the situation as one that calls for help (Latané and Rodin, 1969; Bickman, 1972), attribution of responsibility to personal or external causes (Schopler and Matthews, 1965; Berkowitz, 1969; Piliavin, Rodin, and Piliavin, 1969; Field, 1974; Gruder, 1974), the presence of others in the situation, leading to increased likelihood of helping through modelling (Bryan and Test,

1967; Macaulay, 1970), or decreased likelihood of helping through diffusion of responsibility (Darley and Latané, 1970). Yet other situational factors that have been found to affect helping are the donor's liking for the recipient (Daniels and Berkowitz, 1963; Baron, 1971; Pandey and Griffitt, 1974), the donor's mood (Aderman, 1972; Rosenhan, Underwood and Moore, 1974), success (Berkowitz and Connor, 1966; Isen, 1970; Isen and Levin, 1972), motivation to repair his or her image after failure (Begin, 1977) and prior reinforcement for helping (Moss and Page, 1972). There are very many more determinants of helping that have been investigated, but that brief description presented above should suffice to indicate the giving of help is clearly determined by multiple factors. Some of these factors may also affect the receiving of help, as will be seen in the discussion that follows. We may now turn our attention to the recipient.

FORMS OF RECIPIENT REACTIONS

In studying how a recipient responds to aid, three major possibilities may be considered:

(i) the recipient may exhibit the immediate reaction of acceptance or refusal of aid;
(ii) he/she may react by expressing varying degrees of liking for the donor, or other forms of affective responses;
(iii) he/she may subsequently return or not return the favour when placed in the role of a potential donor.

Another aspect of recipient reactions is that of help-seeking (DePaulo, 1978; Fisher, DePaulo and Nadler, 1980), which involves a situation in which prior help has not already been given. Fisher, DePaulo and Nadler (1980) have adopted a broad view of recipient reactions, classifying them into three categories: external perceptions, or, perception of the donor's motives in giving the aid, internal perceptions, that is, the recipient's perception of his/her own motives behind, or consequences for himself/herself, of accepting or refusing aid; and behavioural responses, which would include subsequent returning of help or favours. The first two categories would indicate the attributional processes underlying recipient reactions, and have recently become an integral part of the explanation of reactions to aid (Fisher, Nadler and Whitcher, Note 2). The understanding of recipient reactions has been greatly facilitated by empirical research showing that reactions to aid are also affected by a wide variety of factors, the major among which will be reviewed below.

DETERMINANTS OF RECIPIENT REACTIONS

As in the case of the giving of help, the determinants of reactions to aid have been classified into four categories :

Donor characteristics

There does not seem to be any specific information on the effect of demographic variables such as age and race of the donor on recipient reactions, but the donor's sex has been reported to have some effect on acceptance and subsequent return of help in studies by the present author (to be described later). Yet it appears that the donor's sex affects reactions to help only in conjunction with factors such as the recipient's sex and situational factors such as the nature of the task on which help is given and received.

The donor's status relative to the recipient's status has been shown to influence the recipient's perception of the donor's motives in giving help. A high-status donor tends to be attributed friendly and dispositional motives, while a low-status donor tends to be perceived as complying because of coercive power from the recipient (Thibaut and Riecken, 1955).

Physical attractiveness of the donor has been found to have a negative relationship with help-seeking as a recipient reaction. Stokes and Bickman (1974) report that a potential recipient is more willing to seek help from a potential donor who is physically unattractive than from one who is physically attractive. But when help seeking is a requirement in the situation, physical attractiveness has no significant effect on help-seeking. Acceptance of aid has been found to be negatively related also to similarity between the donor and recipient. This has been interpreted as being due to the fact that aid from an attitudinally similar other is perceived as more self-threatening by the recipient than that from a dissimilar other (Fisher and Nadler, 1974). On the same lines, Clark, Gotay and Mills (1974) found that when there was an opportunity to return the favour, the likelihood of acceptance of aid and of future help-seeking by the recipient was lower when the donor was perceived as similar rather than dissimilar.

Recipient characteristics

The recipient's sex has been observed to affect reactions to aid (Gruder and Cook, 1971). In general, women are more willing than men to seek help (Fisher, DePaulo and Nadler, 1980) which is consistent with the idea that females are socialized to be more dependent and 'help-seeking' than males (Whiting and Edwards, 1973). Social class of the recipient is another demographic variable that has been shown to be associated with reciprocal helping. Berkowitz (1966) and Berkowitz and Friedman (1967) found that the norm of reciprocity in exchange of help is more strictly followed by American entrepreneurs than by American or English bureaucrats.

With respect to personality characteristics that affect recipient reactions, in a study by Brewster (1971) comparing giving-oriented and receiving-oriented people on Cattell's 16 PF Questionnaire and the MMPI, it was found that receiving-oriented people were no different from the norms on their scores on these two tests. Thus personality characteristics as measured in this study did not seem to be good predictors of recipient reactions. Among other personality characteristics of the recipient that have been found to affect responses to aid are locus of control, authoritarianism and achievement motivation. An internal rather than external locus of control, as well as low rather than high authoritarianism (Fischer and Turner, 1970) and low rather than high achievement motivation (Tessler and Schwartz, 1972) have been found to be associated with willingness to seek help.

Resource characteristics

The magnitude of aid as a resource characteristic has been consistently shown to affect recipient reactions. The greater the amount of help given, the greater is the amount of help subsequently returned by the recipient (Berkowitz and Friedman, 1967; Frisch and Greenberg, 1968; Wilke and Lanzetta, 1970; Greenberg and Frisch, 1972; Kahn and Tice, 1973), and the more positive the motives attributed to the donor. When the obligation to return the help is low, the greater the amount of help given, the greater is the attraction for the donor (Freeman, 1977) and the greater the expressed willingness to acquire information to help the former donor (Greenberg and Bar-Tal, 1976). However, there may be situations in which the amount of help given is very large and tends to make the recipient feel uncomfortable, obligated and indebted rather than pleased and grateful (Tesser, Gatewood and Driver, 1968; Greenberg and Frisch, 1972).

As in the case of the giving of help, the cost of helping to the donor also seems to affect reactions to aid, but usually in conjunction with the degree of obligation it generates in the recipient. Castro (1974) observed that when high-cost help was given, and there was no opportunity to return the favour, recipients were less willing to request further help than when there was an opportunity to reciprocate the favour. Often it is the perceived cost rather than the actual cost of helping that is a more potent determinant than of recipient reactions. Gergen, Ellsworth, Maslach and Seipel (1975) report that recipients expressed greater attraction toward a donor who was generous even though he had few resources (that is, one who helped at a greater cost to himself) than to a high-resource donor. But they returned more of the resources subsequently to a low-resource donor than to a high-resource donor. Furthermore, the perceived cost of accepting aid (to the recipient) may determine whether or not it is accepted and subsequently returned. These aspects of perceived cost of accepting aid may be classified as situational variables, and will be discussed later.

There is some indication that it is the rewards obtained by the recipient rather than the cost of helping or of accepting help per se that determines a recipient's gratitude (Tesser, Gatewood and Driver, 1968) and subsequent helping (Greenberg, Block and Silverman, 1971). Another resource characteristic that affects responses to aid is the appropriateness of the aid or favour. An appropriate favour (as manipulated by experimental instructions) has been found to be more likely to lead to later reciprocation than an inappropriate favour (Kiesler, 1966).

Situational characteristics

A fairly wide range of situational determinants of recipient reactions has been studied. Help is more likely to be accepted from a donor who is said to be a friend or ally than from one who is said to be a foe (Nadler, Fisher and Streufert, 1974). The closeness of the donor-recipient relationship also affects recipient reactions. Less obligation is experienced in accepting aid when the donor is a parent than when the donor is a stranger (Bar-Tal, Harmon and Greenberg, 1975). A broad class of situational factors pertaining to the recipient's perception of the locus of initiation of help, the donor's motives and powerfulness have also been found to influence reactions to aid. For example, there is evidence that subsequent reciprocation of help is more likely when the recipient is made to believe that the donor helped voluntarily on his or her own initiative, than if they are made to believe that the donor helped because of the experimenter's instructions (Goranson and Berkowitz, 1966), and also when the recipient does not suspect ulterior motives on the donor's part (Schopler and Thompson, 1968). More help is found to be given on a later occasion by a recipient who has been previously helped voluntarily rather than compulsorily (Nemeth, 1970), and when the help has been given deliberately rather than accidentally (Greenberg and Frisch, 1972). The attribution of altruistic or non-altruistic motives to the donor is also coloured by the perception of the recipient's powerfulness (Thompson, Stroebe and Schopler, 1971). Help given to a powerful recipient is seen as being more selfishly motivated than that given to a less powerful recipient. In addition, aid that is given in response to a request is viewed less favourably than aid that is offered spontaneously (Broll, Gross and Piliavin, 1974; Muir and Weinstein, 1962).

Yet another category of situational factors that may affect responses to aid can be described in terms of the degree of obligation or indebtedness generated by the aid. In general, the experience of obligation or indebtedness aroused by help is uncomfortable and the recipient tries his or her best to relieve this discomfort (Greenberg, 1968, 1978). Anticipation of a later opportunity to return a favour decreases the intensity of this discomfort, and thus makes acceptance of aid more likely (Greenberg and Shapiro, 1971). Subsequently, when the opportunity for reciprocation actually arises, recipients are highly likely to actually return the favour (Greenberg and Bar-Tal, 1976; Shumaker and Jackson, 1979). It has been observed that in some situations anticipation of an occasion for reciprocation interacts with other factors such as perception of donor-recipient similarity (Clark, Gotay and Mills, 1974) and feelings of adequacy (Morris and Rosen, 1973).

The self-esteem of the recipient in the situation has also been found to be a powerful determinant of responses to help. Lowered self-esteem in an experimental situation generally decreases the likelihood of acceptance of aid compared to a control condition (Fisher and Nadler, 1974, 1976; Nadler, Fisher and Streufert, 1974, 1976). Similarly, feelings of inferiority or inadequacy lower the likelihood of help-seeking by a potential recipient (Stokes and Bickman, 1974). Nadler, Altman and Fisher (1979) have reported that in the case of positive self-regard induced experimentally through favourable self-evaluation, aid was perceived as more threatening than in the case of situationally induced negative self-regard. These findings have been corroborated in other studies (Tessler and Schwartz, 1972; Wallston, 1976).

Finally, there are situations that affect recipient reactions by generating psychological reactance (Brehm, 1966; Wicklund, 1974) in the recipient. If the aid or favour restricts the recipient's freedom of action (actually or perceptually) by compelling him or her to act in a specified way, the perception of the aid is generally less positive and the likelihood of actual reciprocation of help is lower than if the aid or favour does not have such restrictive effects (Brehm and Cole, 1966; Nemeth, 1970; Wicklund, 1974; Worchel, Andreoli, and Archer, 1976). Another source of reactance may lie in the recipient's expectation that accepting aid may later penalize him or her in some way (DePaulo and Fisher, 1978). Aid that is given with specification regarding the purpose for which it is to be used, or has "strings attached" to it (Gergen and

Gergen, 1974) and aid that is given with a high obligation for return (Gergen, Ellsworth, Maslach and Seipel, 1975; Freeman, 1977) are viewed negatively mainly because they restrict the recipient's freedom of action. In addition, attribution of motives other than helpfulness or altruism may also lead to reactance and thus affect reactions to aid (Goodstadt, 1971).

The brief review presented above serves to indicate clearly that systematic efforts have been made to examine recipient reactions in experimental situation in order to investigate the determinants of responses to aid. Continuing this line of inquiry, the present author conducted a series of investigations of reactions to aid with specific attention to circumstances that have not been examined directly in the studies described above. Some of these experiments are reported below.

STUDY I

The effect of donor's sex, recipient's sex, amount of help, and resource control on acceptance of aid

While the majority of investigations on recipient reactions deal with reciprocity or subsequent reactions to aid, it is intuitively obvious that immediate reactions to help may themselves affect later reciprocity, regardless of other factors. On this rationale, Krishnan and Carment (1981) conducted an experiment which included as independent variables a donor characteristic (donor's sex), a recipient characteristic (recipient's sex), a resource characteristic (amount of help offered), and a situational characteristic (resource control), that is, whether the donor actually owned the resources offered or was merely acting as agent for the experimenter. While there is some evidence on the effects of the first-three factors, resource control does not seem to have been investigated. These four variables were factorially combined into a $2 \times 4 \times 2$ experimental design [Small/Large amount of help $\times$ Sex composition of the dyad (Female donor, female recipient/Female donor, male recipient/Male donor, male recipient/Male donor, female recipient) $\times$ resource control (Ownership/Agency)]. The dependent variables were frequency of acceptance or refusal of help, the amount of help accepted, and the latency of acceptance or refusal.

Subjects

Thirty-three male and thirty-two female undergraduates of McMaster University (Canada) participated in this study along with a male and a female confederate.

Procedure

Subjects were scheduled for the experiment in pairs, but actually one member of each pair was a confederate. The experiment was presented as a part of an "art project"; accordingly, subjects were asked to perform two art-related tasks, the first-one involving art-judgment, and the second-one involving picture-construction using felt-pieces. The first task was meant to form a basis for 'assigning' one person (the confederate) to the donor role in the second task. This was done by giving a slightly higher 'score' to the confederate on the first task which made it legitimate for him or her to choose a box containing more of the resources (felt-pieces) required for the second task. The naive subject thus had the second choice, and got a box containing fewer resources. Once the resources were thus distributed, Ownership and Agency were manipulated through experimental instructions, each pair being randomly assigned to either condition. In the course of the second task, the confederate offered the subject a small or large amount of help (number of felt-pieces). The recipient's acceptance or refusal of the offered resources was recorded, along with the acceptance—or refusal—latency, and the amount of help accepted.

In the absence of unambiguous information pertaining to the effects of the independent variables on immediate reactions to aid, no specific hypotheses were laid down regarding the direction of these effects.

Results and discussion

It was found that the frequency of acceptance of help was significantly greater than that of refusal (Chi-square $= 6.46$, $df = 1$, $p < .05$). The amount of help accepted was significantly and negatively correlated with the amount of help offered (Contingency Coefficient $C = -.30$, $p < .05$), indicating that a proportionately larger amount of the resources was accepted when the amount offered was small, and vice versa. With respect to the effect of the amount of help offered, the likelihood of acceptance of help was significantly greater when a large amount of help was offered, but acceptance and refusal were equally likely when a small amount of help was offered. This could be possibly due to the fact that the generous donor was liked more than the less generous donor which made refusal of aid from such a donor less likely. With regard to resource control, the likelihood of acceptance of help was greater under Agency than under Ownership of resources, but the likelihood of refusal of aid was greater under Ownership (Chi-square = 16.16, df = 1, $p < .01$). This finding can be interpreted as being due to the lower degree of obligation experienced by the donor's 'agent' role relative to the donor's 'owner' role.

Some trends in sex differences in the likelihood of acceptance of aid were also noted. Male recipients who were offered aid by a female donor were less likely to accept aid compared to all other recipients. Possibly due to sex-role stereotypes, it is considered especially inappropriate for a male to accept help from a female.

With reference to the latency of acceptance or refusal of aid, it was found that the mean latency was significantly shorter than that of refusal. Also, latency was found to be jointly affected by resource control, amount of help and sex composition of the dyad ($F = 9.493$, df = 3,48, $p < .001$).

In short, the results of this experiment indicated clearly that resource control, the amount of help offered and the donor's and recipient's sex determine the likelihood as well as the latency of acceptance in different ways.

The next study to be reported here dealt with other situational variables as well as the sex composition of the donor-recipient dyad, and examined not only immediate reactions to aid, but also subsequent returning of help.

STUDY II

The effect of reciprocity, responsibility and reactance on reactions to aid

Several studies have investigated the effect of the norm of social responsibility (Berkowitz and Daniels, 1963, 1964) and the norm of reciprocity (Gouldner, 1960) and some investigators have examined the joint effects of the two norms (Berkowitz and Daniels, 1964; Goranson and Berkowitz, 1966; Greenglass, 1969). In these experiments the need for help was explicitly conveyed to a potential donor in the form of a direct request for help. Helping in response to such a request may often be confounded with compliance. If, however, the need for help were indicated indirectly, would the relative effect of reciprocity and social responsibility emerge more clearly? This question was examined in an experimental study (Krishnan and Carment, 1979) of the effect of prior help, communication of need for help, and donor's/recipient's sex on recipient reactions.

Procedure

Eighty-four subjects participated in same-sex and opposite sex pairs, and were asked to perform two tasks: a 'mechanical' task, on which a confederate helped (or did not help) the naive subject, and then a 'mental' task, in which donor-recipient roles were reversed and the former donor (confederate) communicated indirectly, or did not communicate, a need for help. As dependent variables, on the first task, the frequency of acceptance of aid, the amount of aid accepted, and the latency of acceptance were noted. On the second task, the frequency of helping by the naive subject (who was now the donor) was noted. Four conditions were compared: prior help/communication of need, no prior help/communication of need, prior help/no communication of need, and no prior help/no communication of need. The last-mentioned condition was meant to serve as a control.

Results and discussion

Findings indicated that, as in the first study, acceptance of aid was significantly more likely than refusal. The amount of help accepted did not differ between experimental conditions. The latency of acceptance was longest in the case of those female donor-male recipient dyads, in which help was later reciprocated, and was shortest in the case of those female donor-female recipient dyads in which help was not subsequently reciprocated ($F = 6.496$, $df = 3,31$, $p < .01$). Once again, it appears that sex-role stereotypes make it relatively less appropriate for males to accept aid from a female than for females to accept aid from another female. Moreover, the obligation to return aid if accepted seems to be greater for males who receive aid from a female donor.

In accordance with the reciprocity norm, in this study later helping was significantly more likely when the subjects had received prior help than when they had received no prior help. There was not a single case of 'spontaneous' helping in the 'No prior help' condition. However, with regard to the effect of communication of need, it was found that helping was significantly more likely when there was no communication of need than when a need for help was communicated (Chi-square= 5.53, df=1, $p < .02$). While this finding is contrary to the dictates of the norm of social responsibility which requires that one helps another person in need, especially when such a need is communicated directly, it can be explained on the basis of the notion of psychological reactance (Brehm, 1966; Brehm and Cole, 1966; Wicklund, 1974). It is possible that communication of need aroused reactance in the potential donor, making him or her feel compelled to give help, and thus lowering the actual likelihood of helping in this condition. Reactance did not arise when there was no communication of need.

It is not possible to conclude definitely on the basis of this study which norm—reciprocity or social responsibility—was salient. But one thing that emerged unambiguously was this: social responsibility is not always guaranteed to operate, and there may be occasions in which the awareness of another person's dependency or need may inhibit rather than facilitate one's propensity to help.

Having explored two questions in a task-performance setting, reciprocity was further studied in a situation which had the following features as distinguished from a task-performance setting: there was no structured task to be performed, but instead, certain choices had to be made between alternatives that led to different rewards (payoffs) for the recipient; there was sequential exchange of resources over a number of trials rather than a single exchange; the 'amount' of help given could vary depending on whether a generous or non-generous choice was made, and how frequently such a choice was made; the element of 'need' in this setting did not imply a 'deficiency' of resources, but rather, the resource was needed only for a more efficient attainment of the goal (in this case, the accumulation of rewards). These features were incorporated into an 'Altruism Matrix' which had the following payoffs: the upper number in each cell represents the donor's payoffs and the lower number, the recipient's payoffs :

		Donor	
		A	**B**
Recipient	**X**	1 10	2 2
	Y	1 1	2 2

Choice A by the donor was termed an 'Offer' because it offered the recipient 10 points while giving the donor only 1 point. Choice B, while allowing both persons equal rewards, deprives the recipient of a possible gain of 8 points, and hence was called a 'Withhold' choice. From the recipient's point of view, choice X was called an 'Accept' because it signified an acceptance of 10 points (or 2 points), in contrast to choice Y ('Refuse') which signified a refusal of the donor's offer. These labels were, however, not presented to the subjects. It is clear that in this payoff-structure, the donor can himself or herself never get a large reward, but it is the donor who determines whether or not the recipient gets the reward. The recipient, on the other hand, can only determine his or her own rewards (by accepting or refusing them) but can do nothing to affect the donor's rewards.

For the purposes of the experiments to be reported, only the 'Offer'-related and 'Accept'-related choices were analyzed. Some of the issues left unanswered by previous investigations of reciprocity were examined in the next two experiments, using the Altruism Matrix.

STUDY III

The effect of information about an opportunity for reciprocation, and amount of help on recipient reactions

One of the major determinants of reciprocity mentioned earlier is the anticipation of an opportunity for returning a favour. Greenberg and Shapiro (1971) examined this variable by manipulating anticipation of the forthcoming opportunity for a reciprocation through instructions, but not actually presenting the opportunity. If, as Greenberg proposes (Greenberg, 1968, 1978) indebtedness generated by a favour were truly a mediator of recipient reactions, this fact should be clearly shown when an opportunity for reciprocation is actually presented to the recipient. This possibility has been tested by Shumaker and Jackson (1979) and their conclusion supports Greenberg's proposition of mediation by indebtedness. In order to see whether there would be a similar mediation by indebtedness in a choice situation involving sequential helping, Krishnan and Carment (1980a) investigated the effect of giving information about an opportunity for returning the favour in the setting of an Altruism Matrix in two experiments. In the first experiment, the amount of help given and returned was left to the subjects, but in the second experiment, the amount of help given was controlled.

Experiment 1

Subject : Forty male and female undergraduates participated in this study after random selection from a student list.

Procedure : Subjects were told that they were participating in an interactive situation in which the reward that each person obtained (by way of points representing some money) depended on the joint choices of two persons, and not on the choice made by one person alone. They were scheduled for the experiment in same-sex pairs, and upon arrival for the experiment were randomly assigned to the donor ('Yellow') role and recipient ('Red') role. Choices were to be made successively, the donor making the first choice. This sequential choosing is parallel to what happens in a typical helping situation.

Half of the subject-pairs were told at the start of the

experiment that they would be changing their roles mid-way through the experiment (Information condition) while the other half were given no such information (No Information condition). All subject-pairs did, however, change their roles. There were 50 trials in the session, out of which the first 25 trials were treated as the 'prior situation' and the later 25 trials as the 'subsequent situation'.

Results and discussion : Overall, while the F-ratios between various experimental conditions were statistically at chance-level, some interesting trends were observed. In the prior situation (first-half of the experiment), there were more Offer-related choices in the Information condition than in the No Information condition. But in the second-half this trend was reversed, and there were more Offer-related choices in the No Information condition than in the Information condition. This might be indicative of reactance caused by specific information about the later opportunity for reciprocation (that is, the recipient might have perceived this information as restricting freedom by making it mandatory to return the favour). In terms of recipient reactions, as expected, there tended to be more Accept-related choices in the Information condition than in the No Information condition, in both the prior and subsequent situations. The trends in sex differences indicated that males in general tended to make fewer Offer-related as well as Accept-related choices than females. This is what would be expected on the basis of sex-role stereotypes.

However, an explanation was called for in view of the ambiguous effects of information. An examination of the proportion of the Offers made 'naturally' (in the absence of information about future reciprocation) showed that, on the average, this proportion was fairly small (32-33%). It is possible that this proportion of generous choices was too small to be perceived as indicating helpfulness or generosity, so that the question of returning 'help' did not arise.

Whether or not this was an explanation for the findings which could be verified by controlling the amount of help given, and this was done in the second experiment which is described below.

Experiment 2

Subjects : Forty-eight male and female undergraduates served as subjects in this experiment, along with a male and a female confederate of the same age as the subjects.

Procedure : The only respect in which this experiment differed in procedure from Experiment 1 was that a confederate was used to control the amount of help given. Donor-choices, therefore, were no longer of interest to the experimenter. In addition to being informed or not informed that they would change roles midway through the experiment, subjects were either given a small amount of help (32% Offers) or were given a large amount of help (80% Offers). The magnitude of the 'small amount' was deliberately kept equivalent to the small amount of help given 'naturally' (see Experiment 1), while the magnitude of the 'large amount' was chosen so as to be obvious enough as a generous amount, but at the same time not so high as to arouse suspicion in the recipient.

Results and discussion : The main results are presented in Table 4.1

In this experiment there was clear support for Greenberg's proposition that indebtedness mediates the acceptance of aid. Recipients accepted more help when they were informed about a later opportunity for reciprocation than when they were not informed about such an opportunity. Also, when the opportunity actually arose, those who were previously informed made more Offers than those who had not been informed previously. Also, more help was accepted in the Large amount condition than in the Small amount condition, possibly because the more generous donor was perceived as being truly and intentionally more helpful than the less generous donor. Later, in keeping with the reciprocity norm, more help was returned in the Large amount condition than in the Small amount condition. However, it was noticed that while the amount of help returned in the latter condition was equivalent to that received, in the Large amount condition the magnitude of help returned was much less than that received (that is, about 55 per cent compared to the 80 per cent received earlier). This could be due to the effect of a change of the recipient from a position of high reward to one of almost no reward (in the

TABLE 4.1 : **Mean proportions of choices and F-ratios in various experimental conditions**
(Experiment 2)

Choice	Infor-mation	No infor-mation	F(1,40)	Sex Composition $M_d - M_r$	$F_d - F_r$	F(1,40)	Amount of Help Small	Large	F (1,40)
Prior Situation									
Accepts	.75	.64	6.99**	.69	.68	0.205	.57	.80	21.78**
Accepts following an Offer	.76	.59	10.37**	.67	.68	0	.55	.79	21.93**
Accepts following an Offer-Accept	.68	.55	3.53	.65	.58	0.89	.45	.78	24.68**
Subsequent Situation									
Offers	.46	.44	0.04	.51	.39	1.47	.34	.56	5.15*
Offers following an Accept	.46	.43	0.05	.49	.39	1.29	.34	.56	5.44**
Offers following an Offer-Accept	.38	.37	0.59	.46	.29	2.31	.22	.53	8.40**

**$p<.01$ *$p<.05$

donor role). Sex differences were statistically non-significant, but there was a trend for females to both accept and return less help than males.

In short, the two experiments in this study indicated that acceptance and subsequent reciprocation of aid is mediated by feelings of indebtedness which can be relieved by information about an opportunity for returning the favour. They also indicate the importance of amount of help as a determinant of recipient reactions. One characteristic of Study III was that in both experiments, the donor made choices without first declaring his or her intentions or plan of action. However, in many real-life settings helpful exchanges often start with an agreement or a promise to give aid. The next study described below examined the effect of statement of an intention by the donor on recipient reactions.

STUDY IV

The effect of stated intention and amount of help on recipient reactions

In a situation in which a donor states an intention to give a certain amount of help to the recipient, he or she may or may not actually carry out this stated intention. How the recipient reacts to aid given under these two circumstances was examined by Kahn and Tice (1973). In the first of their two experiments, female subjects received a large or small amount of help from a fictitious 'supervisor' who had earlier stated an intention to help, not to help, or had stated no intention. While the amount of help actually given in these conditions was found to affect the amount of help returned later to the donor, the statement of intention itself did not have a significant effect. But in the second experiment, ostensibly unknown to the 'supervisor,' her intention was 'discovered' by the subjects instead of being directly conveyed to them. Here, the amount of help returned to the donor was found to be influenced both by the stated intention to help and the actual amount of help given.

The statement of an intention to give help is also a form of communication between the donor and recipient. In this context, there is some evidence on the effects of stated intention in choice-settings. Deutsch's (1958) study, for example, which involved a mixed-motive game, found that there was more cooperation when subjects communicated their plans of action to each other than when there was no such communication between them. This was probably because communication established a trust relationship between the participants. Other investigators have also reported that various levels of communication (Loomis, 1959) and making a promise versus not making a promise regarding choices to be made by one player (Evans, 1964) affect prosocial behaviour, mainly cooperation, in specific choice-settings. On the basis of this information, Krishnan and Carment (1980b) examined the effect of communicating an intention to give a certain amount of help, and actually giving or not giving that amount of help, on recipient reactions, using an Altruism Matrix.

Subjects

Forty males and females participated in same-sex pairs in this experiment, along with a male and a female confederate.

Procedure

The procedure adopted in this study was identical to that adopted in Experiment 2 of Study III, with additional manipulations of the new variable (Stated Intention) and an omission of the 'Information' variable. Stated Intention was manipulated as follows: the donor was 'allowed' to send a written message to the recipient, indicating his or her intention to give a small amount or large amount of help (in terms of the proportion of Offers to be made). The message was sent after the donor checked one of the two alternatives indicating the amount of help. Since both of the alternatives were on the same slip of paper, the recipient could know which of them was chosen as well as which one was not chosen. Unknown to the recipient, however, the donor had been instructed to choose a particular alternative, depending on the experimental condition. After the experiment began, the donor gave either a small amount or a large amount of help. Thus there were four experimental conditions: Stated Intention (Small)/Amount given (Small), Stated Intention (Large)/Amount given (Large), Stated Intention (Small)/Amount given (Large), and Stated Intention (Large)/Amount given (Small). Although subjects were given no prior information regarding a change of roles, all of them did change donor-recipient roles midway through the experiment.

It was expected that more help would be accepted when the donor stated an intention to give a large amount of help rather than a small amount of help, and subsequently a large amount of help would be returned in the former condition. In the absence of empirical evidence related to similarity and discrepancy between Stated Intention and Amount given, no specific predictions were made about these factors. As in the previous experiments, sex differences were expected with respect to the new variables.

Results and discussion

Table 4.2 shows the major findings of this experiment.

With regard to the effect of Stated Intention, while there was a non-significant difference between the two conditions of Stated Intention, there tended to be more acceptances in the Stated Intention (Large) condition than in the Stated Intention (Small) condition, and more Offers (and Offer-related choices) in the Stated Intention (Small) condition. The effect of Amount given corroborated the earlier findings, that more help was accepted when a large amount of help was given than when a small amount was given; similarly, more help was returned when a large amount of help was given. The difference was significant, however, only in the case of Offer related choices. In short, it can be said that in the present experiment, acceptance of help tended to be affected both by stated intention and the actual amount of help given, but the subsequent return of aid was affected by the actual amount given rather than by the stated intention. This finding is not difficult to explain if it is borne in mind that it was only at the end of the prior situation (before the change of roles) that it became clear to the recipient whether or not the donor has acted on his or her stated intention. Subsequent return of help came only after this stage, and was therefore based on the donor's actual behaviour. Finally, sex differences in this study were found to be statistically significant, females making fewer Accept-related as well as Offer-related choices than males. This observation continues the trend found in the previous experiments using the

TABLE 4.2 : **Mean proportion of choices and F-ratios in various experimental conditions (Study IV)**

Choices	Stated Intention		F(1,32)	Amount of Help Given		F(1,32)	Sex Composition		F(1,32)
	(Small Amount)	(Large Amount		Small	Large		$M_d - M_r$	$F_d - F_{rr}$	
Prior Situation									
Accepts	.64	.74	2.52	.67	.70	0.22	.75	.62	4.36*
Accepts following an Offer	.60	.69	1.35	.61	.69	1.23	.69	.60	1.49
Accepts following an Offer-Accept	.48	.64	3.02	.52	.61	1.02	.66	.46	4.87*
Subsequent Situation									
Offers	.55	.51	0.21	.40	.65	10.08**	.61	.44	4.69*
Offers following an Accept	.55	.50	0.50	.42	.63	9.54**	.62	.43	6.94*
Offers following an Offer-Accept	.47	.45	0.04	.31	.62	9.63**	.56	.37	3.74

**$p<.01$; *$p<.05$

same setting, and while it appears to contradict sex-role prescriptions, is consistent with sex differences found in some other choice-settings (Wiley, 1972; Carment, 1974).

To summarize the present author's findings, there was unambiguous evidence of the operation of the reciprocity norm in a task-performance setting as well as in a choice-setting. The experiments reported above do not represent a single research question pertaining to recipient reactions; rather, they have been reported here to illustrate the fact that some questions in this aspect of helping behaviour can be systematically investigated not only in the conventionally used task-setting, but also in a choice-setting. The recipient reactions found in both kinds of settings with respect to many independent variables are quite similar. Thus the present author found, as had some other investigators, that recipients tend to respond positively to a donor who gives a large amount of help rather than to one who gives a small amount of help. Similarly, feelings of indebtedness caused by an offer of aid have been found to be alleviated, and consequently to affect recipient reactions, when the recipient anticipates an occasion for returning the favour. The same thing emerged in one of the present author's experiments using a choice-setting. A new factor, namely, resource control, was also investigated, the effect of which suggests that indebtedness or obligation is probably less intense when the donor does not actually own the resources given, but rather acts merely as the agent for giving them away. The findings related to the effect of stated intention perhaps modify those reported earlier. In a choice-setting such as the Altruism Matrix, the amount of help actually given by the donor, despite his or her promises, is the crucial determinant of the amount of help returned subsequently. Finally, the picture with respect to sex differences is not very clear in the case of task-setting, but is slightly more definite in the case of a choice-setting. In the latter setting, females tend to both accept less help and return less help than males, a finding which does not accord with the effect of sex-role stereotypes with respect to giving and receiving help, but is not surprising in view of findings on prosocial (cooperative) exchange in other choice-settings.

Up until this point, we have examined some of the determinants of recipient reactions that have been experimentally investigated. For a more thorough understanding of the effects of these factors, it would be necessary to examine the major theoretical propositions that attempt to explain reactions to aid. We next turn our attention to this aspect of recipient reactions.

THEORETICAL BASES OF REACTIONS TO AID

Most of the theories of recipient reactions explain or interpret acceptance of aid, subsequent return of aid, and other reactions mainly in terms of specific intervening states between the offer of aid and the recipient's response. Four major theoretical propositions may be considered in the present context :

(1) The norm of reciprocity
(2) Indebtedness
(3) Self-esteem
(4) Attribution

The norm of reciprocity

The basic postulate of the reciprocity norm as stated by Gouldner (1960) is that people should help, and should not harm, those who have helped them. To illustrate the prevalence of this norm, Gouldner cites instances of exchange in various primitive and modern societies that involve giving and receiving gifts. Gouldner also describes two kinds of reciprocity : (a) homeomorphic, in which the resources returned are equivalent in form to those received, and (b) heteromorphic, in which the resources are different in form but equal in value. The former kind of reciprocity is described as "tat for tat" reciprocity, as distinguished from the second kind which may be termed "tit for tat" reciprocity.

According to Gouldner, the reciprocity norm serves certain social functions. First, it defines and maintains status relationships by requiring all members of society to carry out responsibilities associated with their status. Secondly, it accounts for mutual dependence among members of a society. Dependence on one another ensures that a transaction between the two persons concerned continues as long as each reciprocates the other's services. This dependence then gets extended to other aspects of social life. However, a few exceptions to this idea of dependent transactions may be found, leading to unilateral 'giving', as in the case of certain power and emotional relationships (for example, the mother-child relationship). Thirdly, the norm of reciprocity serves as a 'starting mechanism' for interpersonal relationships. This happens because the person who has first received help is obliged to repay this kindness, and this knowledge makes the donor more confident that he or she will be repaid. Thus the donor is also more willing to part with his or her resources.

In the context of helping, then, the reciprocity norm makes it imperative that the recipient return the aid, but, as Bar-Tal (1976) has pointed out, all reciprocal acts may not be necessarily 'prosocial' in motive, since reciprocal aid may often be given under external pressure.

Finally, Gouldner states that the norm of reciprocity is universal, but adds that it does not operate unconditionally. As has been suggested earlier in the present paper, pressure to reciprocate aid may lead to psychological reactance and lower the likelihood of actual reciprocation. Barring such circumstances, there is empirical evidence that the reciprocity norm operates consistently.

Indebtedness

One aspect of the reciprocity norm is that the recipient of aid is obliged to return the favour. This feeling of obligation or indebtedness has been elaborated on by Greenberg (1978) who states that indebtedness is an aversive state which the recipient would either try to avoid altogether by refusing aid, or relieve if aid has been accepted. It is also suggested that indebtedness is uncomfortable probably because it creates an inequitable situation between the donor and recipient. Following the equity formulation (Homans, 1961; Adams, 1965; Walster, Berscheid and Walster, 1973), when aid is given by the donor to the recipient, the reward/cost ratios of the donor and the recipient become unequal and are in favour of the recipient. Restoration of equity then becomes necessary, and can be effected by returning the favour, by terminating interaction with the donor, or by cognitive means (for example, 'rationalizing' the helping act or devaluing the reward act aspect of receiving aid).

In any case, until equity is restored to the situation, the recipient undergoes an uncomfortable experience which has been called indebtedness. There is evidence that the recipient often considers ways to avoid or minimize indebtedness even before accepting aid.

Bar-Tal (1976) states that the extent of indebtedness is determined :

(a) the relative differences or ratio between the rewards of the donor and recipient, as well as the differences or ratio between the costs of the donor and recipient. Thus there would be more intense indebtedness when there is a great discrepancy between the rewards obtained by the recipient and the costs incurred by the donor, as a result of the helping act;

(b) the locus of initiation of help as perceived by the recipient. If the help is perceived as being spontaneously initiated by the donor, there would be less indebtedness than if the help is perceived as being initiated by the recipient;

(c) the perception of the donor's motives in giving help. The recipient would feel more indebted when the donor gives intentional and personal aid than when aid is given accidentally and is impersonal;

(d) social cues provided to the recipient indicating obligation. The degree of obligation is greater when others indicate to the recipient that he or she has been done a favour which should be returned, than when there are no such indications.

Self-esteem

Self-esteem as a mediator in recipient reactions to aid has been proposed by Fisher, Nadler and Whitcher, (Note 2). In a society or culture which consistently stresses independence and reliance on one's own resources, accepting aid would be typically perceived as implying incapability, incompetence or inferiority of the recipient. Under such circumstances, therefore, accepting aid would be damaging to the recipient's self-esteem. Other theories pertaining to self-esteem as a personality component (Coopersmith, 1967; Wylie, 1962) have indicated that individuals cannot normally continue in a state of lowered self-esteem and attempts are made to maintain an attitude of self-worth by reacting to any experience that challenges or threatens their self-esteem. It would follow that in situations of helping when the acceptance of aid has threatening consequences for the recipient's self-esteem, reactions to aid will be affected accordingly.

In the formulation of a 'threat to self-esteem' model of recipient reactions, Fisher, Nadler and Whitcher include two major aspects of self-esteem, namely, self-support and self-threat. The idea of self-support implies that there may be situations in which aid is perceived positively by the recipient because it is believed to enhance self-esteem. On the other hand, in other circumstances, aid may be perceived as lowering or threatening self-esteem. Two clusters of recipient reactions may thus be identified, one resulting from high absolute or relative self-support for the recipient, and the other resulting from high absolute or relative self-threat to the recipient. The first cluster of reactions would include positive affect, positive evaluation of the donor and the help, low negative and high positive reciprocity, high help-seeking, low refusal of offers of aid, and low degree of subsequent self-help. In contrast, the second cluster of reactions would include negative affect, negative evaluation of the donor and the help, high negative and low positive reciprocity, low help-seeking, high refusal of offers of aid, and high degree of subsequent self-help.

Elaborating on their model, Fisher, Nadler and Whitcher further state that self-support and self-threat may develop through dependency relationships in the course of socialization, that self-support and self-threat are experienced in a specific helping situation because of donor, recipient, resource and situational characteristics, that self-support and self-threat experiences determine reactions to aid, that self-support and self-threat intervene between these four categories of factors on one hand, and recipient reactions, on the other, and that the magnitude of self-support and self-threat experienced affects the intensity of the two clusters of reactions mentioned above.

Attribution

Attribution of motives to the donor of aid is yet another way of explaining reactions to aid. Schopler (1970) discusses the importance of attribution in responding to aid, and mentions three primary criteria that a recipient might use in judging the donor's motives: if there are no extraneous rewards for the donor, if the help synchronizes with the recipient's need, and if the help is appropriate in the context, then the recipient would attribute no ulterior motives to the donor. When these criteria are not fulfilled, and the aid is perceived as being given for reasons other than helpfulness or altruism, recipients are either less likely to accept it or are less likely to subsequently return it, than when aid is perceived as being altruistically motivated. Fisher, Nadler and Whitcher point out that, on the basis of the theory of correspondent inferences proposed by Jones and Davis (1965) the recipient would be expected to attribute dispositional motives to helping only when there is no indication that the aid was given due to situational requirements or by other constraints. In other words, the theory of correspondent inferences proposes the conditions under which the recipient would make attributions about the donor's intentions in view of the presence of situational constraints on helping.

In addition, Kelley's (1967) theory of external attribution attempts to explain the circumstances in which an individual attributes behaviour to external or environmental causes versus internal or personal-dispositional causes. This theory can be applied to helping contexts from the point of view of the recipient. Two major sources of information are used in attributing motives, one related to expectations regarding personally caused behaviour, and the other related to specific conditions within the context in which attribution is made. The behaviour of the other person is then evaluated in terms of three dimensions, namely, distinctiveness, consistency, and consensus. When the behaviour shows a high degree of distinctiveness, a high degree of consensus, and a high degree of consistency across situations, the attribution is made to external causes; when the behaviour shows a low degree of consensus, a low degree of distinctiveness, and a high degree of consistency, an internal attribution results.

In the context of recipient reactions, there is some empirical evidence cited by Fisher, Nadler and Whitcher that shows that Kelley's propositions are generally borne out with respect to help-seeking and reciprocity, although there is still insufficient information regarding the specific conditions under which the need for giving or receiving aid will be attributed to external or internal causes by the recipient. It has been observed that acceptance of aid, help-seeking and reciprocity would be less likely when there is an internal attribution than when there is external attribution, for the need to receive aid.

It must be clear at this stage that most of the research and theory on recipient reactions that has been reported and discussed relates primarily to western societies. This leads very naturally to the question of cultural variations in reactions to aid. In fact, Bar-Tal (1976) suggests a separate category of cultural determinants of helping behaviour, implying that cultures and societies do vary in helping behaviour. This idea may be extended to reactions to aid. It is possible that cultural variations in the latter may be affected by those in the former. Therefore, two major queries will be answered in the present context with reference to cultural variations in giving and receiving aid: first, do cultures differ essentially in their propensity to give and receive aid ? If so, what are the factors underlying cultural differences in helping and reactions to help ?

CULTURAL DETERMINANTS OF HELPING BEHAVIOUR AND REACTIONS TO AID

Several investigations dealing with helping behaviour involve a comparison between at least two cultures or societies (Mauss, 1954; Carment, Note 1; Gergen, Morse and Kristeller, 1973; Gergen, Ellsworth, Maslach and Seipel, 1975; L'Armand and Pepitone, 1975) between two nations (Berkowitz, 1966; Berkowitz and Friedman, 1967; Feldman, 1968), or between social classes within a society (Ugurel-Semin, 1952; Muir and Weinstein, 1962; Berkowitz, 1966; Berkowitz and Friedman, 1967; Dreman and Greenbaum, 1973). All of these studies report differences between cultures, nations, classes or urban-rural settings in some aspect of giving and/or receiving aid. What is not very clear, however, is the determinant(s) of such cross-cultural variations in helping and recipient reactions. It would therefore be useful to consider certain features of cultures which might possibly explain these differences.

First, the determinants of helping and reactions to aid might have varying degrees of importance and salience in different cultures. For example, age and sex are two demographic factors which either as donor characteristics or as recipient characteristics, might differ in their effects between cultures. In eastern cultures such as the Indian culture, age generally plays an important role in social interaction. While very old people are supposed to be the object of respect and deference, and may therefore be considered more worthy recipients of aid than younger people in the same situation, it may not always be in good taste to give older people gifts of any sort at any time in these cultures. Rather, it may be the privilege of the elders to bestow gifts as well as benedictions on younger recipients. In western cultures, sex-role stereotypes persist despite modernization, and the emphasis on equal rights for men and women. Stereotypically women would be expected to give help as well as receive aid to a greater extent than men; yet empirical evidence does not bring out this difference very unambiguously in the context of western cultures, but it is possible that sex-role stereotypes are more clearly maintained in non-western cultures.

Secondly, the norms that have been proposed as a major basis of helping behaviour and response to help may differ between cultures in terms of the strictness with which members of specific cultures adhere to them. Evidence on class-differences in helping in western cultures shows that reciprocity is most commonly a middle-class norm while the social responsibility norm is often but not always found in lower economic levels. There does not appear to be parallel information with respect to norm-differences across cultures. It may be speculated that cultures that stress fairness and justice would be likely to follow reciprocity and equity principles more strictly than would cultures in which fairness and justice are not very important. Moreover, it is possible that social norms within a society are prescribed through traditional customs rather than immediate behavioural rules. In such cases, there may be a discrepancy between traditional prescriptions and actual social behaviour.

Thirdly, because of the first-two sources of cultural differences the intervening states between giving and receiving aid, such as feelings of indebtedness or obligation, lowered or heightened self-esteem, or motives attributed to the donor, would also be expected to have differential effects between cultures. Since most of these factors have been found to be influenced by situational factors more than by any other class of determinants, it may be difficult to generalize for a whole culture the relationship between any particular causal variable and the resultant cognitive or affective state in the recipient.

We may now examine the case of one specific culture, namely, the Indian culture, considering certain characteristics of this society and empirical evidence related to helping behaviour and recipient reactions. This will illustrate the fact that western theory and research may not without qualification explain and predict giving and receiving aid in non-western societies.

Giving and receiving aid in India

Students of Indian culture (Taylor, 1948; Narain, 1957; McClelland, 1973; Sinha, 1978) have frequently pointed out, as discussed at the very beginning of the present paper, that traditional Hindu culture contains 'giving' as a consistent theme. Often, however, underlying this stress and value placed on 'giving' is an essential power motive rather than an altruistic motive, which implies that the donor is more powerful than the recipient. Also, there may be a lurking expectation of reciprocity on the donor's part, or a feeling of 'do ut des'—I give that you may give (McClelland, 1973). From the point of view of reactions to aid, stories that are presented to children often include characters such as King Shibi who offered his own flesh to a hungry hawk in order to protect a dove, or the sage Dadheechi who willingly offered his bones for universal good, or Karna of Mahabharata who was known for his extreme generosity. All of these characters represent a glorification of self-sacrifice with the sole purpose of 'giving', presumably selfless giving.

To what extent these philosophical principles conveyed in traditional Hinduism are actually found in practice can be known only through empirical investigations of helping behaviour, and these are summarized below. In a study comparing Canadian and Indian university male students with respect to their choices on an Altruism Matrix, Carment (Note 1) found that Indian males made a smaller proportion of offers of help than did Canadian males, but also accepted less help than the Canadian students. In a recent investigation using the same choice-setting, while the proportion of acceptances was found to be slightly lower among Indian males than among Canadian males, there was virtually no difference in the proportion of offers of help (Krishnan, Note 3).

A lower level of altruism among Indians has also been reported by L'Armand and Pepitone (1975). In this study, Indians and Americans were compared on a decision-making task that involved helping at a high or low cost. In general the results indicated that American subjects were more altruistic than Indian subjects, but only when helping involved low costs. When the situation involved competition, the Americans were less helpful than in the non-competitive situation, and were more competitive than the Indians while the greater competitiveness of the Americans can be attributed to the predominant values in their culture, it is difficult to explain the lower level of helpfulness of the Indians in terms of cultural values, since the cultural prescription in India is clearly for 'giving' and helping.

This discrepancy between observed behaviour and cultural prescription has been explained by L'Armand and Pepitone in terms of the 'image of limited good' (Foster, 1965). Essentially, the concept of the 'image of limited good' implies that members of some societies (especially the economically underdeveloped ones which are supposedly deprived of necessary resources in life) view the world as a place in which all resources—concrete as well as abstract, universalistic as well as particularistic (Foa and Foa, 1974)—are limited and constantly in short supply. Therefore, any person who obtains a reward is perceived as having got it necessarily at the cost of someone else. In other words, social interaction in terms of rewards and costs is viewed as a zero-sum-game in which one person's gains imply another person's losses. This view of the world thus dictates two kinds of behaviour—(1) every individual must watch out for himself or herself, accumulating as many resources as possible, and every individual must ensure that the others do not get the resources before he/she does. Both the accumulation of resources and prevention of others from getting them imply the opposite of altruism.

The effect of the 'limited good' idea was experimentally investigated in a laboratory setting (Krishnan Note 3). There is some indication that when resources are limited, preformance is facilitated through an achievement-motivational set rather than an altruistic or cooperative-motivational set (Sinha and Pandey, 1970). Considering this finding as well as Foster's proposition, the effects of limit-imposition on helping and responses to helping were tested on the Altruism Matrix. Subjects were either told that they should accumulate no more than a certain number of points ('Limit' condition) or were given no specific limit on the accumulated points ('No limit' condition). Results showed that while there was no significant difference in the proportion of offers of help made in the two conditions, there were significantly fewer acceptances in the 'limit' condition than in the 'no limit' condition. Both of these findings go against the proposition of the 'image of limited good'. A lower level of acceptance of help in the 'limit' condition can be explained on the basis of the fact that within this choice-setting the only way in which the limit could be maintained was for the recipient to accept less than what was offered. The findings of this experiment should caution us against applying the 'limited good' idea without first testing its prevalence in a particular culture or society.

Another factor that has been found to affect helping and has also been found to vary cross-culturally is locus of control. Pandey (1979a) investigated the relationship between locus of control and helping behaviour in an Indian setting. In his study there was a call for volunteers among students of an educational institute for participation in a community 'Crisis Intervention' programme. Volunteering for his programme was considered an index of willingness to participate in social action, and of helpfulness. Subjects were classified into three groups: (i) those who volunteered and were active participants, (ii) those who volunteered but later dropped out, and (iii) non-volunteers, who had read the announcement calling for volunteers. Rotter's I-E Scale was administered to these subjects. Results demonstrated that externality increased linearly from the first to the third group. This relationship corroborates Gore and Rotter's (1963) finding that helping behaviour and internality were positively correlated in the American culture. Both sets of findings thus suggest that helpfulness or willingness to help is associated with an internal locus of control. It would follow that cultures found to be low on internality (such as the Indian culture) would be expected to be low also on helpfulness or willingness to help.

Yet another feature characterizing the Indian culture is the importance it gives to status and power-position. That the power motive as well as the motive of dependency are predominant in the Indian society has been observed by Sinha (1978), specifically with reference to giving and receiving aid. Since a donor-recipient relationship might well be conceptualized as an example of a power-dependence relationship (Thibaut and Riecken, 1955), status would be expected to influence helping and reactions to it especially in societies in which it is a salient variable in social interactions. This was demonstrated in Pandey's (1979b) investigation. The rationale for his study was that since status affects feelings of competence and effectiveness (Midlarsky and Midlarsky, 1976), a person having a high ascribed status would be expected to be more likely to help than one having a low status. Students and faculty members cast into the roles of both donor and recipient were asked by a donor of the same or different status to donate money for flood victims. The findings indicated that the status of both the donor and the recipient jointly affected donations. More money was donated by faculty members (in keeping with their higher socio-economic level) than by students, but at the same time, faculty members also received more donations than students presumably because their request was perceived as more genuine than that of students. Furthermore, high status similarity between donor and recipient led to more helping than low status similarity. It was reported that faculty members as high-status recipients also obtained greater mean ratings in terms of being given help willingly and gladly by donors. The implications of these findings have to be considered in the light of the characteristics of Hindu culture that have been mentioned earlier.

With reference to the power of norms in the Indian culture to determine helping and reactions to help, the empirical evidence outlined above demonstrates that despite altruistic teachings in Hindu tradition, the actual behaviour of Indians compared to that of members of other cultures shows less social responsibility. Perhaps this is because Hinduism prescribes 'giving' as a religious obligation without clarifying its direct applicability to routine social exchanges. With respect to reciprocity and equity, while there appears to be no definite empirical evidence on the prevalence of these principles in Indian social life, Gouldner (1960) cites as an example an Indian custom of returning a gift, not merely in terms of the principal, but also with 'interest'.

From the point of view of intervening states between the offer of aid and the recipient's response, there is no evidence pertaining to the occurrence of feelings of indebtedness, lowered or heightened self-esteem, or any particular kind of attribution for giving or receiving aid among Indians. This topic, therefore, needs thorough investigation before cross-cultural comparisons can be made.

The case of the Indian culture was presented in order to illustrate, as pointed out earlier, that much of what is known about giving and receiving aid in western cultures cannot be automatically said to apply to all cultures. Practically, the question of cross-cultural divergences in helping behaviour as a whole becomes important in the context of situations such as those of prosocial exchanges between two nations or cultures. It is clear from the observations of some investigators that foreign 'aid' is not always happily or gratefully accepted by the recipient nation, no matter how generous the donor nation (Dillon, 1968; Andreas, 1969; Gergen, 1974; Gergen and Gergen, 1974), and on this basis an argument has been made against helping poor nations (Hardin, 1974). Whether or not foreign 'aid' can be considered 'aid' at all, to what extent two governments exchanging aid behave like two individuals or two cultures engaged in such an exchange, and to what extent the mediators of interpersonal giving and receiving of aid also mediate international exchange of aid are all issues that need to be resolved through systematic investigations.

CONCLUSIONS : QUESTIONS FOR FUTURE RESEARCH

The present paper focused primarily on reactions to help. Starting with a brief description of research on the giving of aid, which is a prerequisite for recipient reactions, the determinants of reactions to help were discussed under four major categories, namely, donor characteristics, recipient characteristics, resource characteristics and situational characteristics. Among these factors, resource characteristics need to be explored in greater depth. Moreover, while in the case of the giving of aid situational determinants have been found to be more powerful than personality determinants, such a comparison of relative influence on recipient reactions does not seem to have been made. Specifically, an attempt should be made to discover the particular conditions which induce the personal states intervening between the offer and reactions to aid, such as indebtedness, self-esteem and attribution. Thirdly, it is necessary to include a variety of situations or settings in explorations of reactions to aid, in both laboratory and field studies. In this connection, the present author discussed some experiments that used a choice-setting rather than the conventional task-performance setting. Fourthly, the present paper considered cultural differences in giving and receiving aid. One point that emerged from this discussion was that no a priori assumptions should be made regarding the effect of particular factors in various cultures. Also, a research need in this aspect of helping behaviour is to go beyond obtaining cultural differences and examine features of various cultures in order to explain why there is more or less 'giving' and 'receiving' in these cultures.

REFERENCE NOTES

1. D.W. Carment, Giving and receiving in India and Canada. Unpublished manuscript, McMaster University, 1973.
2. J.D. Fisher, A. Nadler, and S.J. Whitcher, Recipient reactions to aid: A conceptual review and a new theoretical framework. Unpublished paper, University of Connecticut, 1980.
3. L. Krishnan, The effect of an imposed limit on giving and receiving aid. Unpublished manuscript, Indian Institute of Technology, Kanpur, India, 1980.

REFERENCES

Adams, J.S. Inequity in social exchange. In L. Berkowitz (ed.) *Advances in Experimental Social Psychology*, Volume **2**, Academic Press, 1965.

Aderman, D. Elation, depression and helping behaviour. *Journal of Personality and Social Psychology*, 1972, **24**, 91-101.

Andreas, C. "To receive from kings. . .": An examination of government-to-government aid and its unintended consequences. *Journal of Social Issues*, 1969. **24**, 1,

Baron, R.S. Behavioral effects of interpersonal attraction: Compliance with requests from liked and disliked others. *Psychonomic Science*, 1971, **25**, 325-326.

Bar-Tal, D. *Prosocial Behavior*. Halsted Press, John Wiley & Sons, 1976.

Bar-Tal, D., Harmon, M. & Greenberg, M. Effect of relationship between donor and recipient, and harmdoer and victim on reciprocity. Unpublished manuscript, University of Pittsburgh, 1975.

Begin, G. Altruisme ou reparation de l'image, de soi? *Cahiers de l'Institute Superieur des Sciences Humaines*, 1977, **6**, 1-27.

Berkowitz, L. A laboratory investigation of social class and national differences in helping behaviour. *International Journal of Psychology*, 1966, **1**, 231-242.

Berkowitz, L. Resistance to improper dependency relationships. *Journal of Experimental Social Psychology*, 1969, **5**, 283-294.

Berkowitz, L. & Connor, W.H. Success, failure and social responsibility. *Journal of Personality and Social Psychology*, 1966, **4**, 664-669.

Berkowitz, L. & Daniels, L.R. Responsibility and dependency. *Journal of Abnormal and Social Psychology*, 1963, **66**, 429-436.

Berkowitz, L. & Daniels, L.R. Affecting the salience of the social responsibility norm: Effect of past help on the response to dependency relationships. *Journal of Abnormal and Social Psychology*, 1964, **68**, 275-281.

Berkowitz, L. & Friedman, P. Some social class differences in helping behavior. *Journal of Personality and Social Psychology*, 1967, **7**, 367-379.

Bickman, L. Social influence and diffusion of responsibility in an emergency. *Journal of Experimental Social Psychology*, 1972, **8**, 438-445.

Brehm, J.W. *A Theory of Psychological Reactance*. New York: Academic Press, 1966.

Brehm, J.W. & Cole, A.H. Effect of a favour which reduces freedom. *Journal of Personality and Social Psychology*, 1966, **3**, 420-426.

Brewster, E.T. Personality characteristics of giving versus receiving-oriented individuals. *Dissertations Abstracts International*, 1971, 2476A.

Broll, L., Gross, A.E. & Piliavin, I. Effects of offered and requested help on help-seeking and reactions to being helped. *Journal of Applied Social Psychology*, 1974, **4**, 244-258.

Bryan, J.H. & Test, M.A. Models and helping: Naturalistic studies in aiding behaviour. *Journal of Personality and Social Psychology*, 1967, **6**, 400-407.

Carment, D.W. Effect of sex role in a maximizing difference game: A replication in Canada. *Journal of Conflict Resolution*, 1974, **18**, 3, 461-472.

Castro, M.A.C. Reactions to receiving aid as a function of cost to donor and opportunity to aid. *Journal of Applied Social Psychology*, 1974, **4**, 3, 194-209.

Clark, R.D. Effects of sex and race on helping behaviour in a non-reactive setting. *Representative Research in Social Psychology*, 1974, **5**, 1-6.

Clark, M.S., Cotay, C.C., & Mills, J. Acceptance of help as a function of similarity of the potential helper and opportunity to repay. *Journal of Applied Social Psychology*, 1974, **4**, 3, 224-229.

Coopersmith, S. *The Antecedents of Self-esteem.* San Francisco: Freeman and Co., 1967.

Daniels, L.R. & Berkowitz, L. Liking and response to dependency relationships. *Human Relations*, 1963, **16**, 141-148.

Darley, J.M. & Latane, B. Norms and normative behaviour: field studies of social interdependence. In J. Macaulay and L. Berkowitz (eds.) *Altruism and Helping Behavior*. New York, Academic Press, 1970.

DePaulo, B.M. Help-seeking from the recipient's point of view. *JSAS Catalog of Selected Documents in Psychology*, 1978, **8**, 62, (Ms. No. 1721).

DePaulo, B.M. & Fisher, J.D. The costs of asking for help. *Basic Applied Social Psychology*, 1980, **1**, 23-35.

Deutsch, M. Trust and suspicion. *Journal of Conflict Resolution*, 1958, **2**, 265-279.

Dillon, W.S. *Gifts and Nations*. The Hague: Mouton, 1968.

Dreman, S.B. & Greenbaum, C.W. Altruism of reciprocity: Sharing behavior in Israeli kindergarten children. *Child Development*, 1973 **44**, 61-68.

Emswiller, T., Deaux, K. & Willits, J.E. Similarity, sex and requests for small favors. *Journal of Applied Social Psychology*, 1971, **1**, 284-291.

Evans, G. Effect of unilateral promise and value of rewards upon cooperation and trust. *Journal of Abnormal and Social Psychology*, 1964, **69**, 587-590.

Feldman, R.E. Response to compatriot and foreigner who seek assistance. *Journal of Personality and Social Psychology*, 1968, **10**, 202-214.

Field, M. Power and dependency: Legitimation of dependency conditions. *Journal of Social Psychology*, 1974, **92**, 31-37.

Fischer, E.H. & Turner, T.L. Orientations to seeking professional help: Development and research utility of an attitude scale. *Journal of Consulting and Clinical Psychology*, 1970, **35**, 79-90.

Fisher, J.D., DePaulo, B.M. & Nadler, A. Extending altruism beyond the altruistic act: The effects of aid on the help recipient. In J.P. Rushton and R.M. Sorrentino (eds.) *Altruism and Helping Behavior*. Hillsdale, N.J.: Erlbaum, 1980.

Fisher, J.D. & Nadler, A. The effect of similarity between donor and recipient on reactions to aid. *Journal of Applied Social Psychology*, 1974, **4**, 230-243.

Fisher, J.D. & Nadler, A. Effect of donor resources on recipient self-esteem and self-help. *Journal of Experimental Social Psychology*, 1976, **1?**, 139-150.

Foa, U.G. & Foa, E. *Social Structures of the Mind*. Charles C. Thomas, Publisher, 1974.

Foster, G. Peasant society and the image of limited good. *American Anthropologist*, 1965, **67**, 293-315.

Freeman, H.R. Reward versus reciprocity as related to attraction. *Journal of Applied Social Psychology*, 1977, **7**, 57-66.

Gaertner, S. & Bickman, L. Effects of race on the elicitation of helping behavior: The wrong number technique. *Journal of Personality and Social Psychology*, 1971, **20**, 218-222.

Gergen, K.J. Toward a psychology of receiving help. *Journal of Applied Social Psychology*, 1974, **44**, 187-294.

Gergen, K.J. & Gergen, M. Foreign aid that works. *Psychology Today*, 1974, **8**, 58-64.

Gergen, K.J., Ellsworth, P., Maslach, C. & Seipel, M. Obligation, donor resources, and reactions to aid in three cultures. *Journal of Personality and Social Psychology*, 1975, **31**, 390-400.

Gergen, K.J., Morse, S.J. & Kristeller, J.L. The manner of giving: Cross-cultural continuities in reactions to aid. *Psychologia*, 1973, **16**, 121-131.

Goodstadt, N.S. Helping and refusal to help: A test of balance and reactance theories. *Journal of Experimental Social Psychology*, 1971, **7**, 610-622.

Goranson, R.E. & Berkowitz, L. Reciprocity and responsibility reactions to prior help. *Journal of Personality and Social Psychology*, 1966, **3**, 227-232.

Gore, P.M. & Rotter, J.B. A personality correlate of social action. *Journal of Personality*, 1963, **31**, 58-64.

Gouldner, A.W. The norm of reciprocity: A preliminary statement. *American Sociological Review*, 1960, **25**, 161-178.

Graf, R.C. & Riddell, L.C. Helping behavior as a function of interpersonal perception. *Journal of Social Psychology*, 1972, **86**, 227-231.

Greenberg, M.S. A theory of indebtedness. In K.J. Gergen, M.S. Greenberg, and R.H. Willis (eds.) *Social Exchange: Advances in Theory and Research*. New York, John Wiley and Sons, 1978.

Greenberg, M.S. & Bar-Tal, D. Indebtedness as a motive for acquisition of "helpful" information. *Representative Research in Social Psychology*, 1976, **1**, 19-27.

Greenberg, M.S., Block, M.W. & Silverman, M.A. Determinants of helping behavior: Person's rewards versus Other's costs. *Journal of Personality*, 1971, **39**, 79-93.

Greenberg, M.S. & Frisch, D.M. Effect of intentionality on willingness to reciprocate a favor. *Journal of Experimental Social Psychology*, 1972, **8**, 99-111.

Greenberg, M.S. & Shapiro, S.P. Indebtedness: An adverse aspect of asking for and receiving help. *Sociometry*, 1971, **34**, 290-301.

Greenglass, E.R. Effects or prior help and hindrance on willingness to help another: Reciprocity or social responsibility. *Journal of Personality and Sociol Psychology*, 1969, **11** (3), 224-331.

Gross, A.E. Wallston, B.S. and Piliavin, I.M. Beneficiary attractiveness and cost as determinants of responses to routine requests for help. *Sociometry*, 1975, 3°, 131-140.

Gruder, C.L. Cost and dependency as determinants of helping and exploitation. *Journal of Conflict Resolution*, 1974, **18**, 473-485.

Gruder, C.L. & Cook, T.D. Sex, dependency and helping. *Journal of Personality and Social Psychology*, 1971, **18**, 294-299.

Hardin, G. Stimulus/Response: Lifeboat Ethics: The case against helping the poor. *Psychology Today*, 1974, **8**, 38ff.

Harris, M.B. A scale for measuring attitudes of social responsibility in children. *Journal of Abnormal and Social Psychology*, 1957, **55** 322-326.

Homans, G.C. *Social Exchange: Its Elementary Forms.* Harcourt, Brace and World, Inc. 1961

Horowitz, I.A. Effect of choice and locus of dependence on helping behavior. *Journal of Personality and Social Psychology*, 1968, **8**, 373-376.

Isen, A.M. Success, failure, attention and reactions to others: the warm glow of success. *Journal of Personality and Social Psychology*, 1970, **15**, 294-301.

Isen, A.M. & Levin, P.F. The effect of feeling good on helping: Cookies and kindness. *Journal of Personality and Social Psychology*, 1972, **21**, 384-388.

Jones, R.A. Volunteering to help: The effects of choice, dependence and anticipated dependence. *Journal of Personality and Social Psychology*, 1970, **14**, 121-129.

Jones, E.E. & Davis, K.E. From acts to dispositions: The attribution process in person perception. In L. Berkowitz (ed.) *Advances in Experimental Social Psychology*, Volume 2. New York: Academic Press, 1965.

Kahn, A. & Tice, T.E. Returning a favor and retaliating harm: The effects of stated intentions and actual behavior. *Journal of Experimental Social Psychology*, 1973, **9**, 43-56.

Kelley, H.H. Attribution theory in social psychology. In D. Levine (ed.) *Nebraska Symposium on Motivation*, Lincoln: Nebraska University Press, 1967.

Kiesler, S.B. The effects of perceived role requirements on reactions to a favor. *Journal of Experimental Social Psychology*, 1966, **2**, 198-210.

Krebs, D.L. Altruism—An examination of the concept and a review of the literature. *Psychological Bulletin*, 1970, **73**, 258-302.

Krishnan, L. & Carment, D.W. Reactions to help: Reciprocity, responsibility and reactance. *European Journal of Social Psychology*, 1979, **9**.

Krishnan, L. & Carment, D.W. Recipient reactions in the Altruism Matrix: The effect of information about an opportunity for reciprocation. Unpublished manuscript, McMaster University, 1980a.

Krishnan, L. & Carment, D.W. Reactions to altruism: The effect of stated intention and amount of help given. Unpublished manuscript, McMaster University, 1980b.

Krishnan, L. & Carment, D.W. The effect of resource control, amount of help, donor's sex and recipient's sex on acceptance of aid. *Psychologia*, 1981, **1**.

Kuppuswamy, B. Concept of begging in ancient thought. *Indian Journal of Social Work*, 1978, **39**, 187-192.

L'Armand, K. & Pepitone, A. Helping to reward another person: a cross-cultural analysis. *Journal of Personality and Social Psychology*, 1975, **31**, 189-198.

Latané, B. Field studies of altruistic compliance. *Representative Research in Social Psychology*, 1970, **1**, 49-62.

Latané, B. & Darley, J.M. Social determinants of bystander intervention in emergencies. In J. Macaulay and L. Berkowitz (eds.) *Altruism and Helping Behavior*. New York: Academic Press, 1970.

Latané, B. & Rodin, J. A lady in distress: Inhibiting effects of friends and strangers on bystander intervention. *Journal of Experimental Social Psychology*, 1969, **5**, 189-202.

Lau, S. & Blake, B.F. Recent research on helping behavior: An overview and bibliography. *Journal Supplement Abstract Services*, 1976, **6**, 2-10.

Liebhart, E.H. Empathy and emergency helping: The effects of personality, self-concern and acquaintance. *Journal of Experimental Social Psychology*, 1972, **8**, 404-411.

Loomis, J.L. Communication, the development of trust, and cooperative behavior. *Human Relations*, 1959, **12**, 305-315.

Lowe, R. & Ritchey, G. Relation of altruism to age, social class, and ethnic identity. *Psychological Reports*, 1973, **33**, 567-572.

Macaulay, J.R. A shill for charity. In J. Macaulay and L. Berkowitz (eds.) *Altruism and Helping Behavior*. New York: Academic Press, 1970.

Macaulay, J.R. & Berkowitz, L. *Altruism and Helping Behavior*. New York: Academic Press, 1970.

McClelland, D.C. Some themes in the culture of India. In H.C. Lindgren (ed.) *Contemporary Research in Social Psychology*. John Wiley & Sons, 1973.

Midlarsky, E. & Bryan, J.H. Training charity in children. *Journal of Personality and Social Psychology*, 1967, **5**, 408-415.

Midlarsky, E. & Midlarsky, M. Status inconsistency, aggressive attitude, and helping behavior. *Journal of Personality*, 1976, **44**, 371-391.

Morgan, W.G. Situational specificity in altruistic behavior. *Journal of Representative Research in Social Psychology*, 1973, **4**, 56-66.

Morris, S.C. III, & Rosen, S. Effects of felt adequacy and opportunity to reciprocate on help-seeking. *Journal of Experimental Social Psychology*, 1973, **9**, 265-276.

Moss, M.K. & Page, R.A. Reinforcement and helping behavior. *Journal of Applied Social Psychology*, 1972, **2**, 360-371.

Muir, D.E. & Weinstein, E.A. The social debt: An investigation of lower class and middle-class norms of social obligation. *American Sociological Review*, 1962, **27**, 532-539.

Nadler, A., Altman, A. & Fisher, J.D. Helping is not enough: Recipient's reactions to aid as a function of positive and negative self-regard. *Journal of Personality*, in press.

Nadler, A., Fisher, J.D. & Streufert, S. The donor's dilemma: Recipient's reaction to aid from friend or foe. *Journal of Applied Social Psychology*, 1974, **4**, 275-285.

Nadler, A., Fisher, J.D. & Streufert, S. When helping hurts: Effects of donor-recipient similarity and recipient self-esteem on recipient reactions to aid. *Journal of Personality*, 1976, **44**, 392-409.

Narain, D. *Hindu Character*. Bombay: Bombay University Press, 1957.

Nemeth, C. Effects of free versus constrained behavior on attraction between people. *Journal of Personality and Social Psychology*, 1970, **15**, 303-311.

Pandey, J. Social participation as a function of internal-external control of reinforcement. *Journal of Social Psychology*. 1979a, **107**, 285-286.

Pandey, J. Effect of status of benefactor and recipient on helping behavior. *Journal of Social Psychology*, 1979b, **108**, 171-176.

Pandey, J. & Griffitt, W. Attraction and helping. *Bulletin of Psychonomic Society*, 1974, **3**, 123-124.

Piliavin, I.M., Rodin, J. & Piliavin, J.A. Good samaritanism: An underground phenomenon? *Journal of Personality and Social Psychology*, 1969, **13**, 289-299.

Pomazal, R.J. & Clore, G.L. Helping on the highway: The effects of dependency and sex. *Journal of Applied Social Psychology*, 1973. **3**, 150-164.

Rosenhan, D.L., Underwood, B. & Moore, B. Affect moderates self-gratification and altruism. *Journal of Personality and Social Psychology*, 1974, **30**, 546-552.

Sawyer, J. The altruism scale: a measure of cooperative, individualistic and competitive interpersonal orientation. *American Journal of Sociology*, 1966, **71**, 407-416.

Schaps, E. Cost, dependency and helping. *Journal of Personality and Social Psychology*, 1972, **21**, 74-78.

Schopler, J. An investigation of sex differences on the influence of dependence. *Sociometry*, 1967, **30**, 50-63.

Schopler, J. An attribution analysis of some determinants of reciprocating a benefit. In J. Macaulay and L. Berkowitz (eds.) *Altruism and Helping Behavior*. New York: Academic Press, 1970.

Schopler, J. & Bateson, N. The power of dependence *Journal of Personality and Social Psychology*, 1965, **2**, 247-254.

Schopler, J. & Matthews, M.W. The influence of the perceived causal locus of partner's dependence on the use of interpersonal power. *Journal of Personality and Social Psychology*, 1965, **?**, 609-612.

Schopler, J. & Thompson, V.D. The role of attribution processes in mediating amount of reciprocity for a favor. *Journal of Personality*, 1968, **10**, 243-250.

Shumaker, S.A. & Jackson, J.S. The aversive effects of non-reciprocated benefits. *Social Psychology Quarterly*, 1979, **4?**, 148-158.

Sinha, J.B.P. Power in superior-subordinate relationship: The Indian case. *Journal of Social and Economic Studies*, 1978, **VI** (II), 205-218.

Sinha, J.B.P. & Pandey, J. Strategies of high n-Ach persons. *Psychologia*, 1970, **13**, 210-216.

Smith, B.M.M. & Nelson, L.D. Personality correlates of helping behavior. *Psychological Reports*, 1975, **37**, 307-310.

Sole, K., Marton, J. & Hornstein, H.A. Opinion similarity and helping: Three field experiments investigating the bases of promotive tension. *Journal of Experimental Social Psychology*, 1975, **11**, 1-13.

Staub, E. A child in distress: The effect of focusing responsibility on children on their attempts to help. *Developmental Psychology*, 1970, **2**, 152-153.

Stokes, S.J. & Bickman, L. The effect of physical attractiveness and role of the helper and help-seeking. *Journal of Applied Social Psychology*, 1974, **4**, 286-294.

Taylor, W.S. Basic personality in orthodox Hindu culture patterns. *Journal of Abnormal and Social Psychology*, 1948, **43**, 3-12.

Tesser, A., Gatewood, R. & Driver, M. Some determinants of gratitude. *Journal of Personality and Social Psychology*, 1968, **28**, 8-11.

Tessler, R.C. & Schwartz, S.H. Help-seeking, self-esteem, and achievement motivation: An attributional analysis. *Journal of Personality and Social Psychology*, 1972, **21**, 318-326.

Thayer, S. Lend me your ears: Racial and sexual factors in helping the deaf. *Journal of Personality and Social Psychology*, 1973, **28**, 8-11.

Thibaut, J.W. & Riecken, H.W. Some determinants and consequences of the perception of social causality. *Journal of Personality*, 1955, **24**, 113-133.

Thompson, V.D., Stroebe, W. & Schopler, J. Some situational determinants of the motives attributed to the person who performs a helping act. *Journal of Personality*, 1971, **39**, 460-472.

Tipton, R.M. & Browning, S. The influence of age and obesity on helping behavior. *British Journal of Social and Clinical Psychology*, 1972, **11**, 404-406.

Ugurel-Semin, R. Moral behavior and moral judgement of children. *Journal of Abnormal and Social Psychology*, 1952, **47**, 463-474.

Wallston, B.S. The effects of sex-role ideology, self-esteem and expected future interactions with an audience on male help-seeking. *Sex Roles*, 1976, **?**, 353-356.

Walster, E., Berscheid, E. & Walster, G.W. New directions in equity research. *Journal of Personality and Social Psychology*, 1973, **25**, 151-176.

Whiting, B. & Edwards, C.P. A cross-cultural analysis of sex differences in the behavior of children aged three through eleven. *Journal of Social Psychology*, 1973, **91**, 171-188.

Wicklund, R.A. *Freedom and Reactance*. Lawrence Erlbaum Associates, Publishers, 1974.

Wiley, M.G. Sex roles in games. *Sociometry*, 1972, 526-541.

Wilke, H. & Lanzetta, L.T. The obligation to help: The effects of amount of prior help on subsequent helping behavior. *Journal of Experimental Social Psychology*, 1970, **6**, 488-493.

Wispé, L.G. Positive forms of social behavior: An overview. *Journal of Social Issues*, 1972, **2f**, 3, 1-19.

Wispé, L.G. & Freshley, H.B. Race, sex and sympathetic helping behavior: The broken bag caper. *Journal of Personality and Social Psychology*, 1971, **17**, 59-65.

Worchel, S., Andreoli, V. & Archer, R. When is a favor a threat to freedom: The effects of attribution and importance of freedom on reciprocity. *Journal of Personality*, 1976, **44**, 294-310.

Wylie, R. *The Self-Concept*. Lincoln: University of Nebraska Press, 1962.

FIVE

R.C. Tripathi

MACHIAVELLIANISM AND SOCIAL MANIPULATION

Two classes of social behaviour can be termed manipulative: ingratiation and Machiavellianism. This paper will focus on the studies relating to the manipulative behaviour of Machiavellians in field settings. The first part of the paper will discuss certain broad conceptual issues, in the second part certain studies on Machiavellianism conducted by us will be reported; and in the last section an attempt will be made to draw inferences and conclusions from the studies discussed in Part II.

PART I

Machiavellianism

Like many psychological terms, Machiavellianism also means different things to different people. We may, therefore, discuss the construct of Machiavellianism at the outset. Machiavellianism as a psychological construct was introduced by Richard Christie and his associates (Christie & Geis, 1970). The construct of Machiavellianism refers to a style of behaviour recommended by Nicollo Machiavelli in his two books, namely, *The Prince* and *The Discourses*. The recommendations contained in these books were made to a prince in 16th century Italy. Christie (1970) describes how the social and political conditions of 16th century Italy were markedly disturbed. There was rampant corruption, cut-throat competition for power and throne, tremendous social inequality, poor economic conditions and tough inter-state rivalry.

Machiavelli, therefore, prescribed to the prince a set of behaviours which would get him in power and enable him to remain in power. The set of behaviours recommended were manipulative of others and were based on guile, deceit and untruth. Roughly about 2000 years back in our own country, a Brahmin by the name of Kautilya had written a treatise called "The Arthasastra" under similar situations which contained recommendations closely resembling the ones made by Machiavelli. It may be recalled that Kautilya was no other than Chanakya, the Prime Minister of Chandra Gupta who put into practice what he had written and was instrumental in the founding of the Mauryan dynastic rule. In popular parlance Machiavellianism like "Kautilya-Neeti" or "Chanakya-Neeti" has become synonymous with political machinations for achieving personal ends. The term, Machiavellianism, therefore, has come to acquire a lot of negative connotation. Through their works, Christie and Geis (1970) have attempted to set right the aberrations in the meaning of the term. Geis (1979) is correct in suggesting that the attitude towards the term depends on who practices it and for what purpose. If you practise it, she says, it is interpersonal skill. However, if Machiavellians use their skills to attain private goals, they are branded as "manipulators". The very same skills if used for achieving approved goals by these individuals bring them the labels of "effective leaders", "master tactician", "interpersonal adept", etc.

Machiavellianism, as used in psychological literature, refers to the construct operationalized by Christie and measured through the various Mach scales. The scale typically contains statements which describe certain beliefs and values derived from the writings of Machiavelli and others. Endorsements of these statements by an individual indicate a Machiavellian orientation. A Machiavel (i.e. a person with high Machiavellian orientation) according to Christie (1970) and Geis (1979) shows the following characteristics :

(i) he shows a lack of concern with conventional morality. The actions are weighed in terms of utilitarianism and not in terms of morality.

(ii) he believes in the manipulability of others because

he thinks that most people have certain weaknesses which can be exploited for personal ends.

(iii) he shows lack of affect in interpersonal relationships and treats individuals as objects.

(iv) he shows very little ideological commitment. This allows him the necessary flexibility in adopting tactics appropriate to a situation.

To get an insight into the functioning of a Machiavel one needs to take a look at the manipulative behaviours he engages in. We will turn to this later. For conceptual clarity of the construct of Machiavellianism let us distinguish it from ingratiation which is another form of manipulative social behaviour. Manipulative social behaviour represented by these two categories of social behaviour may be understood in terms of social influence processes. After all, what is successful manipulation? As Geis (1979) points out it is getting some one to do something, he would not have done otherwise. Although, both in Machiavellianism and ingratiation actors attempt to successfully influence a target person for personal gains, there is a basic difference in their nature and conditions under which they are attempted. Some of the important dimensions on which the two may be differentiated are outlined below :

Nature of the variables

Machiavellianism has been conceptualized by Christie (1970) as an individual difference variable. The type of manipulative behaviour represented by Machiavellianism, therefore, is dispositional in character. On the other hand, ingratiation has been generally conceptualized as a behavioural strategy rather than as a behavioural style. It is conjectured that situational variables account for more variance in ingratiation than the personality variables. There is little empirical support to substantiate that ingratiation is the result of interaction of personality and situational variables. Machiavellian's behaviour, nevertheless, is explained in terms of Machiavellianism and its interaction with certain situational variables.

Nature of interpersonal power relationship

Machiavellianism and ingratiation also differ with respect to the nature of power-relationship which obtains between the actor and the target of manipulative attempt. A precondition for the operation of ingratiation is an asymmetrical power relationship between the actor and the target person. Bohra and Pandey (Note 1) found that individuals ingratiated themselves more when the target person was higher in authority than the actor and did not when the target was at the same level of authority. An actor who ingratiates himself is generally low on power relative to the target in a particular interpersonal influence situation. In the case of Machiavellianism, this power relationship may either be symmetrical or asymmetrical. A Machiavel seeks to manipulate individuals higher up in authority, or possessing more power, or individuals who are lower down in authority, or are less powerful.

Outcome control

It follows from (ii) above that in case of ingratiation, the actor perceives that outcome control is in the hands of the target person. For the operation of Machiavellianism, it is not necessary that the target person is perceived as controlling the outcome. So long as the target person can be used as an instrument for the attainment of a positive outcome, the attempt to manipulate will be made. But not so in case of ingratiation.

Structuredness of situation

A Machiavel operates best when the situation is unstructured, where the rules of the game are not clearly defined and relationships are not formalized (Christie and Geis, 1970). In case of ingratiation, the agent can operate effectively when the situation is structured, that is the authority lines are clearly demarcated, roles are clearly defined, and there is a high degree of formalization.

Degree of openness of agenda

Successful manipulation will not be possible for the Machiavels if they make open their hidden agenda. However, in case of ingratiation, the relation of agenda is not likely to result in total failure of the influence attempt. Such ingratiating tactics as other enhancement or opinion conformity where the intent of the actor is relatively transparent do obtain positive outcomes.

Nature of control exercised

In Machiavellianism as well as ingratiation, both actors and targets exercise mutual behavioural control. However, in case of ingratiation, control is likely to grow after the episode, whereas in case of Machiavellianism it is likely to get reduced. The reason being that a successful ingratiation attempt results in making the agent more attractive to the target whereas attractiveness of the agent for the target person is likely to get reduced, particularly where the target person feels that he has lost face in an interpersonal encounter situation. Ingratiation operates on the principle of non-zero sum game, whereas Machiavellianism on the principle of zero-sum game.

Limiting of behavioural freedom

The tactics used by the Machiavels are different from those of the ingratiators. A Machiavel attempts to limit the behavioural options of the target through his behaviour as well as by providing a "psycho-logic" to the target for his actions. The ingratiator also attempts to do the same, however, he would make it appear to the target that his behavioural freedom instead of being curtailed has actually increased.

Overview of experimental research

Geis and Christie (1970) provide an excellent and probably the only exhaustive review of the experimental studies on Machiavellianism. A later paper by Geis (1979) further summarizes the studies done recently in this area. The studies described here derive primarily from the above two sources. These studies may be broadly categorized under the following two heads:

(i) Machiavels as agents of manipulation.
(ii) Machiavels as targets of manipulation.

Machs as agents of manipulation

The studies which have studied Machs as agents of manipulation have sought to establish the conditions under which Machs turn out to be more successful than others. On the basis of studies reviewed, Geis and Christie (1970) found that three conditions account for successful manipulation by the Machiavels. These are, (i) face to face interaction, (ii) latitude for improvisation, and (iii) irrelevant affect. High Machs have been found to be more inclined to manipulate in the face to face interaction situations (Geis, Christie and Nelson, 1970; Christie and Geis, 1970) and less in situations which are not face to face (Christie, Gergen and Marlow, 1970; Christie and Boehm, 1970). It appears that low Machs get carried away more in situations involving social response processes relative to high Machs who remain cool in such situations. Similarly, no difference is found between high and low Machs when the situation is such which requires choosing out of a set of predefined and prescribed responses. High Machs are found successful where situations require improvisation and individuals are called upon to fabricate tactics to suit a certain situation (Exline, Thibaut, Hickey and Gumpert, 1970). High Machs are able to turn an ambiguous pay-off situation to their advantage (Geis, 1970). Lastly, it appears that high Machs are able to do better than low Machs in situations which arouse emotions or give rise to moral concerns. In such situations high Machs are able to keep themselves emotionally aloof whereas low Machs get entangled emotionally in situations as well as persons (Christie and Geis, 1970; Geis, Weinheimer, and Berger, 1970).

There are other characteristics of Machs which make them successful manipulators. For example, high Machs are unaffected by any beliefs or ideological positions including their own behaviours. This detachment from ideological positions provides the high Machs with the flexibility so essential for winning in an unstructured situation. Their task focus and cognitive orientation enables them to process information independently of their ideological positions and therefore, do better than low Machs who focus more on human relationships than on task at hand. High Machs are shrewd judges of the situations and adapt their tactics to specific conditions of the situation at hand. They persist and pursue their goals single mindedly and do not relinquish. A recent study by Gleason,

Seaman, Jones and Hollander (1978) shows that task-structure and Machiavellianism determine emergence of leadership. It was found that the low task structure condition increased emergence of leadership across Machiavellianism level. High Machs initiate and control group structure and therefore, control the group process and the outcome.

Machs as targets of manipulation

One of the significant characteristics of High Machs is that they resist social influence. High Machs have negative attitude towards men in authority and in police (Keenam and Clarkson, 1977). High Machs may change their attitude only when provided with sufficient justifications and not on the basis of persuasiveness of people. Even in the face of negative feedback, Jones, Gergen and Davis (1962) found that high Machs did not change their self descriptions to ingratiate themselves with the interviewers. Exline et al., (1970) found that high Machs resisted to get implicated in cheating. But once they got involved in cheating they resisted any attempt to interrogate them and elicit confessional statements from them. Unlike low Machs, high Machs are not moved by sheer social pressure. It is for this reason that in face to face situation low Machs lose out to high Machs.

PART II

This section will review studies which throw light on the functioning of Machiavellians. All the three studies reported in this part have been done in the field settings. In conducting the studies in the field settings we have assumed that the analogue between the simulation in the laboratory and happenings in the real life is rarely complete and satisfactory, particularly when such a sensitive behaviour like manipulation or deception is involved. Secondly, it is our belief that manipulation of an independent variable in a field setting under somewhat controlled conditions is likely to be more potent because one operates then on an existing state or condition of the field situation. The set-up of the three studies is the same. The first study relates Machiavellianism to ingratiation. The secon and third relate Machiavellianism with lying and deception practised for financial gain.

STUDY I

Ingratiating tactics of Machiavels

R.C. Tripathi and K. Thapa (Note 2)
The study had three main objectives. First, it sought to correlate Machiavellianism with ingratiation. Second, it attempted to study the relative frequency of different ingratiating tactics employed by the high and low Machs in their attempts to win some "money" in the form of financial-aid. Third, it attempted to investigate whether there would be any difference between the high and low Machs in resisting suggestions to ingratiate. A positive correlation between Machiavellianism and ingratiation was predicted. In other words, it was expected that high Machs will tend to engage more in ingratiation than the low Machs. It was also hypothesized that high Machs will go in for a less transparent tactic of ingratiation such as, "self-devaluation" rather than "other enhancement." Since there was a monetary justification to ingratiate, high Machs were not expected to resist the influence of experimenter when he asked them to engage in manipulation (in this case ingratiation).

Method
Forty-four students of a North Indian University who had applied for financial aid under the Poor Boys Fund (P.B.F.) Scheme of the University served as subjects for the study. Under the scheme, the students who are financially hard pressed are provided financial help by the University to enable them to meet the cost of their education. The grant received by the students is generally utilized by the students to pay off their tuition and examination fees, and purchase of text books. Students whose parents have a monthly income beyond a certain limit are not eligible for the grant. However, some students present forged income certificates to become eligible for the award. The subjects were appearing before a board of interviewers who were to evaluate their suitability for the award. The interview situation was such that called for ingratiation. In the eyes of the subjects the interviewers, if convinced and pleased with them, could award them the financial aid. Since

the aid to be provided was limited, there was strong competition among the aspirants to get it. The interviews were held in the Department of Psychology. Two of the interviewers on the board were teachers belonging to the Psychology Department. The interviews were held on two consecutive days.

The experimental set-up was as follows. On the first day when the subjects arrived they were ushered into a room and seated. After some time the junior investigator walked in and introduced herself as a research student of the Department of Psychology. She told them that one of the interviewers had been held up in some urgent university meeting and therefore, the interviews would begin a little late. She then asked whether they would like to cooperate in a study being conducted by the Department regarding certain attitudes and beliefs of students. After obtaining their approval the investigator administered the Mach IV scale. Students, thereafter, appeared before the interview board. No other manipulation was attempted. The members of the board, both trained psychologists, had been requested to rate the behaviour of each subject with respect to three different tactics of ingratiation, namely, opinion conformity, self-depreciation and other enhancement. The judges were also to note any explicit behavioural act of ingratiation such as touching of feet, crying, etc. The judges were provided a brief description of the tactics and asked to rate on a three point scale the degree of use of a tactic by an interviewee. Towards the end of the interview, the Chairman of the board asked each applicant the leading question, 'why do you think we should grant you the financial aid?' The question was designed to elicit ingratiating behaviour, such as, self depreciation or other enhancement. For eliciting opinion conformity, a different procedure was adopted. During the interview, one of interviewers would express an opinion on some contemporary social situation and would thereafter ask for the opinion of the subject. After some time, the other interviewer also would join in the discussion and would express an opinion contrary to the opinion of the first one. If the subject agreed with the diametrically opposite positions held by the two interviewers he was positively scored for opinion conformity.

On the second day, a fresh set of 21 applicants were administered the Mach IV scale using the same pretext as on the first day. When they were about to complete the Mach IV scale the ingratiation manipulation was introduced. Another research student previously trained in the deception walked in casually exhibiting an air of idle curiosity. After a few minutes of conversation with the research scholar collecting her data, she proceeded to fall into a conversation with the subject nearest to her who had finished by then filling up of his Mach questionnaire. She continued the conversation until the subject asked her who she was. The confederate explained that she was a research scholar and had been in the Department for years and knew all the members of the board inside out. By now, the rest of the subjects had started listening to her. She continued in the same vein and suggested a few tactics in a helpful manner, which would ensure them success at the interview, such as, agreeing with the interviewers by saying 'yes' to whatever they say, telling the interviewers that they were eminent psychologists and, therefore, would know how badly they needed a scholarship; and relating facts about their pitiful existence. She finally told them that the taller of the two interviewers had been an army man and was a nationalist. As such, it would impress him tremendously if at the end of the interview, they said "Jai Hind." After this she wished them all luck in the interview. The subjects, thereafter, as on the first day appeared for the interview. The board members used the same procedure as on the first day for rating ingratiation. Twenty three subjects who appeared on the first day for interview formed the control group. Twenty one subjects who came on the second day for the interview formed the experimental group because of the presence of experimental manipulation inducing them to ingratiate.

Results

The interjudge reliability for ingratiation ratings was found to be 65 per cent and 77 per cent for the control and experimental groups, respectively. This was considered sufficiently high for pooling up of their ratings. A total ingratiation score for each subject based on the judges rating was calculated by aggregation his score for different ingratiating tactics employed.

No difference in the scores of control and experimental groups on Machiavellianism was found, although, the assignment of the subjects to the two groups was incidental and not random. The correlation between Machiavellianism and ingratiation was found to be .77 ($p < .01$) for the control group and .70 ($p < .01$) for the experimental group. After splitting the groups at the median high Machs had a mean ingratiation score of 4.42 and low Machs of 1.55. In the experimental group the mean ingratiation scores were higher in comparison for both high ($M=5.40$) and low ($M=3.10$) Mach groups. The relative frequency for different tactics of ingratiation are given in Table 5.1 below.

TABLE 5.1 : **Frequency of ingratiating tactics employed by high and low Machs**

	(a) Control condition (N=23)		(b) Experimental condition (N 21)	
Tactic	High Mach	Low Mach	High Mach	Low Mach
Opinion conformity	19	10	28	17
Self-depreciation	16	11	22	8
Other enhancement	4	3	4	3

In the control condition, where no specific instructions were given to the subjects to ingratiate themselves, high Machs showed a slight preference for the opinion conformity tactic. Low Machs preferred opinion conformity and self-depreciation about equally. In the experimental condition, the incidence of both opinion conformity and self depreciation was found greater than in the control group. Low Machs, however, opted more for the opinion conformity tactic as opposed to self depreciation. The relative frequency of other-enhancement is found low in both conditions.

Discussion

Two findings of this study appear particularly relevant. First, a positive relationship between Machiavellianism and ingratiation is obtained. This only confirmed our hypothesis. Machiavellianism and ingratiation both being manipulative behaviours, a positive relationship was to be expected. In another study Pandey and Rastogi (1979) had obtained similar results. The experimental situation in this study was such as to encourage operation of both Machiavellianism and ingratiation. The situation was face to face interaction situation and accorded opportunities for improvisation because it was sufficiently ambiguous. It was ideal for Machiavellianism. At the same time, the actor and target formed an asymmetric power relationship within a formal set-up, where the outcomes were largely in the control of the target. Such a situation encouraged ingratiation. It may be because of this reason, that a high positive relationship between these two variables is obtained. One can, nevertheless, visualize situations where high Machs may not necessarily engage in ingratiation, for example, where such attempts are not seen as instrumental in obtaining the derived outcomes.

The second significant finding was that instructions to ingratiate in the experimental condition resulted in higher incidence of ingratiation attempts both in case of high as well as low Machs. In a study done by Jones, Gergen and Davis (1962) instructions to ingratiate resulted in attempts to present themselves more positively. Certain studies notably by Exline et al., (1970), suggest that high Machs resist influence to engage them in manipulative behaviours such as cheating and deception. Since the instruction to ingratiate was not very far off from what is normally practised, as indicated by relatively high incidence of ingratiation under the control condition, high Machs had no reason to resist such influence particularly when they thought it could be a justifiable tactic for attaining their goals.

STUDY II

Machiavellianism and lying for financial gain

R. C. Tripathi and Y. Sinha (Note 3)

Study I revealed that high Machs tend to engage in more frequent attempts to ingratiate in comparison to the low

Machs when there was a possibility of obtaining financial rewards. This raised a question whether in a similar situation, they are also likely to lie more often than the low Machs.

In Study II, therefore, an attempt was made to relate Machiavellianism with lying. Earlier studies by Exline et al., (1970), Bogart, Geis, Levy, and Zimbardo (1970) had shown that low Machs were as prone to lie as high Machs. It was found that when inducements to cheat were increased, high Machs lied and cheated more. Hegarty and Sims (1979) performed a laboratory experiment which involved making an unethical decision for the organization. A marketing decision task was simulated and *S*s were required to make a series of decisions on whether to pay a kickback or not. Although, no personal gains were involved, Machiavellianism was found to relate to unethical decision behaviour. However, in some other studies no difference between high and low Mach subjects were found (Epstein, 1969; Feiler, 1967). In the present study, it was hypothesized that high Machs will tend to lie more frequently than the low Machs when the associated risks of lying were not high, and secondly, a high incentive value was associated with lying.

Method

The same experimental set up of the financial aid interviews for the Poor Boys' Fund (P.B.F.) was made use of. *S*s were 68 male students in their final year of the Master of Arts programme at a North Indian University. Most of the applicants came from the surrounding villages and reported their parental annual income as less than Rs. 3000. Forty-six of the subjects belonged to the high caste group and twenty-two to the low caste.

All the *S*s had filled out a prescribed form for the award of financial aid under the Poor Boys' Fund scheme of the University at the beginning of the session. The interviews were called roughly after six months of the filling out of the forms. On the forms, the applicants provided information about such items as : (i) parental income, (ii) number of dependents, (iii) number of dependents receiving education, (iv) whether the student was self supporting, (v) help received by him in the past, and (vi) special hardships faced by him. An elaborate system for giving weightage to the responses given on the above items is employed by the University. This system has been in force for a long time. Older students of the University, by and large, have knowledge of this system. Therefore, sometimes, they try to exaggerate their financial need by providing wrong information on the application form or during the interview. The fact that the incidence of fudging and lying is high in these interviews was known to the investigators through personal experience.

The procedure for the study was as follows : All students on arrival were seated in a hall by an Assistant of the Chairman of the board of interviewers. He then announced that there would be a slight delay in the commencement of interviews because one of the members of the board was busy elsewhere. In the meanwhile, they could help a research scholar in his research work, if they so desired. It was made clear that there was no connection of this with the actual interview. As in the previous study, the junior researcher introduced himself as one conducting a study of student beliefs and attitudes. Mach IV scale was administered to all those present. There were no refusals.

Lying was measured on the basis of ratings of judges. All three members of the interview board served as judges. Interview was held in the routine fashion. The Chairman of the board first sought information from the applicants on various items. In case of any discrepancy occurring between the written information supplied on the form, and oral information supplied by the subject during the interview, the subject was asked whether any change had occurred since his filling out of the form. If he said yes, he was asked to provide the necessary details. If he said no, he was confronted with the discrepant information and asked to explain the discrepancy. The judges then rated him for lying on a three point scale (0=not lying; 1=somewhat lying; 2=down right lying). Only in 2 out of 70 cases there was complete disagreement among the judges. These cases were eliminated. In the remaining 68 cases, at least two of the three judges agreed on their ratings.

Results

Both individual as well as pooled ratings of the three judges were analyzed. Mach scores of *S*s were correlated against the pooled ratings of the judges. The product moment coefficient of correlation was found to be .57 (df=66; $p < .01$). Even when data were analyzed separately for the judges, it was found that the three judges rated more of the high Machs as lying in comparison to low Machs. Observational data gathered by us during the interview also provided support to our hypothesis that high Machs would lie and cheat more often. During the interview, 11 students were found peeping into the evaluation charts of the judges while marks were being entered. All of these later turned out to be higher Machs. There were five other students who had either brought a letter of recommendation or got some one to put in a word for them. They also were high Mach subjects.

Discussion

In earlier studies where Machiavellianism has been related to lying or cheating, *S*s have been induced or implicated to lie or cheat. The findings of these studies, therefore, have not yielded clearcut results. Geis and Christie (1970) conjecture that because of this, such experiments may have been measuring compliance or persuasion and not lying or cheating. In this experiment, lying in more or less spontaneous fashion has been studied in a naturalistic setting. Our findings suggest that Machiavellianism is related with lying for financial gain. There is one possibility though, which needs to be ruled out. Past studies have suggested that high Machs are successful liars (Exline et al., 1970). How come then they got caught ? It would appear that, at least, in this case high Machs get caught because of the nature of the experimental situation. There was very little escape for them because they were confronted with discrepancy in the objective information they themselves had provided. It can also be argued that some of them may have successfully deceived us and escaped with an honesty rating. If some high Machs escaped our detection, their detection would only bolster up our contention further.

STUDY III

Machiavellianism and deception under moral appeal and punitive threat condition

R. C. Tripathi and Y. Sinha (Note 4)

The study reported in the earlier section showed that Machiavellianism was related to lying for financial gain. It raised two questions. Firstly, what will happen if the associated risks with lying were increased? Secondly, if a moral appeal were to be made to high and low Mach subjects to desist from cheating, how would they respond, particularly, when they are told that they may, deprive some more deserving students from obtaining financial aid through their lying. It was hypothesized that moral appeal will affect the low Mach subjects, according to Christie and Geis (1970) get influenced by "irrelevant affect" much more than the high Mach subjects. The high Mach subjects and low Mach subjects were expected to be influenced to an equal degree by the threat of punitive action.

Method

The sample consisted of 82 male subjects studying in their first year at a North Indian University. The students were applicants for the award of tuition freeships offered by the University. The award is made on the basis of past academic record of the students and their parental income. The reported annual income of the parents of subjects was less than Rs. 6000.

Like in the previous studies, *S*s had filled up an application form similar to the one described in the earlier studies. As in the case of Poor Boys' Fund interviews, so also here, the incidence of providing false information is quite rampant. The award of tuition free studentship is based on the objective information supplied by the applicants on the basis of a predetermined weightage system.

The experiment was conducted on two successive days under three conditions; namely, moral appeal, punitive threat, and control conditions. The control group was expected to be affectively neutral since no moral appeal or punitive threat was made out to them. On the first day, half of the control and the moral appeal groups were run. On the second day, the other half of the control and punitive threat groups were experimented upon. *S*s were assigned to different groups on the basis of their first initials and were not randomly assigned. This was necessary to make the situation look realistic and to avoid any possibility of guessing about the true purpose of experimental manipulation. *S*s were made to fill out the Mach IV forms using the same pretext as in case of the other two studies. The experimental manipulation was introduced in the following manner. Just when the *S*s were completing the Mach IV scale, the Chairman of the committee entered the room along with the forms which the *S*s students had filled out earlier. The following instructions were given to the students forming the control group:

> We are about to begin the interviews. I have with me here the forms you had filled out some time back. I would request you to go over the forms carefully and check the information supplied by you on all times once again. Please make the correction wherever required and return the forms to Miss............(research investigator collecting data).

The Chairman, then went into the other room where subjects belonging to the moral appeal condition were sitting and gave the following instructions:

> We are about to begin the interviews. I have with me here the forms you had filled out some time back. I have been sitting on such committees for many years. During this period, I have discovered that quite a few students try to get their tuition fee waived by providing false information. This is morally wrong. By providing false information, you may succeed in obtaining a tuition freeship for yourself but you may be depriving a more deserving student from obtaining some vital financial help. If a bright student cannot pursue his education because of financial reasons, not only will it be his loss but also a loss to the society, a loss to the nation. I would, therefore, appeal to you to go over the information supplied by you on this form and correct any wrong or false information

> that you may have supplied. After making the corrections please hand over your forms to Miss.........(research investigator).

Thereafter, the Chairman left. The forms were collected by the two research investigators and handed over to the Chairman, the senior author in this case. Next day, again the same procedure was followed. *S*s in the punitive threat conditions and the control conditions were seated in two different rooms. The punitive threat group was instructed as follows:

> We are about to begin the interviews. I have with me here the forms you had filled out some time back. I have been sitting on these committees for a long time now. During this period, I have discovered that quite a few students try to get their tuition fee waived by providing false information. This year we have clear instructions from the University to report such cases to the University Proctor. The Proctor will take whatever disciplinary action he thinks appropriate in such cases. Such students may be fined or even expelled from the University. (There was indeed a notice from the Dean to this effect.) I would, therefore, request you to go over the information supplied by you on the application form and make the necessary corrections. You will not be penalized for corrections made before the interview. After the corrections please hand over the forms to Miss. . . . . . (research investigator).

Thus, there were two control groups for each experimental group. The subject break up for the groups was as follows: Control group (1st day)=12; Control group (2nd day)=12; Moral appeal group=26; Punitive threat group=32. Since the two control groups did not differ with respect to their mean Mach scores, the data for the two control groups were pooled. The control group, thus, had 24 subjects.

The major dependent variable in this study was the changes made by the subjects in their forms after the forms were returned the second time. The nature and amount of change in each variable was noted. The changes made by the *S*s could have been of two types. A subject could have changed the information supplied earlier on in a manner that it could have resulted in financial loss for him (change for financial loss—CFL) or such that it could have resulted in financial gain for him (change for financial gain—CFG). To illustrate, a subject could have opted for financial loss by increasing the reported income of his parents or reducing the number of dependents or the number of dependent receiving education or denying that he supported himself. By changing the information in the positive direction, he could have opted for financial gain.

Results

The two experimental groups and the control group were comparable with respect to Mach scores although they were not assigned to the groups on a random basis. This was also apparent from the fact that when the sample was split into high Mach and low Mach groups on the basis of median of scores of all the *S*s in the study, the split yielded roughly equal number of highs and lows in each condition. After the split, control group had 13 high Machs and 11 low Machs; moral appeal group, 13 high Machs and 13 low Machs; and the punitive threat group, 15 high Machs and 17 low Machs.

Since information sought on the application form was objective, a minimum amount of change could have been expected in respect of various items of the application form after the expiry of only a few months. However, 33 *S*s out of 82, about 40 per cent, changed their form entries in one direction or the other. The percentage of *S*s who changed form entries was 44, 38, and 40 per cent in the control, moral appeal, and punitive threat conditions respectively. Since the *S*s could have changed in either direction, i.e., towards financial loss (CFL) or financial gain (CFG), one could not expect any differences among the groups. When the change was analyzed in terms of Machiavellianism, no significant differences between the different conditions were noticed except that it was found that high Machs changed more under the threat condition than under the other two conditions. When the change was analyzed in terms of financial gain and financial loss, some interesting results were obtained. It was found that under the control condition most *S*s changed their form entries towards financial gain. In the moral appeal condition that split between change for financial loss (CFL) and change for financial gain (CFG) was found to be approximately equal. In the case of threat condition, more *S*s changed for financial loss (CFL) than for financial gain (CFG). This change towards financial gain and financial loss was also analyzed in terms of Machiavellianism. In the control condition most high Mach subjects changed form entry for financial loss, whereas only one subject opted for financial gain. In the moral appeal condition more low Mach subjects opted for financial loss as predicted than did the Mach subjects. Under the threat conditions more high Mach *S*s opted for financial loss than financial gain. The number of high Mach *S*s opting for financial loss was greater in the punitive threat condition than in the moral appeal condition. As a matter of fact, it was also found that Mach scores for subjects opting for financial gain were higher than for those opting for financial loss. However, the statistical significance of these results could not be tested because of large number of cells and small cell entries. The pattern of results, however, was consistent with our predictions.

Discussion

The predictions made by us are borne out by the results of this study. The *Ss* who changed form entries to obtain financial gain had higher Mchiavellianism scores. Also more low than high Mach *Ss* were moved by the moral appeal and consequently opted for financial loss. A study by Harrell and Hartnagel (1976) provides indirect support to some of these findings. These authors found that low Machs did not cheat from a trusting supervisor but the higher Machs did. In our study, moral appeal by the experimenter may have been responsible for generating similar feelings. Also, there is evidence that low Mach indeed consider needs and concerns of others as their own (Geis and Christie, 1970).

PART III

Conclusions

Towards the end of their seminal work, Christie and Geis

(1970) ask "Is there any correspondence between behaviours elicited in controlled laboratory settings and those occurring under the control of forces in the larger society?" and then add "This is a difficult question to answer" (p. 342). They go on to remark, "Although, their (high Machs) ability to adapt their tactics to the specific situation, demonstrated in laboratory studies, would suggest that they might be equally effective in dealing with others to promote their own interests in longer-term situations (such as encountered in real-life), this is more speculative" (p. 342). The studies reported here will remove at least some reservations about the translation of laboratory findings in the real world. The findings of the three studies generally supported the model of Christie and Geis which holds that high Machs are able to manipulate effectively in situations which are (a) face to face interaction situations, (b) loosely structured, requiring improvisation and (c) are characterized by 'irrelevant' affect. The set-up used for the three studies involved face to face interactions between the actors (high Machs) and their targets (interviewers) and, therefore, was appropriate for the operation of Machiavellianism. This variable (face to face interaction) appears to be crucial because manipulations cannot be expected to operate in a vacuum. In another study in which we studied choice-shifts this message came out loud and clear (Tripathi and Sinha, Note 5). High Mach groups showed the largest shift towards the risky end (obtained on the basis of pre and past group discussion scores), while there was no difference on the initial risk scores of high and low Machs. It was when the high Machs were put in groups that they really came alive. Although, the situation of the interviews was a formal situation which cannot be said to be strictly loosely structured, particularly, because the rewards in the situation were tied to 'objective performance', the *Ss* did perceive some latitude for improvisation. This was evident from the different ingratiating tactics they adopted in Study I and also the manipulative attempts they made as described in Study II and III. The general finding of Christie and Geis that low Machs do not perform as well because they get carried away easily got support in Study III where under the moral appeal condition, low Machs changed form entries to incur even personal financial loss.

In conclusion, it may be said that a large number of questions remain unanswered even where manipulative social behaviour is understood in terms of the behaviours of the Machiavellians. It is not clear why Machiavellians manipulate others. Do they have a need to manipulate ? Is it because of the incentives attached with the desired goals ? We need to specifically investigate the cognitive and motivational determinants of Machiavellianism.

REFERENCE NOTES

1. K.A. Bohra & J. Pandey, Ingratiation toward different target persons: A stranger, a friend, and a boss. Unpublished paper, Department of Psychology, University of Allahabad, 1980.
2. R.C. Tripathi & K. Thapa, Ingratiating tactics of the Machiavellianism. Unpublished manuscript, Department of Psychology, Allahabad University, Allahabad, 1977.
3. R.C. Tripathi & Y. Sinha, Machiavellianism and lying for financial gain. Unpublished manuscript. Department of Psychology, Allahabad University, Allahabad, 1975.
4. R.C. Tripathi & Y. Sinha, Machiavellianism and deception in a real life setting. Unpublished manuscript, Department of Psychology, Allahabad University, Allahabad, 1978.
5. R.C. Tripathi & Y. Sinha, Machiavellianism and choice-shift. Unpublished manuscript, Department of Psychology, Allahabad University, Allahabad, 1976.

REFERENCES

Bogart, K., Geis, F., Levy, M. & Zimbardo, P. No dissonance for Machiavellians. In R. Christie & F.L. Geis (eds.) *Studies in Machiavellianism.* N.Y. : Academic Press, 1970.

Christie, R. Why Machiavelli? In R. Christie, & F.L. Geis (eds.) *Studies in Machiavellianism,* N.Y. : Academic Press, 1970.

Christie, R. & Boehm, V. Machiavellians meet Miss Rheingold. In R. Christie & F.L. Geis (eds.) *Studies in Machiavellianism,* N.Y. : Academic Press, 1970.

Christie, R., Gergen, K. & Marlow, D. The penny-dollar caper. In R. Christie & F.L. Geis (eds.) *Studies in Machiavellianism.* N.Y. : Academic Press, 1970.

Christie, R.L. & Geis, F.L. *Studies in Machiavellianism.* N.Y.: Academic Press, 1970.

Epstein, G.F. Machiavelli and the devils advocate. *Journal of Personality and Social Psychology,* 1969, **11,** 38-41.

Exline, R.V., Thibaut, J., Hickey, C.B. & Gumpert, P. Visual interaction in relation to machiavellianism and an unethical act. In R. Christie & F.L. Geis (eds.) *Studies in Machiavellianism.* N.Y. : Academic Press, 1970.

Feiler, J. Machiavellianism, disonance, and attitude change. Unpublished manuscript, New York University, 1967, (As quoted in R.E. Christie & F.L. Geis (eds.) *Studies in Machiavellianism.* New York: Academic Press, 1970.

Geis, F.L. Bargaining tactics in the con game. In R. Christie & F.L. Geis (eds.) *Studies in Machiavellianism.* N.Y. : Academic Press, 1970.

Geis, F.L. Machiavellianism: a cross-cultural perspective of manipulative social behaviour. In L.H. Eckensberger, W.J. Lonner & Y.H. Poortinga (eds.) *Cross-cultural Contributions to Psychology.* Lisse: Swets and Zeitlinger, 1979.

Geis, F.L. & Christie, R. Overview of experimental research. In R. Christie & F.L. Geis (eds.) *Studies in Machiavellianism.* N.Y. : Academic Press, 1970.

Geis, F.L., Christie, R. & Nelson, C. In search of the Machiavel. In R. Christie, & F.L. Geis (eds.) *Studies in Machiavellianism.* N.Y. : Academic Press, 1970.

Geis, F.L., Weinheimer S. & Berger, D. Playing legislature: Cool heads and hot issues. In R. Christie & F.L. Geis (eds.) *Studies in Machiavellianism.* N.Y. : Academic Press, 1970.

Gleason, J.M., Seaman, F.J. & Hollander, E.P. Emergent leadership process as a function of task-structure and Machiavellianism. *Social Behaviour and Personality*, 1978, **6**, 33-36.

Harrel, W.A., & Hartnagel, T. The impact of Machiavellianism and the trustfulness of the victim on laboratory theft. *Sociometry* 1976, **39**, 157-165.

Hegarty, W. & Sims, H.P. Organizational philosophy, policies, and objectives related to unethical decision behaviour: A laboratory experiment. *Journal of Applied Psychology*, 1979, **64**, 331-338.

Jones, E.E., Gergen, K.J. & Davis, K.E. Some determinants of reactions to being approved or disapproved as a person. *Psychological Monographs*, 1962, **76**, (No. 2, Whole No. 521).

Keenam, A. & Clarkson, V. Machiavellianism and attitudes towards the police. *Journal of Occupational Psychology*, 1977, **1**, 15-22.

Pandey, J. & Rastogi, R. Machiavellianism and ingratiation. *Journal of Social Psychology*, 1979, **108**, 221-225.

SIX

Janak Pandey

INGRATIATION AS A SOCIAL BEHAVIOUR

THE PRESENT attempt is to report and integrate findings of recently completed several studies under a research programme *Social-psychological Studies of Ingratiation** (Pandey Note 3). In recent years increasing attention has been paid to study interpersonal behaviour with major focus on interpersonal attraction research (e.g. Byrne, 1971; Byrne and Griffitt, 1973; Duck, 1977; Huston, 1974; Huston and Levinger, 1978). Some of the more tactical or pragmatic features of interpersonal behaviour such as ingratiation (Jones, 1964; Jones and Wortman, 1973), have received relatively less attention from contemporary social psychologists inspite of recognition of its importance (Carnegie, 1936; Gergen, 1969; Jones, 1964; Jones and Wortman, 1973; Pandey, 1978a). The problem of getting along with and influencing people in our everyday business and social contacts concerns everybody. On the basis of research data Gergen (1969) characterizes the human being as a creature of maximization (Chadwick-Jones, 1976; Homans, 1961; Thibaut and Kelley, 1959). A human being searches continuously for ways of increasing his rewards at less and less cost to himself inspite of the norms of dividing rewards and costs among persons on a predictable basis. We are trying to suggest ways in which people calculate their payoffs, assess their social context and manipulate the situation to their benefits, most of the time at the expense of others. One of such tactics is ingratiation which

* This research programme is funded by the Indian Council of Social Science Research.

a person uses to manipulate others' feeling to establish that he, the ingratiator, is attractive and deserves reward.

Ingratiation can be considered as impression-management or attraction-management with a manipulative intent. Jones and Wortman (1973) define ingratiation as "...... a class of strategic behaviours illicitly designed to influence a particular other person concerning the attractiveness of one's personal qualities" (p. 3). The ultimate goal of the ingratiator is to make himself attractive to the target person who may in return reward him in various ways. The ingratiator seeks attraction by manipulating the attributions of friendliness, or perceptiveness or integrity made by the target person and at the same time avoiding attributions of ulterior motivation. According to Jones and Wortman's (1973) analysis "The ingratiator, to be successful, must operate with all the wisdom of an applied social psychologist in trying to manipulate the outcomes of another's attribution process" (p. 3).

Why ingratiation research?

Jones (1964) has tried to justify the decision to study ingratiation. He argues that the omnipresence and importance of ingratiation are confirmed when we frequently observe conversations and actual existence of flattery, manipulation and deceptive social tactics. The presence of such behaviour is widely observed in different social contexts of Indian society (Khosla, 1976; Nayar, 1977; Nandy, 1977). In recent years we have observed that even in daily newspapers and periodicals sycophancy has been a favourite term to describe the ubiquitous social phenomena of flattery. Nandy (1977) has described at length the way ingratiation and flattery are closely related to autocracy and authoritarianism.

In his ingratiation theory, Jones (1964) has mentioned the significance of the perceived legitimacy of ingratiation in the specific situation. A normative consideration plays a role in ingratiation. However, a society in general also could provide normative legitimacy to a particular class of behaviour (Pandey, 1980b). One may argue that in a traditional, feudal and hierarchical Indian society, to function in an ingratiating way and to become successful using such behavioural tactics and strategies is quite understandable. In Pandey's (1980b) study subjects were asked to complete a questionnaire titled as "Social Behaviour Questionnaire" (SBQ). The questionnaire was developed to measure six forms of ingratiation: opinion conformity, self-enhancement, other enhancement, name dropping, changing with situations, and instrumental dependency. The subjects were asked to rate on SBQ their actual behaviour and expected behaviour. Finally, they also rated their behaviour, planned with intention to be successful in Indian society. As predicted, the subjects rated ingratiation as an expected behaviour. Subjects responded in ingratiating way probably as a part of their manipulative strategy for gaining maximum success (Pandey, 1980b). May be the hierarchy ridden traditional Indian society is quite demanding of ingratiating behaviour.

The study of ingratiation may also help in understanding the central mysteries of social interactions. Social psychologists find that studying ingratiation is helpful in our knowledge of other common social phenomena such as group cohesiveness, social influence, conformity, social reinforcement in sequence of social interactions, person perception, leadership, social power, and many other aspects of social behaviour.

Any society requires from its members productivity oriented behaviour to facilitate the process of socio-economic development and change. In Indian society, "where ingratiation tactics are more prevalent and acceptable, individuals may remain engaged in activities which are not necessary for organizational productivity" (Pandey, 1978a, p. 388). Recently, Sinha and Sinha (1974) have examined some of the middle class values under the Indian social context. They have suggested that *aram* (i.e. rest, relaxation) is an important value of the Indian middle class. What we generally observe is that most of the people look for a job which might provide a lot of rest and relaxation. Recently, it has been argued that *aram* emphasizes achievement of prestige and recognition in return for little or no effort (Latané, Weiner, and Pandey, Note 2). Another interlinked prevalent tendency among Indian people like other people of traditional societies, is, dependence proneness (Pandey and Sinha, 1968; Sinha, 1970). This is a tendency "to seek support, help, and protection from superiors in return for compliance and unconditional loyalty" (Sinha and Sinha, 1974, p. 103). Where dependency and liking for rest is widely prevalent, individuals may adopt social strategies other than hard work for their personal success and achievements. Ingratiation may be such a possible strategy. Therefore, in our culture, ingratiation seems to bear an interesting relationship with productivity and change.

Most of the reported research on ingratiation are based on studies conducted in Western societies (Pandey, 1978a). The findings and implications of these studies are difficult to be generalized in our culture. Moscovici (1972) has rightly put the importance of social context in the study of social behaviour: "The proper domain of our discipline is the study of cultural processes which are responsible for the organization of knowledge in a society, for the establishment of inter-individual relationships in the context of social and physical environment, for the formation of social movements (groups, parties, institutions) through which men act and interact, for the codification of inter-individual and inter-group conduct which creates a common social reality with its norms and values, the origin of which is to be sought again in the social context" (pp. 55-56). It seems improper to generalize explanations of ingratiation suggested by Western social psychologists (Jones, 1964; Jones and Wortman, 1973) for the understanding of ingratiation in our society without empirical verification of those explanations. While "buttering up the boss" is commonly observed as the royal road to personal advancement and success, there is a need to study the dynamics behind it empirically rather than blindly borrowing explanations from western studies. Cultural variations in use of ingratiation have been recognized (Jones, 1964; Pandey, 1980b). What is ingratiating behaviour in one culture, may not be considered ingratiating in other cultures. Thus, what is custom, (decency, politeness, courtesy) and what is ingratiation depends on time, place, society, culture, and individual. By definition, ingratiation departs from purely normative etiquette.

Further, Steiner (1970) reports ingratiation as a risk-loaded social strategy. We do not know whether ingratiation is risky in our society. We may argue that some aspects of ingratiation may be quite culture specific and generalizations of research findings based on western studies may involve problems. Therefore, it is important to identify the cultural baselines of ingratiation.

Broadly, three major classes of ingratiation tactics have been suggested by Jones (1964). They are : other-enhancement, opinion conformity, and self-presentation. In their research, Jones (1964) and his associates (Jones and Wortman, 1973) have studied mostly these three ingratiation tactics. It seems, that there may be many other forms of ingratiation used in the social episode which have not been invesitgated. In addition, forms of ingratiation depend on the specific culture. In our recent research, which would be discussed in the later section, we have been able to identify various ingratiation tactics other than what Jones and his associates have suggested.

The inadequacy of Jones's (1964) theory requires further empirical work for a more inclusive and broad theory of ingratiation. In their theory, Jones (1964) and his associates (Jones and Wortman, 1973; Jones and Baumeister, 1976) have provided cognitive and motivational explanations. Jones and Wortman (1973) argue that three sets of factors affect the use of ingratiation strategy : (1) incentive based determinants, (2) the ingratiator's subjective probability of success, and (3) the perceived legitimacy of engaging in tactics to curry favour. Ingratiation is a motivated behaviour to increase one's attractiveness. There may be several possible reasons to explain why an individual seeks attraction. Firstly, attraction implies that others like him and this helps to realize his worth. Secondly, by making himself attractive, an individual may increase his chances of obtaining a specific goal such as a raise in salary, a promotion or other favours. Alternatively, he may decrease his chances of receiving negative outcomes such as transfer, demotion or any other form of punishment. Jones and Wortman (1973) suggest that ingratiation depends on, (a) value of the goal and (b) perceived uniqueness of the target person as a source of the desired benefit. However, the incentive and motivational aspects cannot be sufficient conditions for ingratiation. One important aspect of such behaviour is the ingratiator's perception of the subjective probability of success of the tactics which he uses. Third major determinant of ingratiation is perceived legitimacy of tactical behaviour. The question of moral justifiability and ethical legitimacy does come in the mind of the ingratiator.

In summary, Jones's (1964) ingratiation theory cannot be generalized for another society unless it is tested empirically. The role of the three major classes of determinants may vary with cultural variations. For example, estimation of subjective probability of success will depend on the ingratiator's perception of target person's liking for ingratiation tactics. As mentioned earlier, it has been observed (Nayar, 1977; Nandy, 1977; Pandey, 1980b) that such behaviour is widely acceptable in Indian society. This by implication suggests, that legitimacy and a generalized probability for success exist for ingratiation tactics in Indian society facilitating its pervasive use. It is not important that the form of ingratiation varies but most important aspect is whether ingratiation in any form is still linked to such broad underlying determinants as incentive value, subjective probability, and perceived legitimacy. In any case, this analysis supports justifiability of ingratiation research.

In addition, Jones's (1964) theory fails to elaborate the psychology of the victim of ingratiation, the target person. The theory explains only the ingratiator's motivation and perspective of the situation which includes target person. The other partner, that is, the target person in such dyadic interaction is important. In our research we have tried to investigate the other side of such social episode. In sum, the present research programme on ingratiation developed due to: (1) socio-cultural relevance, (2) implications for productivity related behaviour, and (3) to answer several theoretical questions.

Ingratiation Tactics

Jones and his associates (Jones, 1964; Jones and Wortman, 1973) suggest three broad categories of ingratiation tactics: Other-enhancement, opinion conformity, and self-presentation. However, they argue that these broad categories are not exhaustive and the ingratiator may adopt any other form to increase interpersonal attraction. In addition, the ingratiator can adopt all or any form of social tactics to increase his influence on the other person. Ingratiation tactics are influenced by variations in cultural and social conditions (Pandey, 1981a;

Pandey, 1980a). For example, in Poland, Olszewska-Kondratowicz (1975) found self-depreciation, a negative way of self-presentation, as ingratiation tactic. He further argues that subjects with high self-esteem prefer positive self-presentation, while subjects with low self-esteem prefer self-depreciation. We would like to argue that due to socio-cultural differences some new ingratiation tactics may be found in our society. Pandey (1981a) suggests that since ingratiation tactics can be influenced by cultural and social variations, categories suggested on the basis of research in western societies should not be considered all inclusive and universal in nature. In recent research we (Pandey, 1980b; Pandey, 1981a; Pandey, 1981b; Bohra and Pandey, Note 1), have observed four other forms of ingratiation tactics in our society: (a) self-degradation, (b) instrumental dependency, (c) name dropping, (d) changing with the situation. Selection of these tactics was based on intuitive observations and findings of previous research. For example, instrumental nature of dependency to seek help and influence people is well substantiated in research findings (Krebs, 1970; Berkowitz and Daniels, 1964; Pandey and Griffitt, 1977; Sinha, 1970). In traditional society, self-degradation or depreciation style of self-presentation does not create threat for the persons in authority and therefore, it becomes a more effective way of attraction management. Schlenkar (1975) has examined how situational variations and changes in the individual's state may influence his methods of self-presentation and impression management. Very briefly, we would like to elaborate the four additional forms of ingratiation suggested above.

(a) *Self-degradation* : In this tactic, the ingratiator emphasizes his weakness rather than his strength. He overplays the superiority of the target person and tries to reduce the chance of being perceived as a competitive threat to him.

(b) *Instrumental dependency* : Acknowledgement of one's dependence on the target person induces a sort of social responsibility in him. Thus, instrumental dependency which is purely tactical is used by the ingratiator to appear totally dependent on the target person and to seduce the target to like and help him,

(c) *Name dropping* : This is a class of behaviour where ingratiator tells the target person about his high connections with important people and thus suggests ways in which he can be useful to the target. Particularly, in a resource-limited developing society, such social connections are highly valued.

(d) *Changing with the situation* : This interactional bribe is related to opportunism practised by the ingratiator to please the target, rather than consistent behaviour based on some principle, value, ideology, or norm.

To substantiate our conceptualization of various ingratiation tactics a 35-item questionnaire (Pandey and Bohra, Note 5), with five-point scale and 5 items for each of the 7 major ingratiation tactics has been developed. Factor analysis of the data based on this questionnaire in general supports the above classification of ingratiation tactics.

Cognitive and motivational factors in ingratiation

When does a person make special effort to become attractive? There may be a number of conditions that enhance the value of becoming attractive for the individual. Jones and Wortman (1973) suggest that some of the conditions are of the dispositional nature. In addition to personality factors, various situational conditions can be identified that increase or decrease tendency of ingratiation. This contention has some support from earlier experiments by Walster (1965); Jacobs, Berscheid, and Walster (1971); Schneider (1969) and more recently by Baumeister and Jones (1978). The incentive to ingratiate is determined by the uniqueness of the target person. If there is only one of many persons who can satisfy the need of the ingratiator, the strength of motive to ingratiate will be higher than in a situation where various persons can equally provide satisfaction (Jones, 1964). In our recently completed studies we have attempted to identify some conditions determining ingratiating behaviour.

Competitive and non-competitive situations

In limited and unlimited resource conditions people behave differently. There is empirical basis to support

(McClelland and Winter, 1969; Sinha, 1968; Sinha and Pandey, 1970) the contention that under limited resource condition behaviour such as resource monopolization emerges. The way we behave in a resource limited society where opportunities and resources are controlled by a few people is an intriguing question. Pandey and Rastogi (1979) planned an experiment to answer this question. More specifically, Pandey and Rastogi (1979) predicted that in a competitive situation individuals will be more motivated to try to win the favour of the target person who controls the reward in comparison to a non-competitive situation. The design of the experiment was a 2×2 factorial with two levels of Machiavellianism and two levels of a situational factor involving competitive/non-competitive hypothetical job interview situations. The subjects were graduating engineering students for whom getting a job was most important. In non-competitive job interview condition subjects were told that number of jobs were more than the number of applicants while in competitive condition they were informed that jobs were fewer than the applicants. They were provided opportunities to respond in ingratiating or non-ingratiating manner. Results revealed that subjects of both the experimental conditions differed only for opinion conformity ingratiating style. Subjects of competitive condition ($M=4.43$) showed their intention to express significantly $F\ (1,28) = 6.61, p<.01$, more values, opinions and attitudinal conformity with members of interview board than the subjects of non-competitive condition ($M=3.54$). The subjects' willingness to ingratiate the target more in competitive than in non-competitive situation explains to some extent the commonly observed phenomena of flattery and ingratiation in a resource limited society. It seems, individuals use skilful social strategy of ingratiation to achieve their goals in such resource-limited condition.

Motivation for power and control

Power may be considered as the capacity of one agent to induce another to incur costs. In case of a slot machine, one is required to insert coins to receive the payoffs it yields. The "machine" maintains a positive correlation between costs and payoffs. Thus, the individual who incurs costs, receives the outcomes. The individual, however, may attempt to cheat the machine by inserting counterfeit coins into its money slot or by inserting coins of wrong denomination. Here, the individual's aim is to obtain the desired outcome without incurring the required normal costs. When a human being takes the place of the machine, there is a behavioural way of cheating and getting payoffs which he controls. One of many such behavioural ways and tactics -is called ingratiation (Steiner, 1970; Pandey, 1978a). The ingratiator aims to get reward payoffs by means of flattery or similar other deceptive manoeuvres. In a way, the ingratiator attempts to control and limit decision freedom of the other person who has power to give payoffs. Ingratiation in such conditions becomes mechanisms of controlling the person in power to get desired reward from him. Thus, in reality, the ingratiator becomes more powerful because in such situation he limits decisions of the powerful person holding resources. In earlier research, we have examples in support of such propositions. Jones, Gergen, Gumpert, and Thibaut (1965) demonstrated that ingratiation occurred when a worker felt it difficult to improve his outcomes within the task system itself, and when he was led to believe that the supervisor had some freedom to develop and modify his standards of performance evaluation.

Pandey (1981b) designed a study to show how an individual without resources, but motivated to get benefits, attempts to control and limit decision freedom of the other person who has power to give payoffs. He uses ingratiation power in exchange of influence. Subjects were seventy six male workers. The design of the study was a 2×2×2 factorial involving two levels of technical/non-technical background, two levels of seniority of workers as between factors, and two levels of experimental instructions as, within factor. Dependent measures were six styles of ingratiating behaviours: opinion conformity, self-enhancement, other-enhancement, name dropping, changing with situation and instrumental dependency. First, the subjects were asked to complete the dependent measure questionnaire to represent their actual behaviour in work situation. Then, they were asked to complete it in a manner which would help them to maximize their control over their boss on the basis of their behavioural skills. Means of the six ingratiating styles as a function of power and control instructions are presented in Table 6.1. Differences of responses between actual behaviour and power control instructions conditions reached significance level for items related to self-enhancement, other-enhancement, name dropping, and instrumental dependency. When subjects were instructed to think of a situation in which they would like to maximize their control over their boss on the basis of their behavioural skills, they responded in a more ingratiating manner.

In another study on tribal and non-tribal samples in Northern India, Pandey and Kakkar (Note 6) found lack of cultural variation in ingratiation. The findings, however, further support our earlier results that subjects responded significantly more in an ingratiating manner when they were asked to behave in a way that made them more effective, influential and successful in their own community. It is obvious that subjects increased their ingratiation responses due to strategic considerations (Pandey and Bohra, in press). The findings clearly implicate that motivated by experimental instructions subjects used ingratiation to achieve the goal of controlling the authorities' behaviour towards themselves. In effect, ingratiation reduces the decision freedom (Steiner, 1970) of the target person and makes the ingratiator a more powerful person in dyadic interaction due to the increased attraction of the target person towards him (Jones and Wortman, 1973).

TABLE 6.1 : **Means of ingratiating styles as a function of power and control instructions**

Ingratiating styles	Actual behaviour	Power and control instructions	F (1,72)
1. Opinion conformity	13.77	14.05	0.60
2. Self-enhancement	9.67	10.22	5.09*
3. Other-enhancement	12.47	14.13	10.24**
4. Name dropping	7.38	9.93	16.18**
5. Changing with situation	11.76	12.13	2.04
6. Instrumental dependency	7.37	8.84	14.44**

*$p<.05$
**$p<.01$
(Source : Pandey; 1981b)

Organizational characteristics and ingratiation

An extension of reinforcement theory into analysis of social interaction would surely emphasize the shaping of present actions by past reinforcements and, by implication, the shaping of action decisions by expected reinforcements (Berger and Lambert, 1968; Skinner, 1973; Staats, 1975). To some extent the basic concepts such as incentive value and subjective probability of success used by Jones (1964) to explain ingratiation are similar to the reinforcement theory concepts of past-reinforcements and expected-reinforcements. People try to behave in a manner which could bring reward and defer punishment. Thus, when an individual joins or expects to join a new organization or a new social context, he perceives the demands and expectations of the new setting and in return tries to behave according to those demands and expectations. We planned an experiment to investigate the effect of changes in organizational demands and supervisory styles on adoption of ingratiation tactics (Pandey and Bohra, in press). Organizations differ in their emphasis on task variations and on leadership orientations. In some organizations, main emphasis is put on completion of task, while in some other organizations maintenance of good interpersonal relationship is emphasized. Supervisors of organizations may differ in their expectation of ingratiation from the people they supervise. A junior employee remains, to some extent, at the mercy of the more powerful supervisor in organization, and therefore, due to his poor position, he may try to improve it using ingratiation tactics (Jones, 1964, 1965; Kipnis, 1976; Kipnis and Vanderveer, 1971; Jellison and Gentry, 1978; Fodor, 1973a, 1973b, 1974; Michner, Plazewski, and Vaske, 1979). In Pandey and Bohra's (in press) experiment a 2 $\times$ 2 within factorial design with two levels of organizations (relationship-oriented/task-oriented) and two levels of executives (those who encourage ingratiation/those who discourage ingratiation) was employed. According to the design, descriptions of the four hypothetical organizations were prepared. The "Response Questionnaire" used as the dependent measure was subdivided in two parts. The first part included 10 items measuring ingratiation on a 7-point scale. In addition, there were 8 items (7-point scale) to measure subjects' preference to join organization, perceived expected effectiveness, satisfaction, personal success, satisfaction of social needs, satisfaction of personal needs, sense of security, and alienation in the organization. As a part of experimental manipulation, the cover story of joint interview situation developed by the investigators was used (Pandey and Bohra, in press). The subjects were required to consider themselves as job applicants and read the description of the organizations carefully. They were instructed to respond to questions with utmost care to increase their chances of selection in all the four organizations. They were further told that the second part of the questionnaire, containing 8 items, was unrelated to the first part, and would not be considered for selection by the organizations.

Results of the experiment are presented in Tables 6.2 and 6.3. Results reveal that subjects showed more ingratiation in interpersonal process-oriented organizations as compared to task-oriented organizations; and more where management encouraged ingratiation than where management discouraged ingratiation. However, subjects showed more positive preference to join organizations where management discouraged ingratiation in comparison to organizations where ingratiation was encouraged. The findings of the experiment fit with Jones' (1964) theoretical analysis and with the reinforcement theory. Subject's demonstrated ingratiating responses seem to be a function of expected reinforcements. It seems, goals of acquisition and protection (Jones, 1964) motivated the subjects to show ingratiation in experimental conditions with executives encouraging ingratiation. However, when asked, subjects showed less preference for joining such organizations followed by negative evaluations with regard to expected effectiveness, job-satisfaction, personal success and security feelings. Perhaps, the ingratiation encouraging executives were judged less supportive and, therefore, subjects evaluated organization dominated by them negatively. When ingratiation is not encouraged, one might expect to find the type of managerial supportive relationship described by Argyris (1964, 1976) and Likert (1961, 1967) leading to positive evaluation of organizations. In sum, the findings imply that when social circumstances demand ingratiation people may decide to adopt it as a socially

TABLE 6.2 : Means of ingratiation responses as a function of main effects of nature of organization and executive style

	A. *Nature of Organization*			B. *Executive Style*		
	Relationship Oriented	Task Oriented	F(1,19)	Executive encouraging ingratiation	Executive discouraging ingratiation	F(1,19)
1. Supporting views of high position person	4.55	4.60	0.04	5.90	3.25	49.37**
2. Praising superiors	5.90	3.40	8.54**	5.40	2.35	57.67**
3. Telling influential person his importance	4.08	3.83	0.48	5.28	2.63	35.80**
4. Pleasing the boss	5.18	4.85	4.39*	5.90	4.13	16.13**
5. Talking high about own qualities	4.15	3.40	7.43*	4.03	3.53	1.12
6. Indicating weak aspects of an authority is harmful	4.20	3.88	1.40	5.40	2.68	29.94**
7. Following executives uncritically	5.00	4.33	4.21	6.00	3.33	61.61**
8. Changing attitudes with boss attitudes	4.25	4.20	0.04	5.45	3.00	29.45**
9. Changing oneself with changes in boss	4.65	4.38	1.07	5.63	3.40	42.53**
10. Praising to get attention of boss	4.50	3.48	5.90*	5.55	2.93	47.23**

*$p < .05$

**$p < .01$

(Source : Pandey and Bohra, in press)

TABLE 6.3 : **Means of response measures as a function of main effects of nature of organization and executive style**

	A. *Nature of Organization*			B. *Executive Style*		
	Relationship-Oriented	Task-Oriented	F(1,19)	Executive encouraging ingratiation	Executive discouraging ingratiation	F(1,19)
1. Preference to join	4.50	4.35	0.21	2.88	5.98	69.82**
2. Perceived effectiveness	4.90	4.78	0.17	3.68	6.00	51.82**
3. Perceived satisfaction	4.55	4.48	0.07	3.03	6.00	73.53**
4. Chances for personal success	4.55	4.65	0.15	3.30	5.90	71.75**
5. Fulfilment of social needs	5.15	3.55	15.61**	3.88	5.03	15.72**
6. Fulfilment of personal needs	4.35	4.55	0.28	3.88	5.53	20.18**
7. Perceived security	4.60	4.45	0.74	3.18	5.88	43.15**
8. Perceived alienation	3.18	4.08	9.95**	3.95	3.30	1.21

*$p < .05$
**$p < .01$
(Source : Pandey and Bohra, in press)

strategic behaviour but if choice is available, they prefer to avoid such situations.

In another study, Pandey (1981c) attempted to show effects of organizational formalization level on ingratiation. Blau and Scott (1962) have argued that large and complex organizations do not spring into existence of full-blown but develop out of simpler ones. Katz and Kahn (1978) maintain that subsystems of organizations, with regard to the flow of work and the specialized mechanisms for carrying it out, are an organizational growth process. In a way, organizational development is a complex process which definitely involves members' efforts and struggle to find a position of their choice in the organizations. Pandey (1981c) argues that in a less formalized organization, this struggle for advantageous position by the members, will be much more obvious than in a highly formalized organization. In this experiment, (Pandey, 1981c) a less formalized organization was defined as a recently established organization with prospect of its gradual development into larger size. The organizational structure is undefined. Norms and rules are in the process of development. It is obvious that, in such an organization, subjective factors play a role in decision making and a lot of opportunities exist for those who join it. On the other hand, a highly formalized organization is a well established large size organization. This organization is characterized with a defined structure, norms, and policies leading to objectivity in decision making. The environmental and social conditions are most likely to affect the individual's cognitive and motivational state to ingratiate. Therefore, it was hypothesized that in a less formalized organization (developing), individuals may cognitively believe ingratiation to be a better behavioural strategy to achieve success and benefits than in a highly formalized organization (developed). The subjects were graduating engineering students who were likely to join some organizations for jobs. They were told that in any organization one likes to be effective. Subjects were given either a description of a developing organization or of a developed organization. Then, they were required to complete an 'Attitude Survey Scale' in a manner which would prove to be the most effective way to be successful in the organization. As predicted, results of the study revealed that in the less formalized organizational condition, subjects showed more ingratiation than in the highly formalized organizational condition. In post-experimental questionnaire, subjects rated their behaviour highly instrumental and motivational for success.

Individual differences and stability in ingratiation responses

Individual's personal stable motivational and dispositional structure may determine his ingratiating behaviour. For example, because of his personal motivational structure, an individual may make efforts in social situations to be loved and admired. Findings of research and analysis by researchers (Jones, 1964; Jones and Wortman, 1973; Colman and Olver, 1978; Olszewska-Kondratowicz, 1975) suggest that individual differences in ingratiation might correlate with such dispositions as stability of self-esteem, need for affiliation, fear of rejection or failure and strength of dependency needs. There are different standards or models of social conduct, and due to individual personality differences, differences might exist in acceptance of those standards and models. Individual differences in personality can lead to value differences, subsequently determining individual differences in the readiness to accept the legitimacy of tactical social behaviour. Of course, cultural and sub-cultural differences influence the extent to which ingratiation is legitimized by the group, but this does not minimize the role of personality factors. Machiavellianism, a personality disposition, was conceptualized by Christie and Geis (1970) to understand particularly those social behaviours which involve deception and social manipulation. In our society, Tripathi and Sinha (Note 7) have studied Machiavellianism as power orientation and have examined social origins of it. Tripathi (1981) reports evidences based on experiments in naturalistic setting which show how high Mach subjects adopt various tactics to achieve the goal of financial benefits in highly competitive situations. In some earlier studies, attempts to establish the relationship between Machiavellianism and ingratiation were not of much success. For example, Jones, Gergen, and Davis (1962) found no clear evidence that high scores on the Mach scale were more inclined than low scorers to adopt self-presentations for the purpose of gaining approval.

However, in an experiment, Geis, Christie, and Nelson (see Christie and Geis, 1970) found that relative to low Mach subjects, high Mach subjects applied themselves with greater zest and originality to the deception and manipulation of a peer in a pseudo-experimental setting. Probably, high Mach subjects had no problem in accepting legitimacy and justification of manipulation in the situation.

In a recent experiment discussed earlier (Pandey and Rastogi, 1979), high and low Mach subjects were assigned to one of the two experimental conditions representing competitive/non-competitive job interview situations. Results of this study clearly supported the role of Machiavellianism in adoption of ingratiation. Those who were high on Mach scale scores significantly showed more liking for praising and agreeing with target person in comparison to those who were low on Mach scale scores. In addition, high Mach subjects did show liking for effort to get more opportunities for praising the target than low Mach subjects. In another experiment (Pandey, 1981c), Machiavellianism was included as an independent variable to further substantiate its role in ingratiation. It was found that high Mach subjects regarded showing weak aspects of an authority as harmful more than the low Mach subjects. Although, main effects for other dependent measures did not reach significance level, the trend of data consistently indicated more ingratiation by high Mach subjects than low Mach subjects.

TABLE 6.4 : **Mean ingratiation scores as a function of main effects***

Styles of ingratiation	Stranger	Friend	Boss	F(2,218)
Other-enhancement	14.436[a]	15.327[b]	17.327[c]	40.17**
Opinion conformity	14.145[a]	14.054[a]	16.481[b]	24.13**
Self-enhancement	16.018[a]	16.036[a]	17.336[b]	6.29**
Self-degradation	15.027[a]	15.663[a]	16.80[b]	16.254**
Instrumental dependency	11.863[a]	12.572[a]	14.563[b]	15.256**
Name dropping	14.072[a]	13.272[b]	14.854[c]	12.309**
Changing with situation	16.145[a]	17.554[b]	17.663[b]	11.074**

$p < .01$ level

* Means with common subscripts do not differ significantly.

(*Source* : Bohra and Pandey, Note 1).

TABLE 6.5 : **Correlation coefficients of ingratiation scores across target three conditions**

Styles of ingratiation	Stranger and Friend	Stranger and Boss	Friend and Boss
Other-enhancement	.40	.52	.53
Opinion conformity	.35	.29	.30
Self-enhancement	.51	.53	.56
Self-degradation	.39	.42	.45
Instrumental dependency	.35	.52	.47
Name dropping	.68	.64	.65
Changing with situation	.56	.44	.53

All correlations are significant at $p<.01$ level.
(*Source* : Bohra and Pandey, Note 1).

The experimental findings referred suggest that individual variations in ingratiating behaviour are expected. Some persons may behave in a highly ingratiating manner than others, and they also remain consistent in their ingratiating behavioural patterns across different situations. The factors responsible for consistency in ingratiating behaviour across situations may be due to certain personality dispositions some of which are briefly mentioned earlier. Bohra and Pandey, (Note 1) designed a study to show the stability of ingratiation scores across situations. It was argued that high positive correlations among ingratiation scores across different situations will imply that those who were highly ingratiating in one situation will continue to be highly ingratiating in other situations. Similarly a less ingratiating person will remain that way in different situations. A 35-item questionnaire described earlier was used to measure 7 major ingratiation tactics, listed in Table 6.4. One hundred and ten male undergraduates of an engineering institution of Northern India participated in the present study. Subjects were asked to rate their behaviour with three different hypothetical target persons : A stranger, a friend, and a boss. The subjects were instructed to respond in a manner so as to impress the other person and to make themselves attractive. It was found that subjects adopted consistently more ingratiation with the boss, than the stranger and friend. The differences in ingratiating responses related to the stranger and the friend were not clear (Table 6.4). The findings suggest that ingratiating behaviour varies with the changes in the social context. Table 6.5 presents correlations of ingratiation scores for each style in relation to stranger and friend, stranger and boss and friend and boss. Positive correlations of subjects' ingratiating behaviour across different target persons providing different social contexts suggest some stability in ingratiating behaviour which might be due to some stable dispositional characteristics of the individual. The results require more extensive empirical exploration of personality variables to establish its linkages with situational factors for enhancing our knowledge of ingratiation.

Affective and cognitive reactions of target person

So far, we have discussed ingratiation tactics and enumerated some conditions conducive for ingratiating behaviour. We have also briefly mentioned earlier that Jones (1964) and his associates (Jones and Wortman, 1973) in their theory and experimentation have emphasized study of the ingratiator and his perspective of the situation. Maintenance of any social behaviour depends to a great extent upon the social reinforcement and social support (Staats, 1975). In this case, reinforcement for ingratiating behaviour has to be provided by the target person. Thus, a systematic research of ingratiation requires study of the target person and his perspective. In some earlier attempts, effects of praise, conformity or favours on the target person have been studied. At cognitive level, if the target person formulates ideas about reality on the basis of ingratiator's statement then his appraisals of valid reality may be threatened. Jones and Wortman (1973) write "the ingratiator's compliments may lead the target person to draw inaccurate inferences about himself, and the ingratiator's agreement on opinion issues may lead him to draw ill-founded conclusions about the world" (p.45). This statement has far reaching consequences at societal level when the target person is in a position of power. Thibaut and Riecken (1955) argue that a dictator as a head of government mistrusts the citizen's motives for compliance. Why people are loyal to him leads to further mistrust and increased surveillance, finally creating a vicious circle of the two. Strickland (1958) in a later study supported such implicative findings of Thibaut and Riecken (1955). Jones (1964) and his associates (Jones and Wortman, 1973) have summarized other, primarily cognitive, reactions of the target person. In a recent study, Colman and Olver (1978) report that high self-esteem subjects reacted with a far greater liking for the flatterer than did the subjects of low self-esteem who, tended to prefer the neutral evaluator. Colman and Olver's findings suggest the role of the target's dispositional characteristics in his reactions to ingratiation. Several possible personality factors of the target can be identified. For example, the target's authoritarianism (Adorno, Frenkel-Brunswik, Levinson, and Sanford, 1950) might affect his acceptance of the ingratiator. Argyle (1967) writes "The so-called 'authoritarian personality' is submissive to people of greater power or status, and dominant to those of less. He can be found displaying these alternating styles of behaviour in hierarchical organizations. . . ." (p. 23).

It is important to conjecture regarding conditions associated with the target responsible for making him attracted and favourable towards the ingratiator. The straight question is, why does the target person become the victim of the ingratiator's tactics? In one of the most popular personality theories of Roger (1959), the concept of self-enhancement assumes that people are motivated to evaluate themselves favourably and for this reason they get attracted to people who ingratiate them. Other possible explanations to this intriguing question can be found in Heider's (1958) balance theory. However, we would like to provide an alternative explanation to this question using reinforcement-affect-model of Clore and Byrne (1974), and reinforcement-model of interpersonal attraction of Lott and Lott (1974). Clore and Byrne's (1974) model stresses the role of affect and conditioning in liking between people. According to the model, reinforcing events or stimuli that evoke positive affect are liked, and stimuli that evoke negative affect are disliked. In this case, according to the model, a positive personal evaluation from the ingratiator elicits positive affect in the target who in return feels attracted towards the source of positive affect. Similarly, opinion conformity can be positively reinforcing (Griffitt, 1974). The reinforcement properties of similar and dissimilar attitudes, according to Griffitt (1974), are widely assumed to derive from a general motive to be logical, accurate, and correct in interpreting one's environment. The motive involved is thus satisfied by consensual validation (agreement) and frustrated by consensual invalidation (disagreement) (Byrne, 1971). Data from various sources (Huston, 1974; Duck, 1977) has consistently reported the effect of agreement on interpersonal attraction. The ingratiator's opinion conformity is a means of attracting the target towards himself provided it is reinforcing. Thus, positive affect induced in the target by ingratiation tactics mediates with his attraction and subsequently, it might mediate with other forms of positive social behaviour such as helping the ingratiator (Pandey and Griffitt, 1974; Pandey, 1978b; Lott and Lott, 1972; Isen and Levin, 1972; Berkowitz, 1972).

TABLE 6.6 : **Means of dependent measures as a function of main effects of ingratiation**
Ingratiation manipulation effect

Dependent Measures	A. *Ingratiation*	B. *Non-Ingratiation*	$F(1,28)$
1. Intelligence	5.18	3.87	21.59**
2. Morality	5.75	4.25	14.93**
3. Adjustment	6.06	3.93	31.85**
4. Personal Feelings	5.93	3.93	28.22**
5. Working together	5.56	4.31	11.49**
6. Attraction	11.49	8.24	25.03**
7. Working in the same section	5.62	4.00	8.86**
8. Interpersonal climate	5.37	3.87	30.54**
9. Productivity	5.87	4.62	10.21**
10. Helping	6.06	4.93	14.00**
11. Success	5.93	4.50	18.42**
12. Promotion	5.37	4.37	6.94**
13. Wages	7.62	5.56	10.25**

**$p<.01$
(*Source* : Pandey and Kakkar, in press)

To test our above formulation, Pandey and Kakkar (in press) designed a simulation experiment in which the target person (real subject) played the role of a work-supervisor. As a work-supervisor, the target person was required to write a detailed note to explain a job which a worker was supposed to learn. In two experimental conditions, supervisor's instructions were either evaluated in other-enhancing or in a negative manner (in reality evaluated by the experimenter). The worker's (confederate) evaluation was presented to the supervisor, and immediately after he had completed reading the evaluation, his (supervisor's) feelings were measured on 8-item semantic differential 7-point scale. Later, the supervisor recorded his reactions towards the worker on Interpersonal Judgement Scale (Byrne, 1971) which included some additional items (see Table 6.6). The results of the study are summarized in Table 6.6. Subjects in the experimentally manipulated other-enhancement ingratiation condition showed significantly high self-reported positive affect (M=47.25) than the subjects of negative evaluation condition (M=26.68), $F(1, 28)=153.16$, $P<.01$. In addition, ingratiation condition subjects felt more attracted towards the worker, and evaluated him positively in his (worker's) role in improving interpersonal climate and productivity, than subjects of non-ingratiation condition. Ingratiation condition subjects rated the worker highly in terms of success and personal promotion in organization. They showed more willingness to help and awarded higher wages to the worker than the subjects of non-ingratiating condition. Thus, the findings of Pandey and Kakkar's (in press) experiment clearly suggest that ingratiation possibly produces positive affective state in the target and subsequently, his positive affective state mediates in making decisions which are rewarding for the ingratiator. The results of a more recent experiment by Singh (1980) support Pandey and Kakkar's findings that ingratiation influences the target both affectively and cognitively. In addition, Singh (1980) reports that affect induced as a result of ingratiation, produces higher power feeling. Affect and power feeling were found to be positively correlated.

Individuals may differ in their reactions to ingratiating overtures due to personality disposition differences. For example, high and low Machiavellians may respond differently to ingratiating and non-ingratiating workers. Singh's (1980) findings reveal the influence of ingratiation on both high and low Machs, with more pronounced affective and cognitive changes in low Mach subjects. There are many other personality variables such as authoritarianism which need to be studied in this context.

The bystander's perception of the ingratiator

The target person and a bystander may react differently towards the ingratiator. Jones, Gergen and Jones (1963) report, though slim but suggestive evidence, that a bystander and the target of ingratiation differ in their evaluation of the ingratiator. A bystander was found to evaluate suspected conformists more negatively. Probably, a bystander who just has information regarding other person's ingratiating overtures, and who does not receive compliments, remains more alert than the target in perceiving manipulative intent of the ingratiator. He has information, however, about the manipulative intent of the ingratiator leading to his (ingratiator's) negative evaluation. Pandey and Bohra (Note 4) use this interpretation for understanding the data of a recently completed experiment. The subjects in Pandey and Bohra's experiment, who were not the target, evaluated ingratiator negatively and showed greater liking for the non-ingratiator. Earlier, Kleinke Staneski and Weaver (1972) studied evaluation of the person who was either using proper name of the interviewer or not using proper name under ingratiating and non-ingratiating situations. It was found that when the name user was in the ingratiating situation he was evaluated more negatively than the non-name user. In non-ingratiating situation reversal of this result was found. These findings suggest that since a bystander's perspective of the situation remains different from the target, his reactions to the ingratiator are bound to be different.

Criticisms and directions for future research

In the present paper, we have tried to discuss recently conducted experiments to account for the determinants of ingratiation and its consequences. However, we must admit that the tactical side of interpersonal behaviour is quite complex and our recent attempts may help to stimulate further research in ingratiation area. One common criticism to some of our experiments may be related to 'making the horse drink' phenomenon. One may criticize that our experimental manipulation was managed through experimental instructions in which the subjects were required to ingratiate or not to ingratiate. The role-playing variety of experiments have their own problems. One may suggest various problems of demand characteristics type in simulation experiments. In our experiment, we had all these three approaches (Pandey, 1980b; Pandey and Bohra Note 5, Pandey and Kakkar, in press; Pandey and Rastogi, 1979). Consistency of our findings across different methodological approaches adopted in our research is a major defense in our favour. We did not confine our research to easily available student sample. Findings of a completed study on workers (Pandey, 1981b) and results of some projects in real work-situation (Bohra, 1980) suggest generalizability of our results. Methodological problems need to be handled in constructive ways by constantly reviewing one's approach and improving upon it. Experimentalists in social psychology, who are blamed to be simulators of fun games happen to be sincere self critics. This has helped the methodology to grow with improved scientific rigour. We have examples of social psychology experimentation which could not receive lasting popularity as studies based on those experiments failed to provide results with external validity. Generally, experimental social psychologists have been extra careful on this matter. For example, in recent years Jones and Sigall's (1971) method of "bogus pipelines" simulation has been criticized and improved (Jones and Sigall, 1973; Ostrom, 1973; Sigall and Page, 1972). We subscribe to our conviction that no methodology is perfect in social sciences and it is only a question of relative preference and superiority and therefore, our approach has been of constant vigilance, critical review, and improvement on the past.

It is not an easy task to prescribe directions for future research. However, we would like to suggest some aspects of ingratiation which are inadequately studied. For example, the effect of ingratiation on the ingratiator's and the target's self-perceptions (Bem, 1967, 1972) need to be studied. Probably, in the process of such tactical interactions both of them go through changes in their self-perceptions. As discussed earlier, it is important to study the target's social-psychological characteristics and his perspective of the situation. Authoritarianism and social power are considered to be closely linked with ingratiation but they are least studied. The present paper is not intended to create an erroneous impression that ingratiation possesses only negative consequences. Ingratiation may function like a social lubricant and facilitate interactions. May be it provides social support and effective group functioning under certain circumstances. The specific conditions under which ingratiation has positive or negative consequences may be investigated in future research.

In recent years, social psychology has been criticized for being too individualistic in its treatment of social behaviour (House, 1977; Steiner, 1974; Taylor and Brown, 1979). Steiner (1974) argues that F.H. Allport's (1924) influence has been so profound that social psychology has lost its "groupy" flavour. Two of the most influential theories of recent years, attribution and dissonance, are the best examples. In no way is 'individualistic approach' irrelevant. However, we need to balance the development in social psychology by giving due emphasis to sociological social psychology (Cartwright, 1979; Gergen, 1973; Taylor and Brown, 1979; Tajfel, 1979). Specifically, we would like to suggest that variables related to ingratiation should be also investigated in the political system, socio-cultural milieu, economic system and historical antecedents of our contemporary society for acquisition of a more comprehensive knowledge of the tactical and manipulative class of social behaviour.

REFERENCE NOTES

K.A. Bohra, & J. Pandey, Ingrtiation toward different target persons: A Stranger, A Friend, and A Boss. Unpublished paper, Department of Psychology, Allahabad University, 1980.

B. Latané, Nan, Weiner, & J. Pandey, Social loafing in the United States and India. Proceedings of the American Psychological Association, Annual Convention, 1981.

J. Pandey, Social-psychological study of ingratiation, Project Report, Indian Council of Social Sciences Research, New Delhi, 1980.

J. Pandey, & K.A. Bohra, Factor-analytic study of ingratiation tactics. Unpublished paper, Department of Psychology, Allahabad University, 1980.

J. Pandey, & K.A. Bohra, Attraction and interpersonal reactions as a function, of ingratiating/non-ingratiating style of target person, subjects' control of reinforcement and executive non-executive role. Unpublished paper, Department of Psychology, Allahabad University, Allahabad, 1979.

J. Pandey, & S. Kakkar, Cross-cultural differences and similarities in ingratiation tactics as social influence and control mechanism. Paper presented at the 5th International Congress of Cross Cultural Psychology, Bhubaneshwar, Dec. 1980.

R.C. Tripathi & Y. Sinha, Certain social correlates of machiavellianism in India. Proceedings of the Fourth Congress of International Association of Cross-Cultural Psychology, Munich, Germany, July 28-August 5, 1978.

REFERENCES

Adorno, T.W., Frenkel-Brunswik, E., Levinson, D.J., & Sanford, R.N. *The Authoritarian Personality.* New York: Harper. 1950.

Allport, F.H. *Social Psychology.* Boston: Houghton Mifflin, 1924.

Argyle, M. *The Psychology of Interpersonal Behaviour.* London: Penguin Books Inc., 1967.

Argyris, C. *Integrating the Individual and the Organization.* New York: Wiley, 1964.

Argyris. C. *Increasing Leadership Effectiveness.* New York: Wiley, 1976.

Baumeister, R.F., & Jones, E.E. When self-presentation is constrained by the target's knowledge: Consistency and compensation. *Journal of Personality and Social Psychology*, 1978, **36**, 608-618.

Bem, D.J. Self-perception: An alternative interpretation of cognitive dissonance phenomena. *Psychological Review*, 1967, **74**, 183-200.

Bem, D.J. Self-perception theory. In L. Berkowitz (ed.), *Advances in Experimental Social Psychology.* Vol. 6. New York: Academic Press 1972.

Berger, S.M. & Lambart, W.W. Stimulus-response theory in contemporary social Psychology. In G. Lindzey & E. Aronson (ed.), *The Handbook of Social Psychology* (2nd ed.) Vol. 1. Reading Mass: Addison-Wesley, 1968.

Berkowitz, L. Social norms, feelings and other factors affecting helping and altruism. In L. Berkowitz (Ed.), *Advances in Experimental Social Psychology*, Vol. 6. New York: Academic Press, 1972.

Berkowitz, L. & Daniels, L.R. Affecting the salience of the social responsibility norm: Effects of past help on the response to dependency relationships. *Journal of Abnormal and Social Psychology*, 1964, **68**, 275-281.

Blau, P.M., & Scott, W.R. *Formal Organizations.* San Francisco: Chandler, 1962.

Bohra, K.A.A. Study of Social Power, Need dimension, Incentive and Ingratiation. D. Phil Thesis, Allahabad University, 1980.

Byrne, D. *The Attraction Paradigm*. New York: Academic Press, 1971.

Byrne, D. & Griffitt, W. Interpersonal attraction. In P. Mussen (ed.) *Annual Review of Psychology*. Palo Alto: Annual Review Inc., 1973.

Carnegie, D. *How to Win Friends and Influence People*. New York: Simon & Schuster, 1936.

Cartwright, D. Contemporary social psychology in historical perspective. *Social Psychology Quarterly*, 1979, **42**, 82-93.

Chadwick-Jones, J.K. *Social Exchange Theory: Its Structure and Influence in Social Psychology*. New York: Academic Press, 1976.

Christie, R. & Geis, F.L. *Studies in Machiavellianism*. New York: Academic Press, 1970.

Clore, G L. & Byrne, D. A reinforcement affect model of attraction. In T.L. Huston (ed.), *Perspectives on Interpersonal Attraction*. New York: Academic Press, 1974.

Colman, A.M., & Olver, K.R. Reactions to flattery as a function of self-esteem: self-enhancement and cognitive consistency theories. *British Journal of Social and Clinical Psychology*, 1978, **17**, 25-29.

Duck, S. *Theory and Practice in Interpersonal Attraction*. New York: Academic Press, 1977.

Fodor, E.M. Disparagement by a subordinate, ingratiation and the use of power. *The Journal of Social Psychology*, 1973a, **84**, 181-186.

Fodor, E.M. Group stress, ingratiation and the use of power. *The Journal of Social Psychology*, 1973b, **91**, 345-346.

Fodor, E.M. Disparagement by a subordinate as an influence on the use of power. *Journal of Applied Social Psychology*, 1974, **59**, 652-655.

Gergen, K.J. *The Psychology of Behaviour Exchange*. London: Addison Wesley, Publ. Co., 1969.

Gergen, K.J. Social Psychology as history. *Journal of Personality and Social Psychology*, 1973, **26**, 309-320.

Griffitt, W. Attitude similarity and attraction. In T.L. Huston (ed.), *Foundation of Interpersonal Attraction*. New York: Academic Press, 1974.

Heider, F. *The Psychology of Interpersonal Relations*. New York: Wiley, 1958.

Homans, G.C. *Social Behaviour: Its Elementary Forms*. New York: Harcourt, 1961.

House, J.S. The three faces of social psychology. *Sociometry*, 1977, **40**, 161-177.

Huston, T.L. *Foundations of Interpersonal Attraction* New York; Academic Press, Inc., 1974.

Huston, T L. & Levinger, G. Interpersonal attraction and relationships. *Annual Review of Psychology*, 1978, **29**, 115-156.

Isen, A.M. & Levin, P.F. Effect of feeling good on helping: Cookies and kindness. *Journal of Personality and Social Psychology*, 1972, **21**. 384-388.

Jacobs, L. Berscheid, E. & Walster, E. Self-esteem and attraction. *Journal of Personality and Social Psychology*, 1971, **17**, 84-91.

Jellison, J.M. & Gentry, K.W. A Self-presentation interpretation of the seeking of social approval. *Personality and Social Psychology Bulletin*, 1978, **4**, 227-230.

Jones, E.E. *Ingratiation: A Social Psychological Analysis*. New York: Appleton-Century-crofts, 1964.

Jones, E.E. Conformity as tactics of ingratiation. *Science*, 1965, **149**, No. 3680, 114-150.

Jones, E.E., & Baumeister, R.F. The Self-monitor looks at the ingratiator. *Journal of Personality*, 1976, **44**, 654-674.

Jones, E.E., Gergen, K J. & Davis, E.E. Some determinants of reactions to being approved or disapproved as a person. *Psychological Monograph*, 1962, **76**, Whole No. 521.

Jones, E.E. Gergen, K.J. & Jones, R.G. Tactics of ingratiation among leaders and subordinates in a status hierarchy. *Psychological Monograph*, 1963, **77**, Whole No. 566.

Jones, E.E. Gergen, K.J., Gumpert, P. & Thibaut, J.W. Some conditions affecting the use of ingratiation to influence performance evaluation. *Journal of Personality and Social Psychology*, 1965, **1**, 613-625.

Jones, E.E. & Sigall, H. The bogus pipeline: A new paradigm for measuring affect and attitude. *Psychological Bulletin*, 1971, **76**, 349-364.

Jones, E.E. & Sigall, H. Where there is *ignis*, there may be fire. *Psychological Bulletin*, 1973, **79**, 260-262.

Jones, E.E. & Wortman, C. *Ingratiation: An Attributional Approach*. Morristown N.J. : General learning Press, 1973.

Katz, D., & Kahn, R.L. *The Social Psychology of Organizations*. (2nd ed.) New York: John Wiley, 1978.

Khosla, G.D. A *Chamcha* is a *Chamcha*. *Surya India*, 1976, December issue, 41-44.

Kipnis, D. *The Powerholders*. Chicago: The University of Chicago Press, 1976.

Kipnis, D. & Vanderveer, R. Ingratiation and the use of power. *Journal of Personality and Social Psychology*, 1971, **17**, 3, 280-286.

Kleinke, C.L., Staneski, R.A. & Weaver, P. Evaluation of a person who uses another's name in ingratiating and non-ingratiating situations. *Journal of Experimental Social Psychology*, 1972, **8**, 457-466.

Krebes, D.L. Altruism: An examination of the concept and a review of the literature. *Psychological Bulletin*, 1970, **73**, 285-302.

Likert, R. *New Patterns of Management*. New York: McGraw Hill, 1961.

Likert, R. *The Human Organization*. New York: McGraw Hill, 1967.

Lott, A.J. & Lott, B.E. The power of liking: Consequences of interpersonal attitudes derived from a liberalized view of secondary reinforcement. In L. Berkowitz (ed.), *Advances in Experimental Social Psychology*. Vol. 6. New York: Academic Press, 1972.

Lott, A.J. & Lott, B.E. The role of reward in the formation of positive interpersonal attitudes. In T.L. Huston (Ed.) *Foundation of Interpersonal Attraction.* New York: Academic Press, 1974.

McClelland, D.C. & Winter, D.G. *Motivating Economic Achievement.* New York: Free Press, 1969.

Michner, H.A., Plazewski, J.G. & Vaske, J.J Ingratiation tactics channeled by target values and threat capability. *Journal of Personality,* 1979, **47**, 1. 36-56.

Moscovici, S. Society and theory in social psychology. In J. Israel & H. Tajfel (ed.) *The Context of Social Psychology: A Critical Assessment,* London: Academic Press, 1972.

Nandy, A. The psychology of loyalty. *Seminar,* 1977, **210**, 12-13.

Nayar, K. *The Judgement: Inside Story of the Emergency in India.* New Delhi: Vikas, 1977.

Olszewska-Kondratowicz, A. Self-image as a regulator of tactical variations in ingratiation. *Polish Psychological Bulletin,* 1975, **6**, 73-79.

Ostrom, T.M. The bogus pipeline: A new *ignis fatus. Psychological Bulletin,* 1973, **79**, 252-259.

Pandey, J. Ingratiation: A review of literature and relevance of its study in organizational setting. *Indian Journal of Industrial Relations,* 1978a, **13**, 381-393.

Pandey, J. Dependency similarity, attraction and perceived helpfulness. *Social Behaviour and Personality,* 1978b, **6**, 37-41.

Pandey, J. Authoritarianism. *Seminar,* 1980a, **255**, 12-15.

Pandey, J. Ingratiation as expected and manipulative behaviour in Indian society. *Social Change,* 1980b, **10**, 15-17.

Pandey, J. Ingratiation tactics in India. *The Journal of Social Psychology,* 1981a, (in press).

Pandey, J. A note on social power through ingratiation among workers. *Journal of Occupational Psychology,* 1981b, **54**.

Pandey, J. Effects of Machiavellianism and degree of organizational formalization on ingratiation. *Psychologia,* 1981c, **24**, 41-46.

Pandey, J. & Bohra, K.A. Ingratiation as a function of organizational characteristics and supervisory styles. *International Review of Applied Psychology,* (in press).

Pandey, J. & Griffitt, W. Attraction and helping. *Bulletin of Psychonomic Society,* 1974, **3**, 123-124.

Pandey, J. & Griffitt, W. Benefactor's sex and nurturance need, recipient's dependency and the effect of number of potential helpers on helping behaviour. *Journal of Personality,* 1977, **45**, 79-99.

Pandey, J. & Kakkar, S. Supervisor's affect: Attraction and positive evaluation as a function of other-enhancement. *Psychological Reports,* (in press).

Pandey, J. & Rastogi, R. Machiavellianism and ingratiation. *The Journal of Social Psychology,* 1979, **108**, 221-225.

Pandey, J. & Sinha, J.B.P. Dependence proneness and perceived problems of adjustment. *Journal of Psychological Researches,* 1968, **12**, 3, 104-110.

Roger, C.R. A theory of therapy, personality and interpersonal relationship as developed in the client-centered framework: In S. Koch (ed). *Psychology: A Study of Science*, New York: McGraw-Hill, 1959.

Schlenker, B.R. Self-presentation: Managing the impression of consistency when reality interferes with self-enhancement. *Journal of Personality and Social Psychology*, 1975, **32**, 1030-1037.

Schneider, D.J. Tactical self-presentation after success and failure. *Journal of Personality and Social Psychology*, 1969, **13**, 262-268.

Sigall, H. & Page, R. Reducing attenuation in the expression of interpersonal effect via the bogus pipeline. *Sociometry*, 1972, **35**, 629-642.

Singh, Purnima. Target's reactions towards the ingratiator as a function of Machiavellianism, power and other enhancement. Masters' Thesis, Allahabad University, 1980.

Sinha J.B.P. The n-Ach/n-Cooperation under limited/unlimited resource condition. *Journal of Experimental Social Psychology*, 1968, **4**, 233-246.

Sinha, J.B.P. *Development Through Behaviour Modification*. New Delhi: All. Pub., 1970.

Sinha, J.B.P. & Pandey, J. Strategies of high n-Ach persons. *Psychologia*, 1970, **13**, 210-216.

Sinha, J.B.P., & Sinha, Mira. Middle class values in organizational perspective. *Journal of Social and Economic Studies*, 1974, **2**, 95-114.

Skinner, B.F. Conversation with B.F. Skinner. *Organizational Dynamics* 1973, **1**, 31-40.

Staats, A.W. *Social Behaviourism*. Illinois: The Dorsey Press, 1975.

Steiner, I.V. Perceived freedom. In L. Berkowitz (ed.), *Advances in Experimental Social Psychology*. Vol. 5, New York: Academic Press, 1970

Steiner, I.D. Whatever happened to the group in social psychology? *Journal of Experimental Social Psychology*, 1974, **10**, 94-108.

Strickland, L.H. Surveillance and trust. *Journal of Personality*, 1958, **26**, 200-215.

Tajfel, H. Individuals and groups in social psychology, *British Journal of Social and Clinical Psychology*, 1979, **18**, 183-190.

Taylor, D.M. & Brown, R.J. Towards a more social psychology? *British Journal of Social and Clinical Psychology*, 1979, **18**, 173-180.

Thibaut, J.W. & Kelley, H.H. *The Social Psychology of Groups*. New York: Wiley, 1959.

Thibaut, J.W., & Riecken, H.W. Some determinants and consequences of the perception of social causality. *Journal of Personality*, 1955, **24**, 113-133.

Tripathi, R.C. Machiavellianism and social manipulation. In J. Pandey (ed.), *Perspectives on Experimental Social Psychology in India*. New Delhi: Concept Publisher, 1981.

Walster, E. The effect of self-esteem on romantic liking. *Journal of Experimental Social Psychology*, 1965, **1**, 184-197.

SEVEN

Sasi Misra

EXCURSION FROM THE PURE TO THE APPLIED IN EXPERIMENTAL SOCIAL PSYCHOLOGY*

THE TITLE hints at the diverse foci of the author's work summarized here. Three criteria have been used to determine inclusion of research findings in this paper : (a) the work must have used the experimental method accepted in psychological research; (b) the hypothesis tested must have been explicitly derived from distinctive theoretical and empirical generalizations in social psychology; and (c) the study must either have been conducted in an applied context or have implications for some practical issues. Thus, applied research built on a historical, humanistic perspectives, and using non-experimental methods are outside the scope of the discussion to follow. Consequently, this paper draws upon five different experimental studies, two focusing directly on theoretical processes of interest to main line social psychology with broad implications for practical concern and the remaining three studies dealing with problems of applied nature. Each study (except the fifth**), however, is rooted in a distinctive middle-range theory of social psychology. Each of these theories operates in a separate domain focusing on different processes of social behaviour. The objective of each experiment described here was to map out some specific

* Writing of this paper was supported by the Indian Institute of Management, Ahmedabad. The paper was revised during the author's tenure as Fellow, Alexander von Humboldt Foundation at Ludwig-Maximilians—University of Munich, West Germany.

** The fifth experiment was an exploratory one. Obviously, it could not meet the second criterion stipulated above.

segment of the social behaviour terrain as it occurred consistently among a number of people. One of the primary tasks of this paper is to delineate what this mapping process has produced. What real world significance do they have in addition to yielding hypothesized statistical significance?

To cover the experiments and their related research fully in a paper such as this is unnecessary. Each of these experiments has been published as a journal article and the reader is referred to the source for fuller coverage.

Accordingly, the approach taken is to summarize each experiment according to the following outline:

1. Title indicating the general problem area
2. Basic ideas leading to specific hypotheses
3. The type of experiment performed and design/procedure
4. Main results
5. Conclusions and implications, if any.

EXPERIMENT I

The effects of attributional instability on conformity and affiliation (Misra, 1973)

The experiment summarized below was guided by two convergent approaches to the study of social influence—social comparison theory approach (Festinger, 1954) and attribution theory approach (Kelley, 1967).

Humans have a drive to evaluate themselves. From this simple assumption, Festinger's theory of social comparison processes (1954) derived a coherent theoretical structure which could treat a wide range of phenomena such as, interpersonal attraction and rejection, affiliation and isolation, conformity and deviancy. Festinger reasoned that people's desire to evaluate themselves arises out of a need to know as to where they stand with respect to such personal attributes as abilities and opinions. Central to Festinger's line of reasoning are three assumptions: (1) People seek to satisfy their need for self-evaluation by comparing themselves with other people (when direct physical standards for comparison are absent or meagre), (2) such social comparison can be perceived as an accurate and stable self-evaluation when people compare themselves with similar others with respect to attributes in question, (3) therefore, people will seek out others who are similar to themselves; try to change others in order to make them similar to themselves; or change themselves to be closer to others (in terms of the attribute being evaluated) who are perceived as similar along salient dimensions. To this may be added the extension: the drive for self-evaluation is an increasing function of the degree of uncertainty concerning the particular aspect of the self being evaluated and this drive can be reduced by the acquisition of relevant information regarding the attribute (Gerard, 1963). As mentioned above, under certain conditions social comparison becomes the primary means by which relevant information is acquired. Thus what people really want is not merely knowledge but certainty. The individual while comparing the level of his attribute with others takes intraindividual variability into account. The basic theoretical statement therefore is: (1) relative uncertainty is the prime mover in social comparison; (2) variability comparison takes precedence over level comparison; (3) finally, there exists a rough isomorphism between the concepts of uncertainty and attribution instability when applied to self-evaluation. The last point needs explanation.

Social comparison: An ANOVA cube analysis

According to Kelley (1967), the individual validates his inferences corresponding to a particular attribute by the application of four criteria: (1) distinctiveness of the entity, (2) consistency of his reactions over time, (3) modality, and (4) consensus. Kelley assumes that both the person's own direct evidence of consistency and the evidence supplied through social consensus contribute to the stability of his own reactions. The greater the consistency, the more stable his attribution. If, however, the person's own consistency evidence is meagre and unreliable, i.e., his variability in reaction is high, he will be rendered uncertain as to the validity of his own reactions. In order to reduce the discomfort associated with uncertainty, he will be receptive to relevant information through social consensus. Social comparison may be viewed as one of the processes whereby information from others is used in order to make stable attribution. The process is set into motion when the information the person has from his own direct interaction with the world (inner or outer) is poor and ambiguous.

Operationally, the greater the variability of an attribute, the greater the attribution instability. In the case of an ability, the performance of a relevant person may be utilized as comparison information. In the event of a sharp discrepancy between the person's performance and the performance of others, he will be more susceptible to influence, since his self-attribution is likely to be unstable. He will tend to exhibit a lack of confidence in his ability and/or longer latency of response. It is also expected that he would show increased dependence upon the others for comparison information. This is likely to manifest both in a tendency to affiliate and to conform to judgments of others that are based upon the ability in question. In a self-evaluation context, it is assumed that both tendencies to conform and affiliate are based on generalized expectation of the positively and negatively reinforcing quality of interpersonal relationships and have similar reinforcing properties for the individual where uncertainty reduction (or the reduction of attribution instability) is the issue. It was, therefore, decided to use both of these dependent measures in order to triangulate better on the following hypothesized effects of attribution instability.

Hypothesis 1

Given a situation in which a person finds his performance discrepant from that of a comparison group, the tendency toward social comparison will be greater the more variable his own performance on the task. Thus, with ability level held constant, greater variability in performance will lead to : (a) lowered subjective confidence in own judgments; (b) increased latency in judgmental responses; (c) greater conformity to group norms; (d) increased tendency toward affiliation.

Hypothesis 2

The effect of level of ability on tendencies toward social comparison as manifested in conformity and affiliation will be more pronounced when the person's ability is of a medium level, less so when the ability level is either high or low.

Design : Thirteen college women were randomly assigned to each of the six cells of a 2×3 factorial design. Three ability levels were induced and counterbalanced against two variability levels. The two main dependent variables were (a) conformity and (b) affiliation.

Procedure

The experiment was run under the guise of "a study of information processing ability". Subjects (UCLA students) run in groups of four were given an elaborate explanation of the importance of information processing ability, with quotations attributed to the Presidential Address of the American Association of Scientists.

Having established the ability-evaluation context, self-attributed level and variability were manipulated by having the subjects first complete a judgmental task over a series of 18 trials and providing each person scores on each trial as well as the mean score. In this manner, each subject's ability was rated "excellent", "average" or "very poor" depending on her ability treatment and the variability in her performance was rated being "extremely consistent" or "extremely inconsistent" depending on the variability treatment to which she was assigned. High variability in ability meant a bogus score distribution that was platokurtic (variance=5.08). Low variability in ability meant a score distribution that was leptokurtic (variance=0.36).

Having manipulated the level and variability in attributed ability, the first set of dependent variables (conformity, subjective confidence, and latency of response) was measured in an Asch-type situation. In order to do so, a highly sophisticated electronic device with electronic stooges were used. This has been described in detail elsewhere (Misra, 1973).

Affiliation, the second main dependent variable was measured by the subject's decision to participate in a future group discussion. The ostensible purpose was to "generate some original ideas that could be put to use in teaching methods for both Head Start and deprived children."

Results

Table 7.1 summarizes mean subjective confidence, latency, conformity, and affiliation tendencies for six experimental groups.

Analysis of variance performed on these data supported the major hypothesis that variability within one's own level of ability is an important determinant of conformity. The variability effect is more pronounced in the conformity and confidence

TABLE 7.1 : **Mean subjective confidence[a], latency of response[b], conformity[c], and affiliation tendencies[d]**

Measures	Variability in attributed ability	Level of ability attributed to self		
		Low	Medium	High
Confidence	Low	77.57	81.38	90.72
	High	77.25	74.13	72.03
Latency	Low	32.33	37.47	51.28
	High	53.60	40.19	56.93
Conformity	Low	3.77	4.46	4.07
	High	6.38	6.46	5.46
Affiliation	Low	1.62	2.08	3.23
	High	2.62	2.92	2.62

[a]Scores ranged from "0—least confident" to "100—most confident."
[b]The unit of measurement was millisecond.
[c]Number of times the subject conformed to incorrect group norm in the 13 critical trials.
[d]Higher scores indicate greater interest in joining the discussion group.

data and less so in the latency data. The data did not bear out the predicted higher degree of conformity in the medium level conditions as compared with the high and the low levels. It appears that reference group influence becomes effective only when the intraindividual variability is low.

A significant Variability × Level interaction in the affiliation data showed that affiliation tendencies decreased for low variability conditions only as the level of attributed ability decreased. The maximum tendency to affiliate was shown by subjects in the high ability-low variability (i.e., consistent-excellent) condition. Does this mean that we affiliate with others who could provide us with self-enhancement?

Implications : Evidently, my experiment did not consider the larger social context in which the social comparison process operates. I conducted this experiment in a hardcore experimental social department addressing myself to theoretical issues and "similar others"! However, the experiment did succeed to some extent in specifying some of the conditions under which persons are more likely to choose similar others as referents and be influenced by them. Are these conditions not fairly common in everyday life?

EXPERIMENT II

The meaning of trust in prisoner's dilemma (Misra and Kalro, 1979)

Non-zero sum games, particularly the Prisoner's Dilemma, have spurred hundreds of experiments in the past two decades. A criticism often levelled against them is that conclusions drawn from research with PDG cannot be generalized to conflicts and cooperations in real life settings. However, it is recognized that the PD game simulates the very important class of social interaction setting, which is relatively free from situational constraints of social roles and structure. It is, therefore, rich in person information and the response strategies of subjects in this game reflect the orientations they tend to adopt in a wide variety of their social relationships. Thus, to put the point rather strongly, the little transactions we engage in this interpersonal game have important and far reaching implications for the way we relate to others and share with them. Specifically, it is assumed that by studying behaviour in PDG, we learn something about how one person's perceptions about another determine his own strategies to respond either cooperatively or competitively. It is assumed that the reader is familiar with the structure of PDG in which both players have a simultaneous and independent choice between a "cooperative" and "non-cooperative" alternative. The crucial feature of such a game is that one player can gain the most by choosing to be non-cooperative when the other chooses to be cooperative; he loses most when the reverse is true. However, for each player, mutual cooperation is a better strategy than mutual non-cooperation. Since a true PD game is a one-play game without repetition, a player's strategy reflects his trust in the other player.

Deutsch (1960) appears to be the first social psychologist to recognize the appealing relevance and implications of this game for studying cooperation-competition and attribution of trust in social situations. Figure 7.1 presents the matrix exemplifying Deutsch's classical version of the PDG.

The experiment (Misra and Kalro, 1979) described above dealt with the relationship between behaviour of subjects in PD to their perceptions of and beliefs about the "other

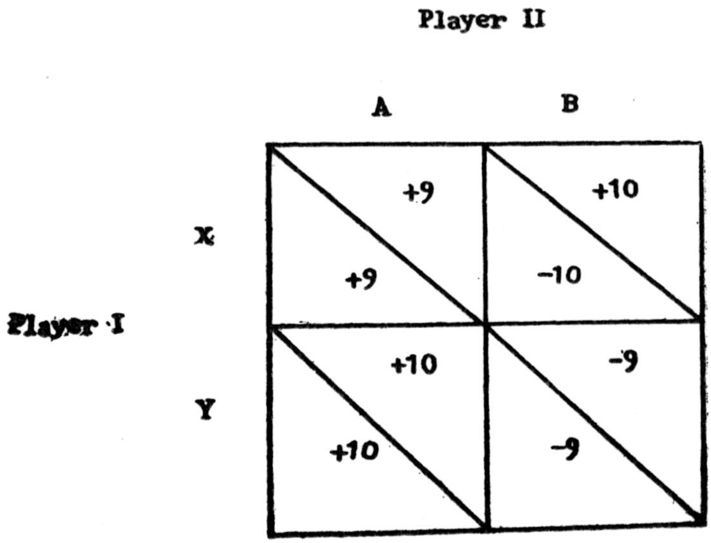

FIG. 7.1 : *The classical version of the PDG matrix used by Deutsch*

Note : Player I chooses between rows X and Y, Player II chooses between columns A and B. The lower left values in each cell are for Player I and the upper right values in each cell are for Player II.

player". It is a hypothetico-deductive experiment and a cross-cultural one at the same time. The impetus for this experiment stemmed from certain empirical generalizations drawn from Kelley and Stahelski (1970) concerning the basis of cooperators' and competitors' beliefs about others.

Based on evidence derived from the extensive literature employing mixed-motive games, Kelley and Stahelski (1970) have drawn the following empirical generalizations : Basically, there are two stable types of individuals which may be approximately described as cooperative and competitive; these two types have different views of what other people are like with respect to this typology; the different views are indirectly caused by their personalities. Further, Kelley and Stahelski have shown that individuals with competitive orientations to social relationships believe the world to be composed homogeneously of competitive individuals. By contrast, those with cooperative orientation construe the world to be more heterogeneously composed of both competitive and cooperative people. The first purpose of our study was to test the cross-cultural generality of the heterogeneity of expectations by cooperators and homogeneity of expectations by competitors about others, by using the familiar one-trial alternating play procedure with PDG (Deutsch, 1960).

		Trusting (Cooperative)				Suspicious (Competitive)
	Trusting	X	X	X	X	X
Own			X	X	X	X
Orientation				X	X	X
	Suspicious				X	X
						X

FIG. 7.2 : *The triangle hypothesis—expectation as to others' orientations*

Kelley and Stahelski have represented the relationship between a person's own orientation in the game and his expectations about the other's orientation by a triangular plot (see Figure 7.2) termed the triangle hypothesis. The extent to which data conform to the triangle pattern is given by the triangularity index (*TI*), which can be computed by the following formula: $TI = (D—C)—|A—B|$, where *A*, *B*, *C* and *D* refer to the percentage of subjects falling into various cells in terms of their own behaviour vis-a-vis their expectations of the typical "other player" (see Figure 7.3).

The index becomes larger the more *D* exceeds *C* and becomes smaller as there is any difference in either direction between *A* and *B*. The index is positive for a triangular pattern oriented in the expected direction. A perfect triangular pattern of the type expected would yield a *TI* of 100 ($A = B = 50\%$ and $D = 100\%$). However, the triangularity indices computed for several western studies reported by Kelley and Stahelski ranged from 28 to 71.

		Expected typical	
		Cooperative	Competitive
Self	Cooperative	A	B
	Competitive	C	D

FIG. 7.3 : *Subjects failing into various cells in terms of their own behaviour vis-a-vis their expectations of the typical "other player".*

Note : **The values A, of B, C and D are in percentages.**

The triangle hypothesis is valid to the extent that the expectations of cooperative subjects are evenly distributed across the top row and the expectations of competitive subjects pile up at the extreme right side of the bottom row. The implication of the triangle hypothesis is that while trusting *S*s will expect the other to be either trustworthy or untrustworthy, most of the suspicious *S*s will expect the other to be untrustworthy. Thus, our first hypothesis was:

Hypothesis 1

With respect to the relationship between a player's own choice and his expectation of the other's move, the expectations of trusting (cooperative) *S*s, about the "typical other" will be substantially more evenly distributed across the top row as compared with the expectations of the suspicious (competitive) *S*s, yielding a highly positive triangularity index.

The second purpose of the study was to explore whether cooperators and competitors attach qualitatively different meanings to the behaviour of the other player. It was assumed that cooperators and competitors would differ with respect to their definitions of the same objective situation (in this case, a nonzero-sum situation). Consequently, there will be differences between the two types in perceiving and evaluating the "other player" (in this case the cooperator) in the situation.

Particularly, we expected to find systematic differences between trusting and trustworthy subjects (cooperative choices at both first and second position play) on the one hand and suspicious and untrustworthy subjects (competitive choices at both positions) on the other in terms of their connotative meanings of cooperative behaviour. These differential indices might be sensitive to their different beliefs about others, as suggested by the triangle hypothesis.

Kelley et al., (1970), in a transnational study of bargaining, found remarkable site differences with respect to the meanings given to the dimensions of cooperation versus competition which influenced negotiation outcomes and subsequent interactions. As measured by Semantic Differentials, at some sites this cooperation-competition dimension was given an "evaluative" meaning (*E*), i.e. good versus bad; at other sites it was given a "dynamism" meaning (*D*), i.e. weak and passive versus strong and active.

It is apparent from the structure of the game used in our experiment that a trusting and trustworthy subject is concerned about joint welfare and is essentially egalitarian in orientation. This could lead him to treat the nonzero-sum game as a setting to demonstrate his basic honesty and fair-mindedness. Perhaps based on this premise, his move on the first trial is a trusting one. On the second trial, those who follow this by a trustworthy move in response to the other player's trusting move do so presumably because they feel it is wrong not to return the trust placed in them. Consequently, their assessment of the other person is more likely to be in evaluative terms such as moral, honest, peaceful, etc. This is also consistent with their opinion of themselves. Conversely, the player whose first move is suspicious treats the nonzero-sum game setting as a zero-sum game in which he can demonstrate his superiority and one-upmanship by maximising his individual gain. On account of his egoistic and rivalrous orientation, his second move in response to the player's trusting move is untrustworthy, because this maximises the differences between his pay-off and the other player's pay-off to his own advantage. Accordingly, he perceives the other player as a weakling and a coward; chicken for his plucking.Thus it was hypothesized:

Hypothesis 2

*S*s who make trusting and trustworthy choices will rate the other trusting player high on the Evaluative (*E*) and low on the Dynamism (*D*) dimension as measured by Semantic Differentials. The reverse trend in ratings of the cooperator will be obtained for suspicious and untrustworthy (competitive) *S*s.

Method

The subjects were 249 male postgraduate students of Management at the Indian Institute of Management, Ahmedabad. Each *S* participated in a two-person, nonzero-sum PD game in which the amount of gains or losses incurred by each player in terms of imaginary money was a function of his move and that of the "other" player who, in fact, was fictional. The pay-off matrix was identical to the one reported by Deutsch (1960) except that the pay-offs were in rupees instead of dollars.

The *S*s participated in two trials. On the first, each *S* made his choice after first indicating what he expected the other player to choose. On the second trial, each *S*, presumably playing with a different person from the first, was asked to indicate what he thought the other person expected him to choose. At this point, each *S* was provided with the choice presumably made by the other person (this always being the trusting or cooperative choice) in a similar game conducted earlier on a sample of similar graduate students and was asked to make his own choice.

Postgame attitude measures

After each *S* finally made his move, he was asked to guess whether the other person was a male or a female, following which he answered the "first impression" questionnaire which consisted of seven adjective pairs on bipolar scales (the semantic differential). The connotative meanings of three pairs (dishonest-honest, hostile-peaceful, and immoral-moral) were Evaluative and the remaining four (passive-active, weak-strong, cowardly-brave, and foolish-wise) represented the Dynamism factor. The positive pole of the Evaluative factor was represented by honest, peaceful and moral and that of the Dynamism factor by active, strong, brave and wise. Scores on the three evaluative pairs were summed up to form an index of evaluative definition (*E*) attributed to trust (cooperation) and composite scores on the four dynamism adjective pairs yielded the dynamism definition (*D*) of trust.

Results

The data concerning the relationship between choices in the two positions showed that *S*s who made the "trusting" choice in the first position tended to be "trustworthy" in their second position choice; on the other hand, *S*s who were "suspicious" to begin with tended to be "untrustworthy" when they played the second time ($\chi^2 = 29.5\ p < .001$).

Inferring sex of the other player

Most provocative here was the result that while 36 out of 70 (51%) "trusting" *S*s thought that the other player was a female, 145 out of 177 (81%) "suspicious" *S*s indicated that the other player was a female.

The triangle effect

Hypothesis 1 predicted that with respect to relationship between a player's own choice and his expectation of the other's move, the expectations of "trusting" *S*s about "typical other" would be more evenly distributed across the top row as compared with the expectations of the "suspicious" *S*s. The *TI* obtained for our data was as high as 54.

Trust and the connotative meaning of cooperation

The data (see Table 7.3) did clearly bear out this prediction and the reverse trend was obtained in ratings of the other player by the "suspicious" and "untrustworthy" *S*s. The difference was statistically significant ($F = 11.48$, $df = 3{,}245$, $p < .001$; $F = 24.12$, $df = 3{,}245$, $p < .001$ respectively).

Discussion and Implications

The results of our study provided clear support for the triangle hypothesis and hypothesis pertaining to the connotative meaning of trust attributed by the trusting and trustworthy subjects

TABLE 7.2 : **Means and standard deviations of responses to measures of meaning of trust/cooperation**

	Evaluative		Dynamism	
	M	*SD*	*M*	*SD*
Trusting/Trustworthy	18.33	2.62	19.49	4.74
Trusting/Untrustworthy	14.86	2.82	16.23	4.58
Suspicious/Trustworthy	16.33	2.15	16.61	5.07
Suspicious/Untrustworthy	15.62	3.28	12.43	5.26
F	11.48*		24.12*	

*$df=3,245$, $p<.001$

on the one hand and the suspicious and untrustworthy subjects on the other.

Comparing the expectations of trusting and suspicious subjects with respect to the typical other in the first position play, it was clear that the suspicious subjects indeed showed a tendency to be blind towards the true variability and uniqueness of people and things. They preferred to categorize things as polar opposites: you vs. me; union vs. management: we vs. they. The trusting subjects, on the other hand, tend to reflect greater heterogeneity in outlook with respect to their expectations about others.

Secondly, our results clearly showed that in the estimation of the trusting and trustworthy subjects, the "trusting other" was one who was described as honest, peaceful and moral. In contrast, for the suspicious and untrustworthy subjects, the "trusting other" was passive, weak, cowardly, and foolish. It is, therefore, not surprising that 81 per cent of the suspicious subjects considered the fictional other person in the game as a female. It is entirely consistent with their traditional role expectation for females to be passive, weak, and dependent.

Our subjects being trained to become professional managers, do perform key roles and occupy, in good time, policy-making position in competitive organizational settings. What attitudes and feelings are our competitive subjects likely to harbour toward a woman in executive position whose formal role may require her to be assertive and directive, which is different from what our subjects expect her to be? How are these people likely to perceive the union point of view across the negotiation table? The detrimental consequences of having managers performing certain categories of functions, such as, personnel and industrial relations, whose beliefs about people are like those of our competitors' are too obvious to elaborate further.

EXPERIMENT III

Organizational choice : dissonance reduction and self-perception (Misra and Kalro, 1972)

This study dealt with attitude of members toward an organization induced by their very act of choice for its membership. The study consisted of two separate experiments. The first experiment tested predictions from dissonance theory (Festinger, 1957) and the second experiment tested the self-perception theory (Bem, 1967). Incorporated within the study was a hypothesis relating to the two-factor theory of job satisfaction (Herzberg, Mausner, and Snyderman, 1959).

Rationale

According to dissonance theory, when an individual decides by choice to transact with one subject or situation and to forgo the other alternatives that may be available, he must begin to come to terms with his act or to reduce his dissonance. In so doing, he views the chosen alternatives more positively than before and the unchosen alternatives more negatively than before. Dissonance increases as the importance of the decision, the number of cognitions involved, and the proximity of predecisional differences among the attractiveness of alternatives increase. Thus, our first hypothesis was:

> After a choice is made between two "equally attractive" alternative organizations, the attractiveness of the chosen organization will increase and the attractiveness of the unchosen organization will decrease.

Secondly, Herzberg et al., talk about motivational (advancement, autonomy, prestige, etc.) and hygiene (salary, security, etc.) job factors as primary determinants of job satisfaction and dissatisfaction, respectively. Thus, they argue that these two sets of factors cater to the different needs of the employees. We reasoned that while it may be reasonable to maintain the broad distinction between the two sets of factors (motivators and hygienes) catering to the different needs of the employees, it may be useful to understand the direction and extent of changes in the attitudes of the individual towards these factors induced by the very act of choice of one organization as over some others. In other words, the instrumentality of chosen and unchosen jobs may undergo changes, so that the cognitive representations of outcomes on the job are in line with their subjective expectations of outcomes. Therefore, based on the premise of the two-factor theory of job satisfaction, it may be possible to predict postdecisional changes in job goals in accord with dissonance theory.

The individual as a postdecisional maneuver, will tend to play up the desirability of the motivators (satisfiers) of the chosen job in order to compensate for the dissatisfaction arising from the absence of adequate hygienes (dissatisfiers). Further compensation may take place by playing up the undesirability of the hygienic factors of the unchosen job. The expected directions of changes in the instrumentality of the two sets of job factors, as a consequence of organizational choice, were hypothesized as follows:

> After a choice is made between two equally attractive alternative organizations, (a) the positive change in the attractiveness of the motivators associated with the chosen organization will be greater than the corresponding changes in the attractiveness of the hygienes associated with the chosen organization, and (b) the negative change in the attractiveness of the hygienes associated with the unchosen organization will be greater than the corresponding change in the attractiveness of the motivators associated with the unchosen organization.

Design

Two realistic job descriptions were constructed each featuring 12 job factors (goals) in such a manner as to include six motivators and six hygienes. These job factors were differentially manipulated so that subjects (MBA students in the final year who were in the job market) perceived significant differences in their conceptions of the extent to which each job satisfied each of the 12 job goals; and did not perceive any significant difference in overall attractiveness of the two jobs. This manipulation was effective.

Procedure

The experiment was run in two sessions. Session II was two weeks later than Session I. In the first session under the guise of a job-analysis study subjects rated the two junior executive job announcements from the point of view of their own career goals. In the second session, they were to terminate their job-search by selecting one of them.

Having performed this experience, a second experiment was conducted on a different sample of similar students as an "interpersonal replication" *à la* Bem (1967). The derivation tested from Bem's self-perception model was: observer subjects should be able to discriminate the circumstances controlling the behaviour of involved subjects in "real" dissonance experiments and to estimate accurately the attitude of involved subjects at the end of the experimental procedure.

Results

Tables 7.3 and 7.4 give results of the dissonance experiment and Table 7.5 gives the results of the "interpersonal replication".

TABLE 7.3 : **Mean attractiveness ratings for chosen and unchosen organizations before and after choice**[a]

Organization	Before Choice	After Choice	Change	t^b
Accepted	7.56	8.03	+ .59	1.39*
Rejected	7.32	6.32	−1.00	3.05**

[a]N=34.

[b]All significance levels are based on one-tailed tests.

*$p<.10$

**$p<.001$

TABLE 7.4 : Mean postdecisional chanegs in the instrumentality of motivational and hygienic factors for chosen and unchosen organizations[a]

Organization	Mean changes in factors		Difference[b]	t^c
	Motivators	Hygienics		
Chosen	3.29	− .62	3.91	2.39*
Unchosen	−2.44	−2.12	−.32	.20

[a]N=34.
[b]Refers to mean change in motivators-mean change in hygienes.
[c]All significance level are based on one-tailed tests.
*$p<.01$.

TABLE 7.5 : Mean displacement in attractiveness ratings from control group means for chosen and unchosen organizations in each condition[a]

Organization	Chosen		t^b	Unchosen		t
	Control	Displacement		Control	Displacement	
HEPL	7.25	+1.45	3.81**	7.25	−.46	1.14*
IEC	7.00	+1.38	3.36**	7.00	−.19	.53

[a]N=16 in the control and 28 in each experimental conditions. Scores range from 1 to 11, where higher number indicates greater attractiveness; positive and negative displacements indicate increased and decreased attractiveness, respectively.
[b]All significance levels are based on one-tailed tests.
*$p<.10$
**$p<.001$

EXPERIMENT IV

Choosing a name and preparing a slogan for your product for increasing brand awareness (Misra and Jain 1971).

This experiment addressed itself to the questions: (1) In order to create better brand awareness, how should the advertiser go about choosing a brand name and a slogan? (2) Are there differences in naming different types of products so far as brand awareness is concerned?

Our work primarily drew upon two sources: Kanungo (1968) and postwar experiments in mass communication at Yale (Hovland, Lumsdain, and Sheffield, 1949).

We argued that brand awareness is essentially learning of

brand-product association. Among multi-brand products, the successful ones are those which have great awareness among consumers. Indeed, the near omnipresence of certain brands of consumer products has led to effective monopoly and reduced the concept of "perfect competition" to the status of a myth.

Various factors to seemed affect the learning of brand-product association. For the purpose of this experiment we chose three. First, appropriate brand names are likely to be more meaningful to the consumers. Hence, easier to learn and recall. This is the well tested and time honoured principle of learning. Second, the strength of brand-product association might be differentially influenced by the nature of product. Because, advertisements of relatively high priced and infrequently purchased consumer durables (shopping goods : radio, crockery, etc.) would be more salient and important than the advertisements of low priced, frequently purchased convenience goods (e.g. soap, talcum powder, etc.). Third, we examined the so-called delayed action effects of two types of slogans, unqualified vs. qualified, on brand awareness. In attitude change literature, the former refers to one-sided communication and the latter to two-sided communication. Simply put, an unqualified persuasive communication contained arguments that only favoured its conclusion, whereas a qualified communication added some secondary qualifications and reservations against the main argument. We hypothesized that products described by unqualified slogans would show greater brand awareness immediately after their exposure as compared to products described by qualified slogans. However, the net impact of the two types of slogans might be the same after a delayed time interval of appreciable length.

In sum, the experiment examined the effect of : (a) fitting vs. non-fitting brand names, (b) shopping vs. convenience goods, and (c) qualified vs. unqualified slogans on immediate brand awareness and its persistence over time.

Hypotheses

(1) Fitting brand names would produce greater brand awareness than non-fitting brand name; (2) brand awareness would be superior for shopping goods than for convenience goods;

and (3) an unqualified slogan describing a particular product would show better brand awareness than a qualified slogan describing the same product, although the superiority of unqualified slogans with respect to brand recall would tend to dissipate over time.

Design and procedure

Seventytwo male *S*s were run in a factorial experiment testing the above hypotheses. Construction of brand names, slogans and choice of products were done by following an elaborate procedure with a variety of operational criteria. This has been described in detail elsewhere (Misra and Jain, 1971).

Results

Table 7.6 gives the results of the experiment in a nutshell. It can be seen that the results confirm hypotheses 1 and 2 and fail to support hypothesis 3.

TABLE 7.6 : **Analysis of variance of recall scores**

Source of variation	*df*	*MS*	*F*
Fittingness (F)	1	340.01	31.69**
Type of Slogan (Q)	1	35.05	3.26*
Time (T)	2	1.56	.15
F×Q	1	18.37	1.71
F×T	2	1.24	.09
Q×T	2	1.05	.12
F×Q×T	2	6.16	.57
Within cell (error)	204	10.73	
Total	215		

*$p<.10$
**$p<.001$

EXPERIMENT V

What makes an effective salesman ? (Rao and Misra, 1976)

Salesmen by and large have a negative public image. Stereotype views about them such as glib-tongued, deceitful, lying, etc. are widespread. Nevertheless, effective salesmen are of enormous value to any organization.

Many decision makers in commercial organizations tend to believe that a good salesman must be of a "certain type" thereby implying that individual differences variables underlie the success of a salesman. The emphasis here is on what salesmen are. We reasoned, another profitable approach might be to examine what salesmen do rather than what they are. In order to do so, our attention had to be focused not on particular people as unique individuals with idiosyncratic characteristics, but on the particular process of interest (in this case, the patterns of interaction between the salesman and the buyer).

To test some of our ideas in this regard, we designed an exploratory experiment in the following manner.

Our line of reasoning was, in any sales situation primarily two parties are involved: the salesperson and the customer. The salesperson generally tries to influence the customer's attitude towards his product and presumably his choice behaviour through various ways and means. This may be called his sales style. We thought of four different sales styles: product centred style wherein he emphasizes the superiority of his product over others; company centred style wherein his company's name and fame (image) is the unique selling proposition; consumer centred style where he attempts to influence the perspective customer by highlighting the benefits the latter might derive by acquiring the product; self-centred style wherein the salesperson emphasizes how many of the given product has been sold by him and how well he was received by others.

Against these four sales styles we introduced four levels of consumer needs such as, strong need, marginal need, no need, and negative need. Thus, the experiment was designed to examine the relative impact of four different sales styles on four categories of consumers with varying need strengths for the product.

Design

A salesperson-customer interaction exercise developed earlier was used in this experiment. It was administered on two different samples: student and actual salespersonnel. In each sample the salesperson-customer roles were played in three groups. Each group had 12 members : four playing the four different salesperson role, another four playing the roles of four categories of customers, and the remaining four were observers (one observer per dyad of salesperson-customer). Each salesperson had to interact with each of the four categories of customers, one after the other, for a duration of 10 minutes. Thus, there were 16 interaction patterns in each group. Each salesperson was to sell a radio manufactured by a fictitious company to the customers.

Procedure

Salespersons and customers were given thorough role briefings verbally as well as in writing before the experiment began. All through the exercise, neither the customer nor the salesperson knew about each other's orientation.

The observers were trained to judge whether the dyads played their respective roles satisfactorily. The main dependent variables were: (1) customer tendencies to buy the radio, and (2) liking for the salesperson.

Results

Data from the student sample and the actual salesperson sample were similar and therefore were combined for analysis purposes. Results showed that product-centred salespersons made a more positive impact on consumers followed by the customer-centred and the company-centred salespersons. Self-centred salespersons made a relatively low impact. Furthermore, product-centred salespersons made a greater impact on low need customers while company-centred salespersons made a greater impact on high-need customers. Customer-centred salespersons showed more consistency in the impact they made than the other three types of sales-persons, indicating that they are likely to be consistently effective irrespective of the need patterns or customers.

Implications for marketing

This experiment dealt with one product only, viz., the radio. Also it was conducted under controlled conditions. It is agreed that the type of the product, the levels of prior contact between the buying and selling establishments, prior experience of the client with the brand, product, and company, company image, etc., are significant in influencing the client and determining the outcome of the transaction. The authors found this exercise pedagogically useful for training salespersons. New variables like those suggested above could be incorporated while using this exercise as a training device. Clearer conclusions can be drawn when results of the differential effects of sales styles are available under a variety of selling situations and market conditions.

In sum, the results suggest that no single strategy of influencing the customer is uniformly effective. Different types of customers are receptive to different sales styles although customer-centredness is generally harmless. The success of a salesperson lies in his skill in making a correct diagnosis of client-orientations and then using responsive sales styles. A combination of sales styles may be more effective than mutually exclusive styles like those presented in this exercise. Results of experiments of this kind are likely to provide useful clues for marketing, advertising, and sales strategies.

CONCLUSION

Out of the five experiments described in this paper, the first two dealt primarily with conceptual issues. Direct applicability of results was of secondary importance. It is realized that leaps between the laboratory and the real world are always loose and tentative. But the central contentions of various theories hold and alert us to look for clearer statements and propositions underlying behaviour. In the remaining three experiments, users of knowledge, in addition to our professional colleagues, were kept in mind. These experiments may be evaluated with respect to their perceived functionality.

In general, my experimental work conforms to the set pattern of the hypothetico-deductive approach slavishly followed by psychologists. The fifth experiment was an exception. But, would the *Journal of Applied Psychology* have accepted it? What might be considered a contribution in the wider context does not necessarily have scholarly impact on the academically oriented social psychology.

Finally, the reader needs to bear two points in mind while evaluating the values and limitations of the experiments described in the preceding pages.

(1) These experiments were carried out by the author(s) with the realization that experimental situations seldom resemble naturally occurring situations. Experiments only permit us to look more closely at some problems. It is the experimenter's theoretical preference and preconceptions that define the range of problems for his inquiry.

(2) There exists a pervasive prejudice against applied research among academically oriented social psychologists, based on the assumption that such research is ephemeral. The merit of this assumption is dubious because generalizations from "pure" research do not generally endure either. Those that endure are more provocative than right.

REFERENCES

Bem, D.J. Self-perception: The dependent variable of human performance. *Organizational Behavior and Human Performance*, 1967, **2**, 105-121.

Deutsch, M. Trust, trustworthiness, and the F scale. *Journal of Abnormal and Social Psychology*, 1960, **61**, 138-140.

Festinger, L. A theory of social comparison process. *Human Relations*, 1954, **7**, 117-140.

Festinger, L. *A Theory of Cognitive Dissonance*. Stanford, Calif: Stanford University Press, 1957.

Gerard, H.B. Emotional uncertainty and social comparison. *Journal of Abnormal and Social Psychology*, 1963, **66**, 568-573.

Hovland, C.I., Lumsdaine, A.A. & Sheffield, P.D. *Experiments on Mass Communication*. Princeton: Princeton University Press, 1949.

Herzberg, F., Mausner, B. & Snyderman, B. *The Motivation to Work* (2nd ed.). New York: Wiley, 1959.

Kanungo, R.N. Brand awareness: Effects of fittingness, meaningfulness, and product utility. *Journal of Applied Psychology*, 1968, **52**, 290-295.

Kelley, H.H. Attribution theory in social psychology. In Levine, D. (ed.), *Nebraska Symposium on Motivation*. University of Nebraska Press, 1967, 192-238.

Kelley, H.H. & Stahelski, A.J. Social interaction basis of cooperators' and competitors' beliefs about others. *Journal of Personality and Social Psychology*, 1970, **16**, 86-91.

Kelley, H.H., Shure, G.H., Deutsch, M., Faucheux, C., Lanzetta, J.T., Moscovici, S., Nuttin, J. N., Jr. & Rabbie, J.M. A comparative experimental study of negotiation behaviour. *Journal of Personality and Social Psychology*, 1970, **16**, 411-438.

Misra, S. Instability in self-evaluation, conformity, and affiliation. *Journal of Personality*, 1973, **41**, 361-375.

Misra, S. & Jain, S. Effect of fittingness, type of goods, and type of slogan on brand awareness. *Journal of Applied Psychology,* 1971, **55**, 580-585.

Misra, S. & Kalro, A. Simulated organizational choice: Postdecision dissonance reduction and self-perception, *Journal of Applied Psychology*, 1972, **56**, 461-466.

Misra, S. & Kalro, A. Triangle effect and the connotative meaning of trust in prisoner's dilemma: A cross-cultural study. *International Journal of Psychology*, 1979, **4**.

Rao, T.V. & Misra, S. Effectiveness of varying sales styles on consumer orientations. *Vikalpa*, 1976, **1**, 19-26.

SECTION THREE

CRITICAL ASSESSMENT

EIGHT

Durganand Sinha

EXPERIMENTAL SOCIAL PSYCHOLOGY
Verbal or Real ?

THE AIM of social psychology is to understand and explain the social reality, and in the process it is expected to predict social behaviour and hopefully through various interventional means to control it also for the benefit of mankind. Some of the European social psychologists like Henri Tajfel (1972) and others regard it as a discipline which should be able to contribute a great deal to the understanding and interpretation of contemporary social phenomena. We may not be very keen at this stage about the objectivity of prediction or control of social phenomena. But the least that one expects of this discipline, if its claim as a science is legitimate, is to help understand and explain social life of the individual and groups, both large and small. It is within this framework that the present status of experimental social psychology should be judged. If it has failed to help us to understand the social phenomena it should be regarded as futile as well as sterile.

With this criterion in mind, a large bulk of what goes on in the name of experimental social psychology falls short of our expectation. Allport's famous dictum that if one wants to know about a person's attitude, how he feels and what are his opinions, why not ask him, has provided the main prop for a lot of our exercises in experimental social psychology. Instead of manipulating the experimental variable and observing what takes place, many social psychologists have taken refuge in the verbal creations of social situations and introducing the independent variable verbally and then analysing what the subject says he would do. In effect, a large amount of experimental psychology has become purely verbal and inevitably cognitive. The only justification for it seems to be its convenience. It appears that confronted with the complexity of social phenomena, and finding them difficult to control and manipulate, the experimentalist has resorted to this very dubious and artificial procedure of verbalising the social situation and analysing verbal reactions to it and thereby deluding himself that the outcome is good social psychology. Confronted with a high degree of complexity which is generally the basic characteristic of man's social behaviour and his interactions in society the proper strategy should have been not to avoid it but to devise appropriate procedures for analysing and experimentally studying it rather than confining himself to problems to which existing methods are suited or following a Procrustean bed policy of forcing everything into the same mould. But in his anxiety to operationalize the variables, induce effective experimental control and fit the whole thing into a neat experimental design so that the data yielded can be subjected to sophisticated statistical treatment, what has been produced, to quote the expression of Moscovici (1972), is anything but social. In fact, the kind of social psychology that it has generated has neither managed to study social conduct as an interaction between Man and society, nor to study Man in society. The findings obtained through this kind of verbal strategy have hardly any external validity and are thereby inadequate because it is difficult to generalize on their basis to social reality. As Harre and Secord (1976) have aptly pointed out "the experimental set-up destroys the possibility of the study of the very features that are essential to social behaviour in its natural setting". Any random sample taken from the studies generally published in this area, especially in the American journals, would make the point clear. When Rettig (Rettig and Sinha, 1966; Rettig, 1979) tried to study ethical risk-taking, what he did was to depict verbally a situation with socio-moral connotations and presented verbally a number of alternatives, each representing various possible actions of an individual in facing such a situation. On the basis of the choices made by the subject and their analysis various inferences concerning ethical risk-taking were made.

This is a common example of studying social behaviour purely on the verbal plane, and I am sure the researchers concerned with this kind of study had no objective of understanding the actual social reality involved in risk-taking behaviour, ethical or otherwise.

Another typical example of this *verbal* social psychology is provided by the mushrooming studies inspired by Byrne's work on interpersonal attraction. The main thrust of the studies conducted by Byrne and his associates concerns the relation between liking a person and the amount of similarity between the liker and the target person he is judging. A person is asked to read a set of attitude items representing the responses of a hypothetical stranger, and to make a judgment about probable liking of him and probable enjoyment of working with him, as well as variety of other attributes. For different hypothetical stimulus persons, the proportion of attitude statements congruent with the individual's own attitudes is varied. Proceeding with such studies, Byrne and his associates (Byrne, Griffit, and Stefanik, 1967) have come to the conclusion that the larger the proportion of similar attitudes depicted as belonging to the hypothetical stranger, the greater the interpersonal attraction of the individual towards him as deduced from the answers to another questionnaire. Let us see what the experimentalists of this brand have done. First, for the sake of proper manipulation of experimental variable, the situation of interpersonal attraction has been sheared off from actual life and reified on a verbal plane which is convenient to the experimentalists. Thus, the dubious experimental ideal of simplification of stimulus situation was achieved, thereby thinking somewhat naively that the responses would be studied in a controlled situation. Limited information about the similarity or otherwise of the hypothetical target person was provided to the subject one at a time because otherwise the manipulation of variables would have got disturbed. Now the question that inevitably comes to mind is do we get attracted to a person simply on the basis of one or two isolated information about him. If we did that in actual life, I am sure we would not only be displaying gross social ineptitude but would also put ourselves frequently in a socially risky situation. In actual life, information do not drip drop by drop. Whole set of information about a person comes as soon as we encounter him : his dress, manners, appearance and what not. Getting attracted or not towards a person is a reaction to the total stimulus situation. This "one-plus-one-plus-one information" situation about similar qualities of a stranger just does not exist in actual life and is, to say the least, highly artificial. In fact, through this limited information technique, we are creating a deprivation situation for the subject by keeping him away from the rich inputs of actual social life involving interpersonal attraction. So in effect, what has been studied : factors of interpersonal attraction as it occurs in normal social life, or factors artificially produced in an abnormal and a-real situation which the experimentalist has contrived in his laboratory so that the rigours of experimental design and demand of operationalization of variables and applications of sophisticated statistical treatment are met? What comes out of the magical hat of the so-called experimental social psychologist? It is just a nice pink rabbit that is attractive to look at and amusing to the receptive audience of children but not good enough for mature adults to bother about. To stretch the simile a little further, the very process by which the rabbit got produced was a kind of trick and a gimmick which should not be of serious concern to a hard-boiled scientist. It has often and quite correctly been remarked about the type of experiments Byrne and his colleagues have perpetuated in social psychology that they have forced the subject to act as a passive information-processing machine rather than as an active agent who is information-seeking and information-generating. It amounts to a gross distortion of reality. The net outcome of such experiments is fragmentation of social phenomenon, creation of a vital gap between the sample of behaviour that is analysed by the social psychologist and the actual social reality, which inevitably results in artificiality of the laboratory situation. This reminds me of the very wise statement made a long time ago by Professor Bartlett on the growing popularity of the so-called "exact method" proposed by Ebbinghaus for the study of memory. Referring to the inherent weaknesses involved in

Ebbinghaus' techniques, Bartlett (1932) remarked that "his ideals were the simplification of stimuli and the isolation of response. He secured the first by using nonsense syllables as his memory material, and the second, he curiously thought, followed immediately". Overawed by the demand of objective constancy, Ebbinghaus ruled out the use of meaningful material as the stuff to be remembered, because they tended to set up an endless stream of associations and cross-associations which significantly differed from person to person. Therefore, in order that all subjects began on a level, he used material which would initially signify nothing and therefore, so he naively thought, would signify the same for everybody. Obviously this was an erroneous assumption and a dangerous procedure. To quote Bartlett (1936) again, "the ideal of simplifying the response by cutting it off from others with which it is normally combined is all very well in its way, but it is a dangerous and slippery ideal in psychology". We merely simplify the stimulus but leave the responding mechanism as complex as ever so that the individual mobilizes all the resources at his disposal by setting up a mass of diverse associations. As we know, the kind of procedure that Ebbinghaus recommended has produced enormous volume of experiments in memory but the bulk of them only relate to a very special type of phenomenon, namely, establishment and maintenance of repetition habits and rote recapitulation the results of which are not always applicable to real-life remembering. I need not point to the inevitable artificiality that such a procedure which shunned complexity of memory process created.

What I have remarked about the Ebbinghaus' "exact method" is largely applicable to what goes by in the name of experimental social psychology these days. Instead of narrowing the gap between laboratory conditions and actual social phenomena, the same is tending to become unbridgeable. These so-called experiments may enable us to produce papers which could be readily accepted in one of the prestigious journals in the United States thereby swelling the publication component of curriculum vitae and making it very impressive. But their implications in understanding and interpreting social phenomena are minimal, if not non-existent. Nevitt Sanford's comment

(Sanford, 1965) is revealing. "Psychology is really in the doldrums right now. It is fragmented, over-specialised, method-centred and dull. I can rarely find in the journals anything that I am tempted to read. And when I do read psychological papers. . . . I become very unhappy; I am annoyed by the fact that all have been forced into the same mould in research design and style of reporting, and I am appalled by the degree to which an inflation of jargon and professional baggage has been substituted for psychological insight and sensitivity."

Some other problems regarding the verbal technique in experimental social psychology should be kept in mind. The first question that arises is that the experimentalist takes for granted the competence of the subject to operate on a verbal level. It is not, therefore, surprising that the victims of such experiments are conveniently available among the average American college sophomores who possess fairly high degree of verbal comprehension and verbal facility. Studies on this very select group have circumscribed the limits of this kind of experimental social psychology. Further, even if the subject is able to verbalise, how is one sure about the fact that he gives a true response ? Apart from the operation of factors collectively called the "demand characteristics", there is always the possibility of the response being based on some implicit theory that the subject may have about social interactions or his response is mediated by processes of what is likely to accrue rather than what he would actually do. There is frequently a gap between what one thinks he would do in a situation and what he actually does. I would illustrate this by giving a very simple example from my own experience. As a student in Europe, I became enthusiastic to learn ice-skating. I went to Switzerland and took some training. I was, after some preliminary training, asked to make a figure 8 on the ice. I could convince my guide that my conceptualization of what I would do on the skating rink was perfect. When I actually set about to describe the figure 8 on the ice, my performance was nowhere near what I said I would do, and the inevitable consequence was a very painful ankle-sprain and jeering laughter of my friends. Therefore, it is one thing to make a choice among verbal alternatives and another to face such alternatives realistically in a situation of interpersonal interaction or ethical risk-taking. As a result, it is not at all surprising that a wide gap has existed between what is studied in the name of experimental social psychology and actual social phenomena. Obviously, one needs to do more hard-boiled thinking rather than deluding oneself by playing about purely with verbal behaviour.

Further, social psychologists routinely ask their subjects in their experiment as to why they behaved in the manner they did, or would like to do. In fact, some social psychologists have advocated the abandonment of social psychology experiment and its deceptive practices, (Brown, 1962; Kelman, 1966) and have urged that subjects simply be asked how their cognitive processes would work if they were to be confronted with particular stimulus situations. Apart from what I have already pointed out, there are many more basic pitfalls inherent in this kind of cognitive approach that Nisbett and Wilson (1977) in their very interesting paper entitled "Telling More Than One Can Know : Verbal Report on Mental Processes" have lucidly outlined them. There is always the question whether there is a direct access to the higher order mental processes involved in the analysis and appraisal of the cognitive situation which go on mainly at the unconscious level. My reaction to this kind of verbal report technique is illustrated with the help of a simple example. While studying the use of various physiological and psychological cues in making judgements of depth, there is no point in asking whether the subject relied on the convergence of parallel lines or texture gradient or the relative sizes of objects. The judgement of depth is usually made automatically and the child has hardly any inkling into the processes involved and the particular cues that he had used. No amount of verbal procedure can unravel the reality. The only way this can be done is to put the child in a situation where he is to judge distance or depth and observe what he does and how he goes about. It is my contention that only through this kind of objectification rather than through verbalization that the correct picture about the psychological processes involved in making choice in actual social situation can be revealed.

It is not surprising that there is growing dissatisfaction about the kind of social psychology that is prevalent particularly in the United States. If our objective is to understand and explain the social phenomenon as it exists in real life, the dissatisfaction expressed by many social scientists including Americans is inevitable. The question of external validity of research is always important. The question of referent is very pertinent in this context. If the referent constitutes some real social problems, economic development, population growth, or anything that is socially significant and relevant, obviously these experiments have nothing to do with them, because the experimental relationship studied here has no counterpart outside the laboratory. It in no way contributes towards increased social psychological knowledge. Therefore, despite the development of an impressive methodology, many social psychologists have rightly felt that these studies have neither contributed substantially to the improvement of social life nor succeeded in developing a coherent scientific discipline (Shaver, 1974). Jahoda's (1974) reaction is that this kind of social psychology is "not getting us anywhere". He remarks that "many people no longer fully believe in what they are doing and feel that they may be on the wrong track". Feeling the need that social psychology should comprehend social reality in all its complexities, and realizing the problems involved in devising and conducting experiments therein and the tendency of many social psychologists to readily take refuge in the rarefied atmosphere of the laboratory and the conveniences of verbal techniques, McGuire (1973) has suggested that at this point we should not emphasize so much the hypothesis-testing and strictly laboratory type of research which has given us a very narrow data base, and whose representativeness cannot be checked against broader reality. On the other hand, it may be more fruitful to emphasize hypothesis-generation rather than hypothesis-testing. He very rightly suggests that we should move methodologically more towards systems theory and multivariate correlational designs. In any case, the factor that underlies our current dissatisfaction with social psychology is the feeling that "our collective and cumulative research efforts do not have important and clearcut implications for the significant social problems of the day" (Kiesler and Lucke, 1976).

So far I have taken a somewhat negative attitude and have tried to point out some of the inadequacies inherent in experimental social psychology which leans heavily on verbal techniques. From its very beginning, social psychology has given us experiments which are good analogues of social reality in the controlled conditions of the laboratroy. Sherif's (1967) famous experiment on the formation of social norms does not only mark the beginnings of experimental social psychology but is an excellent example of how a social phenomenon can be simulated under laboratory conditions and variables properly manipulated. Asch's (1956) experiment on social conformity is another good example. Modifying Bartlett's (1932) method of serial reproduction, Allport and Postman (1948) have successfully analysed the psychodynamics of rumours in the laboratory without sacrificing their true character. Coming nearer, we have the most ingenious experiments by Zimbardo (1960), and by Milgram (1963) and many others who have been highly innovative in marvellously simulating the real life situations. Nearer home, a nice example is provided by J.B.P. Sinha's experiments (Sinha, 1968) on need for achievement under limited and unlimited resource conditions and cooperative and competitive orientations. These experiments have demonstrated how operationalization of variables, and manipulation of factors under laboratory conditions are possible without sacrificing the implications to some vital social phenomena. These studies reveal that under limited resource condition need for achievement was not very conducive to total output of the group and that it generated negative evaluation of the work partners. In another study of a similar nature which simulated closely real life situation (Sinha and Pandey, 1970), it was observed that egoistic high need for achievement subjects resorted to hoarding and were more concerned about maximising their achievement by whatever means possible, fair or foul. I have mentioned these examples to indicate that one does not have to resort to verbal techniques in experimental social psychology to conform to the rigours of experimental design and get results which are publishable. Sherif's and his associates (1961) famous Robber's Cave experiment on groups in harmony and in tension provide another example where it is possible to remain close to social reality as well as resort to careful experimental manipulation of variables. Therefore, looking at these excellent examples of simulation studies in experimental social psychology and the growing dissatisfaction with the kind of so-called social psychology experiments published in various journals, there appears to be distinct hope that some of social psychology will be reconstrued in the near future with exciting prospects.

Another ray of hope comes from the area of intervention studies where effort is made to manipulate one or more social variable in a real life situation to produce a desired outcome. Examples of such intervention studies that are available from organizations, classroom settings and small communities convincingly point out that concepts can be defined precisely, variables can be operationalized, adequate control groups can be formed without compromising the demands of scientific rigour, and at the same time maintain a link with social reality and having obvious implications for interpreting social phenomena. It is my firm belief that experimental social psychology, specially in our context, is meaningful only when conducted with reference to social reality and that there is need for constant feedback between laboratory and non-experimental findings from the field. If scientific endeavour has to have any meaning, there has to be a feedback loop between science and society. Unfortunately, in bulk of experimental social psychological researches of the verbal variety such a link is absent. Fortunately in many of the experiments where social phenomena have been simulated for experimental analysis or in intervention studies, such a feedback loop is built into them.

As a last point I would mention that simulation and intervention experiments have some dangers inherent in them. If one operates too close to social reality with the expressed purpose of doing something about it, there is always the danger of being swept away by good ideas, and in his zeal, scientific rigour tends to get sacrificed. This danger is always there. It can be guarded against if one is clear about his role as a scientist and as a citizen, and keeps them distinct. On the other hand, those who have conceived their scientific endeavour in conservative terms they have taken an "ivory-tower" attitude and values methodological and statistical sophistication even at the risk of irrelevance, there is the obvious tendency to forget the reality. It appears that a social psychologist faces a dilemma. He has to make a choice between the two extremes of social relevance and scientific rigour. To my mind, these two extremes are not irreconcilable. The choice is not necessarily between neatness with triviality and coarseness with meaning and relevance. It is possible to have scientific neatness with social relevance if the scientist accepts the challenge of complexity posed by social phenomena, and instead of escaping from the same into the unreality of a laboratory, he faces the problem squarely, and brings his inventiveness in designing his experiments which while being acceptable from the point of view of precision, measurement and other demands of science are at the same time meaningful and not divorced from reality.

REFERENCES

Allport, G.W., & Postman, L. *The Psychology of Rumour.* New York : Henry Holt, 1948.

Asch, S.E. Studies of independence and conformity : A minority of one against a unanimous majority, *Psychological Monograph*, 1956, **70**, No. 9.

Bartlett, F.C. *Remembering*. London : Cambridge University Press, 1932.

Bartlett, F.C. In C. Murchison (ed.), *History of Psychology in Autobiographics*. Clark University Press, 1936.

Brown, R. Models of attitude change. In R. Brown, E. Galanter, E.H. Hess, and G. Mandler (eds.) *New Directions in Psychology* (Vol. 1) New York : Holt, Rinehart and Winston, 1962.

Byrne, D., Griffit, W. & Stefanik, D. Attraction and similarity of personality characteristics. *Journal of Personality and Social Psychology*, 1967, **5**, 82-90.

Harré, R., & Secord, P.F. Experimentation in psychology. In L.H. Strickland, F.E. Aboud, & K.J. Gergen (eds.), *Social Psychology in Transition*. New York : Plenum Press, 1976, 51-67.

Jahoda, G. The context of social psychology : A critical assessment. *European Journal of Social Psychology*, 1974, **4**, 105-112.

Kelman, H. Deception in social research. *Transaction*, 1966, **3**, 20-24.

Kiesler, C.A., & Lucke, J. Some metatheoretical issues in social psychology. In L.H. Strickland, F.E. Aboud, & K.J. Gergen (eds.), *Social Psychology in Transition*, New York : Plenum Press, 1976, 141-151.

McGuire, W.J. The yin and yang of progress in social psychology. *Journal of Personality and Social Psychology*, 1973, **26**, 446-456.

Miligram, S. Behavioral study of obedience. *Journal of Abnormal and Social Psychology*, 1963, **67**, 371-378.

Moscovici, S. Society and theory in social psychology. In J. Israel & H. Tajfel (eds.) *The Context of Social Psychology : A Critical Assessment*, London : Academic Press, 1972, 17-68.

Nisbett, R.E., & Wilson, T.D. Telling more than we can know: Verbal report on mental processes. *Psychological Review*, 1977, **84**, 231-259.

Rettig, S. Risk-shift and information flow in relation to predicted ethical risk-taking. *Journal of Social* and *Economic Studies*, 1979, 7, 237-247.

Rettig, S., & Sinha, J.B.P. Bad faith and ethical risk hypothesis. *Journal of Personality*, 1966, **34**, 275 286.

Sanford, N. Will psychologists study human problems? *American Psychologist*, 1965, **20**, 192-202.

Shaver, P. European perspectives on the crisis in social psychology. *Contemporary Psychology*, 1974, **19**, 356-359.

Sherif, M. *Social Interaction : Process and Products*. Chicago : Aldine, 1967.

Sherif, M., Harvey, O.J., White, B.J., Hood, W.R., & Sherif, Carolyn W. *Intergroup Conflict and Co-Operation : The Robber's Cave Experiment*. Norman : Institute of Group Relations, University of Oklahoma, 1961.

Sinha, J.B.P. The *n*-Ach cooperation under limited/unlimited resource condition. *Journal of Experimental Social Psychology*, 1968, **4**, 233-246.

Sinha, J.B.P. & Pandey, J. Strategies of high *n*-Ach persons. *Psychologia*, 1970, **13**, 210-216.

Tajfel, H. Introduction. In J. Israel & H. Tajfel (eds.) *The Context of Social Psychology : A Critical Assessment*. London : Academic Press, 1972, 1-13.

Zimbardo, P.G. Involvement and communication discrepancy as determinants of opinion conformity. *Journal of Abnormal and Social Psychology*, 1960, **60**, 86-94.

NINE

Ramadhar Singh

EXPERIMENTAL SOCIAL PSYCHOLOGY IS REAL AND SCIENTIFIC

A Reply to Durganand Sinha

IN RECENT years, experimental social psychology has been criticized for its heavy reliance on experimentation as research method. Experimentation, it has often been pointed out, creates artificiality, suffers from several types of behavioural artifacts, and involves ethical problems (cf., Kelman, 1968; Rosenthal and Rosnow, 1969). Also, the very nature of social phenomena is such that experimentation may not provide an adequate and appropriate approach (Gergen, 1973, 1978a, 1978b). In the preceding chapter "Experimental Social Psychology : Verbal or Real?", Durganand Sinha tries to reemphasize some of these criticisms, and appears to agree with Moscovici's (1972) description of social psychology as "anything but social".

In this reply, I take the position that social psychologists are engaged in activity which is called "normal science" (Kuhn, 1962), that the criticisms of experimental paradigms are not as serious as they have been made to appear, and that the demonstrated capacity of experimental social psychologists to respond positively to the methodological and theoretical challenges raises the expectation that social psychology is to grow even more scientific in the years to come. These points will get clearer as I will examine one major and two minor criticisms mentioned in Sinha's paper.

Experimentation as an inadequate approach to complex social phenomena

According to Sinha, the major challenge to experimental approach comes from the very nature of social phenomena. He notes,

> It appears that confronted with the complexity of social phenomena, and finding them difficult to control and manipulate, the experimentalist has resolved to this very dubious and artificial procedure of verbalizing the social situation and analyzing verbal reactions to it and thereby deluding himself that the outcome is good social psychology. Confronted with high degree of complexity which is generally the basic characteristic of man's social behaviour and his interactions in society the proper strategy should have been not to avoid it but to devise appropriate procedures for analyzing and experimentally studying it rather than confining himself to problems to which existing methods are suited or following a Procrustean bed policy of forcing everything into the same mould. But in his anxiety to operationalize the variables, induce effective experimental control and fit the whole thing into a neat experimental design so that the data yielded can be subjected to sophisticated statistical treatment, what has been produced, to quote the expression of Moscovici (1972), is anything but social (p. 218).

It appears that Sinha views social phenomena as complex, social psychologists as confined to problems for which methods already exist, and experimentation as an inadequate approach to social phenomena. The last point also emerges from his acceptance of McGuire's (1973) suggestion that social psychologists should move methodologically more toward systems theory and multivariate correlational designs (p. 224).

The universe of study in any science, be it physical, biological, or social, is always believed to be characterized by complexity which is incomprehensible, unpredictable, and uncontrollable. If there is no complexity, there would be no need to engage in scientific activity at all. Confronted by the threatening and confusing environment in which we live, a scientist narrows his focus, creates artificiality, and tries to simplify the complex. The principal purpose is to facilitate precision, predictability, controllability, and the creation of abstract generalizations.

Confining oneself to problems for which some methods and knowledge exist is a normal scientific activity. By focusing on a small set of problems, one is more likely to come up with an answer that has some utility. Kuhn (1962) points out,

> The areas investigated by normal science are, of course, minuscule; the enterprise now under discussion has drastically restricted vision. But those restrictions, born from confidence in a paradigm, turn out to be essential to the development of science. By focusing attention upon a small range of relatively esoteric problems, the paradigm forces scientists to investigate some part of nature in a detail and depth that would otherwise be unimaginable. (p.24).

As the purpose of any scientific activity is to transform the complex into simple, incomprehensible into comprehensible, unpredictable into predictable, and uncontrollable into controllable, the scientists adopt methods/approaches which are known to have successful history. If a complex problem is attacked by a complex, unknown method, the outcome would be quite incomprehensible, contrary to what science intends to accomplish. Also, handling each new event in a novel way would be dealing with one unknown through another unknown. This approach would hardly take the scientist anywhere. To create abstract generalizations for the purpose of prediction and control, it is essential that the novel events be fit to the existing moulds. Clearly, then, experimental social psychologists are engaged in activity which is called "normal science".

Perhaps Sinha's major emphasis is on experimentation as an inadequate approach to social phenomena. He complains that the experimental social psychologists have "taken refuge in the verbal creations of social situations". They not only manipulate their independent variables verbally but also measure their dependent variables verbally. Findings obtained from such verbal strategy are too far off from the social reality; hence, they lack external validity. To bolster his criticism, he refers to the experiments on ethical risk-taking (Rettig and Sinha, 1966) and on interpersonal attraction (Byrne, Griffitt, and Stefaniak, 1967) where both decision situations and response measures were purely verbal.

Any one who would examine the methods of experiments published in the *Journal of Personality and Social Psychology, Journal of Experimental Social Psychology, Journal of Personality, Journal of Research in Personality*, and *European Journal of Social Psychology*, would find that all experiments are not of the kind Sinha mentions. More importantly, they seem to have high internal validity. Since experiments are performed to make causal statements, internal validity, which relates to whether a relationship between independent and dependent variables is unambiguously causal or not, is of central importance. From this angle, the experiments on ethical risk-taking and interpersonal attraction may be regarded as true experiments.

According to Aronson and Carlsmith (1968), "... where the idea comes from is not terribly important... The important and difficult feat involves translating a conceptual notion into a tight, workable, credible, meaningful set of experimental operations... (p. 37)". Furthermore, "... an experiment is realistic if the situation is realistic to the subject, if it involves him, if he is forced to take it seriously, if it has impact on him (p. 22)". Let us examine the first experiment Byrne (1961) performed on interpersonal attraction from these angles.

The idea that we like a person to the extent he shares views with us has been present in the writings of social philosophers such as Aristotle, Spinoza, and Samuel Johnson (Byrne, 1971). However, it was not clearly known whether liking brings similarity, or similarity engenders liking. To make causal inference, it was necessary that similarity precede liking, that other factors affecting liking be controlled, and that the subjects be assigned randomly to different similarity conditions. The experiment Byrne (1961) did met all the three requirements, although it had a simple paper-pencil manipulation with bogus strangers. Subsequent experiments disclosed that this paper-pencil manipulation of attitudinal similarity involved the subjects so much that their physiological (Clore and Gormly, 1974) and emotional (Singh, 1974) states changed, and that the subjects generalized their affective responses not only to the target person but also to the nonhuman stimuli associated with the experiment (Griffitt and Guay, 1969). These studies show that the experimental manipulation indeed created a realistic situation for the subjects. Accordingly, Byrne's finding that attitudinal similarity determines interpersonal attraction received scientific acceptance. The idea of similarity-attraction relationship was not new, nor did Byrne claim it to be new. However, his simple paper-pencil experiment yielded evidence for an unambiguous causal link between attitude similarity and attraction. No less important, it served as the base for the paradigmatic study of interpersonal attraction (Byrne, 1971).

It is good to have internal validity, statistical conclusion validity, construct validity, and external validity in any causal inference. But in practice it may not be possible to do so. For persons interested in theory-building, therefore, internal validity is of utmost importance. As Cook and Campbell (1976) state,

> . . . most theories do not specify target settings, populations, times, or the like, so that external validity is of relatively little importance. In particular, it can be sacrificed for the statistical power that comes through having isolated settings, standardized procedures, and homogeneous respondent populations. Thus, for investigators with theoretical interests the rank-ordering of types of validity, in order of importance, is probably internal, construct, statistical conclusion, and external validity (p. 245).

Byrne and his associates have not ignored the external validity, however. Their experiments on computer dating (Byrne, Ervin, and Lamberth, 1970), proximity (Byrne, Baskett, and Hodges, 1971; Fisher and Byrne, 1975), visual interaction (Efran, 1969), and behavioural compliance (Baron, 1971; Pandey and Griffitt, 1977) are good examples of not only nonverbal measures but also of great concern for external validity in attraction research. A particular experiment may not have external validity, nor would it be always expected to have. But external validity is not altogether ignored in any social research programme, be it attraction, helping, hurting, attribution, or leadership.

Whether one conducts experiments in controlled laboratory situations or naturalistic field situations (McGuire, 1973) is of little consequence in evaluating status of social psychology. The main criterion should be the significant and substantial advances in knowledge, and experimental methodology has enriched the field appreciably. As Cartwright (1979) rightly states,

> Advances in experimental methodology now permit us to control and systematically vary many of the more important determinants of human behaviour and thus to investigate causal relationships among variables. Our research has been substantially improved by work in the field of statistics on small-sample theory, experimental design, and multivariate analysis. As a result of these methodological developments, we now have a quite respectable body of firmly based empirical findings (p. 87).

Naive experimenters

Sinha's paper seems to create the impression that social psychologists are naive experimenters. This impression arises from his earlier criticism that experimental social psychologists manipulate social situations verbally. It gets confirmed by his two other comments that experimenters assume that subjects know and are willing to tell whatever the experimenter intends to study (p. 221), and that experimentalists assume one-to-one correspondence between what one says and what he does (p. 221).

Both criticisms do not apply to experimental social psychologists. That respondents know and are willing to tell applies more forcefully to survey research than to experimental research. In reality, experimental social psychologists have been arguing that one may not be able to describe how he behaved. And the work of Nisbett and Wilson (1977) which Sinha cites is a good example.

That there is a discrepancy between what one says and what one actually does has drawn the attention of experimental social psychologists ever since La Piere (1934) reported that attitudes (verbal reports) cannot predict actual behaviours. Several psychologists have, therefore, attempted to enhance prediction of behaviour from attitudes, and interest in the subject still remains very high. Any one interested in this topic may look at the articles by Ajzen and Fishbein (1977), Bagozzi and Burnkrant (1979), Norman (1975), Rokeach and Klienjunas (1972), Wiegel and Newman (1976), Wiegel, Vernon, and Tognacci (1974), and Zanna, Olson, and Fazio (1980). These studies illustrate that experimental social psychologists are quite aware of the discrepancy between verbal reports and actual behaviours, and that they are busy searching out variables which may augment prediction of behaviour from attitudes.

Research for publication only

Sinha feels that experimental social psychologists (perhaps he has the small group of five experimental social psychologists in India in his mind) perform experiments "to produce papers which could be readily accepted in one of the prestigious journals in the United States thereby swelling the publication component of curriculum vitae and making it very impressive (p. 221)". This comment implies that experimental social psychologists are doing research solely for an extrinsic reason—to make their vita look impressive, and that the prestigious journals in the United States accept papers readily.

I find it difficult to agree with Sinha's observations. All the experimental social psychologists in India are in relatively better professional positions than any other group of psychologists. Making the vita lengthy cannot be the only motivation for publication in the highest quality journals. In fact, one's list of publications can be made much longer with least effort if he writes articles for journals which have no competition for space or any review system.

It is well known that prestigious journals of social psychology have the toughest competition for space, most stringent review system, and highest rejection rate. The few articles that are accepted also undergo at least one revision. Isn't it painful to receive negative editorial feedback and revise one's own manuscript? If it is, then publishing in a prestigious journal is not intended to decorate one's vita only.

It is my feeling that experimental social psychologists are more interested in answering a question than in increasing the length of their vita. They conduct a number of experiments to answer the question, and they like to publish their articles in a journal which has the highest professional standard and reaches most of the members of the scientific community. After all, articles are written to be read. Publications in prestigious journals should be taken as healthy sign of progress in a field, and I am indeed glad that experimental social psychologists in India are finding good outlets for their research.

Concluding comments

Much of the work in experimental social psychology has been guided by the *natural science model* which requires that psychological laws, to be scientific, must be transhistorical, abstract, and universal. In recent years, dissatisfactions have been expressed with this logical positivist orientation to scientific conduct. Gergen (1973, 1978b), for example, contends that "social psychology is primarily an historical inquiry", and that much contemporary theory appears to lack the capacity to challenge prevailing assumptions regarding nature of social life and to offer fresh alternatives to contemporary patterns of conduct. Similarly, Sampson (1978) argues that the natural science model has been dominating the field since long; the historical model of science must now get equal-status partnership and legitimacy with natural science model.

Those who find merits in the logical positivist approach are not persuaded by these appeals at all. For example, Schlenker (1974) completely disagrees with Gergen, and reaffirms the contention that social psychology is science. And Cartwright (1979) does not share the gloom of those who think that the field has reached a state of crisis. He writes,

> Social psychology is incomparably better-equipped to achieve its basic objectives than it was forty years ago. We have better facilities, better methods for collecting and analyzing data, and a vast store-house of well-established empirical findings, more rigorous conceptual models, and much more sophisticated theory (p. 87).

I personally share the optimism expressed by Cartwright. From the very beginning, social psychologists have been responding to what must have seemed to be almost insurmountable theoretical, methodological, and institutional obstacles. In view of the complex subject matter and youthfulness of the discipline, it is remarkable that so much progress has been made. In addition, the demonstrated capacity of social psychologists to respond positively and constructively to the challenges raises the expectation that social psychology will grow even more scientific in the years to come.

REFERENCES

Ajzen, I., & Fishbein, M. Attitude-behavior relations : A theoretical analysis and review of empirical research. *Psychology Bulletin*, 1977, **84**, 888-918.

Aronson, E., & Carlsmith, J.M. Experimentation in social psychology. In G. Lindzey and E. Aronson (eds.), *The Handbook of Social Psychology* (Vol. 2). Reading, Mass. : Addison, 1968.

Bagozzi, R.P., & Burnkrant, R.E. Attitude organization and attitude-behavior relationship. *Journal of Personality and Social Psychology*, 1979, **37**, 913-929.

Baron, R.A. Behavioral effects of interpersonal attraction : Compliance with requests from liked and disliked others. *Psychonomic Science*, 1971, **25**, 325-326.

Byrne, D. Interpersonal attraction and attitudes similarity. *Journal of Abnormal and Social Psychology*, 1961, **62**, 713-715.

Byrne, D. *The Attraction Paradigm*. New York Academic Press, 1971.

Byrne, D., Baskett, G.D., & Hodges, L. Behavioral indicators of interpersonal attraction. *Journal of Applied Social Psychology*, 1971, **1**, 137-149.

Byrne, D., Ervin, C.R., & Lamberth, J. Continuity between the experimental study of attraction and "real life" computer dating. *Journal of Personality and Social Psychology*, 1970, **16**, 157-165.

Byrne, D., Griffitt, W., Stefaniak, D. Attraction and similarity of personality characteristics. *Journal of Personality and Social Psychology*, 1967, **5**, 82-90.

Cartwright, D. Contemporary social psychology in historical perspective. *Social Psychology*, 1979, **42**, 82-93.

Clore, G.L., Gormly, J.B. Knowing, feeling, and liking : A psychophysiological study of attraction. *Journal of Research in Personality*, 1974, **8**, 218-230.

Cook, T.D., & Campbell, D.T. The design and conduct of quasi-experiments and true experiments in field settings. In M.D. Dunnette (ed.),

Handbook of Industrial and Organizational Psychology. Chicago: Rand, 1976.

Efran, M.G. *Visual Interaction and Interpersonal Attraction.* Unpublished doctoral dissertation, University of Texas, 1969.

Fisher, J.D. & Byrne, D. Too close for comfort: Sex differences in response to invasions of personal space. *Journal of Personality and Social Psychology*, 1975, **32**, 15-21.

Gergen, K.J. Social psychology as history. *Journal of Personality and Social Psychology*, 1973, **26**, 309-320.

Gergen, K.J. Experimentation in social psychology: A reappraisal. *European Journal of Social Psychology*, 1978a, **8**, 507-527.

Gergen, K.J. Toward generative theory. *Journal of Personality and Social Psychology*, 1978b, **36**, 1344-1360.

Griffitt, W., & Guay, P. "Object" evaluation and conditioned affect. *Journal of Experimental Research in Personality*, 1969, **4**, 1-8.

Kelman, H.C. *A Time to Speak.* Jossey Bass, San Francisco, 1968.

Kuhn, T.S. *The Structure of Scientific Revolutions.* Chicago: University of Chicago Press, 1962.

La Piere, R.T. Attitudes vs actions. *Social Forces*, 1934, **13**, 230 237.

McGuire, W.J. The yin and yang of progress in social psychology: Seven Koan. *Journal of Personality and Social Psychology*, 1973, **26**, 446-456.

Moscovici, S. Society and theory in social psychology. In I. Israel & H. Tajfel (eds.), *The Context of Social Psychology: A Critical Assessment.* London: Academic Press, 1972.

Nisbett, R.W., & Wilson, T.D. Telling more than we can know: Verbal report on mental processes. *Psychological Review*, 1977, **84**, 231-259

Norman, R. Affective-cognitive consistency, attitudes, conformity, and behavior. *Journal of Personality and Social Psychology*, 1975, **32**, 83-91.

Pandey, J., & Griffitt, W. Benefactor's sex and nurturance need, recipient's dependency, and the effect of number of potential helpers on helping behavior. *Journal of Personality*, 1977, **45**, 79-99.

Rettig, S., & Sinha, J.B.P. Bad faith and ethical risk hypothesis. *Journal of Personality*, 1966, **34**, 275-286.

Rokeach, M., & Klienjunas, P. Behavior as a function of attitude-toward-object and attitude-toward-situation. *Journal of Personality and Social Psychology*, 1972, **22**, 194-201.

Rosenthal, R., & Rosnow, R.L. *Artifacts in Behavioral Research.* New York: Academic Press, 1969.

Sampson, E.E. Scientific paradigms and social values: Wanted a scientific revolution. *Journal of Personality and Social Psychology*, 1978, **36**, 1332-1343.

Schlenkar, B. Social psychology and science. *Journal of Personality and Social Psychology*, 1974, **29**, 1-15.

Singh, R. Reinforcement and attraction : Specifying the effects of affective states. *Journal of Research in Personality*. 1974, **8**, 294-305.

Sinha, D. Experimental social psychology . Verbal or real? In J. Pandey (ed.), *Perspectives on Experimental Social Psychology in India*. New Delhi : Concept Publishing Co., 1981.

Wiegel, R.H., & Newman, L.S. Increasing attitude behavior correspondence by broadening the scope of the behavioral measure. *Journal of Personality and Social Psychology*, 1976, **33**, 793-802.

Wiegel, R.H., Vernon, D.T.A., & Tognacci, L.N. Specificity of the attitude as a determinant of attitude-behavior congruence. *Journal of Personality and Social Psychology*. 1974, **30**, 724-728.

Zanna, M.P., Olson, J.M., & Fazio, R.H. Attitude-behavior consistency : An individual difference perspective. *Journal of Personality and Social Psychology*, 1980, **38**, 432-440.

TEN

Jai B.P. Sinha

IN SEARCH OF RESEARCH IDENTITY

NOW THAT I am completing two decades of my research activities, I think it is time that I look back and examine the *process* of my doing research. The process is essentially personal and private and has been guided by my conviction that a lively research has to spring from the encounters of a researcher with his environment moderated by his sense of social consciousness. And yet, I have a feeling that the process is also public to the extent that it is shared by those who tend to make research an involved, relevant, and value based undertaking. My retrospective analysis of the process is meant to primarily understand my research identity, but may also help others, I hope, to identify the constraints and resources and the way they have shaped the courses of their research. More specifically, I intend to focus on the following :

(a) The way my research has evolved. Has there been any continuity in my thought, any internal compulsions arising out of the unanswered questions of the previous studies? Have there been any social referents to guide the course of these studies?

(b) What constraints of internal and external validities have I encountered and how have I been coping with them even though they cost at times in terms of guilty conscience, self-esteem, and or external criticisms?

(c) Obviously, I am taking the liberty to expand the scope of the Workshop which is designed to deal with the experimental social psychological research—its past, present and future in India. But I am doing it deliberately because of my increasingly crystallised belief that experimental social research in India can be meaningful only when conducted in a broader framework of non-experimental research which may first map the domain of socially relevant research interests of an investigator. The investigator of course should have the flexibility to move back and forth from experimental to non-experimental, laboratory to field, and quantitative to experiential research in pursuit of tantalizing research questions. In fact varied types of research strategies might provide a better perspective to bring the issue of the exact experimental social research in the central focus. That is what I plan to try in the rest of my paper.

My indoctrination into experimental social research with a heavy dose of quantitative methods started in the early sixties at the Ohio State University; and I did go through the motion of publishing three papers in collaboration with Professors Wherry and Rettig (Rettig and Sinha, 1966; Sinha, 1967; Sinha and Wherry, 1965). All three papers systematically tested some of the aspects of the ethical risk hypothesis which was the on-going research of Professor Rettig. We introduced paid confederates who either reported pre-arranged sequence of tastes in drops of coloured water which was plain or violated specific experimental instructions at pre-determined intervals. We paid naive subjects who were induced by the confederate to perform unethical risk taking behaviour. We took precautions of having all necessary control conditions, and checked meticulously the adequacy of all manipulations. We in fact spent about two years and thousands of dollars to prove that "unethical risk taking behaviour varies predominantly with perceived risk" (Sinha, 1967, p. 267). It was alright for a beginner to get drilled in the process of rigorous experimental social psychological research. Yet I had the nagging feeling that I was more of a mercenary than an internally directed researcher.

For a while I did try to identify the variables which might reflect my interest and toyed with the concepts such as "independence" and "initiative taking" (with Dr. Usha Kumar) but could not finalize any worthwhile study. During those years, McClelland's (1961) achievement motivation was a craze and he was recruiting psychologists for his Indian experiments

(McClelland and Winter, 1969). My two days of prolonged discussions with McClelland and his colleagues at Harvard in the early part of 1965 led me to conclude that achievement motivation is not conducive to national development in the Indian conditions where resources are limited and the Protestant Ethic almost missing. In such a situation, it was argued, "individual members tend to become inter-dependent for means, and their heightened n-Ach may turn into what was called contriently inter-dependent behaviour" (Sinha, 1968a, p. 234). It took me a year and a half to design a 2×2 factorial study (Sinha, 1968a) in which the effects of competing orientation was contrasted with that of cooperating orientation under conditions of limited versus unlimited resource availability. The results clearly indicated "the limited usefulness of the competitive orientation in a limited-resource situation. Indeed, it was found to be most conducive to output maximization when resources are abundant and hence chances of clash for resource acquisition are low. But when resources are limited, not only is the total group output reduced, but experiences on the task result in lessened liking for the group and for the task, and in more negative evaluations of the partners. Even one's own self-esteem suffers" (p. 244).

When this paper was brought to the notice of McClelland, he wrote a long letter to me.* Let me quote the relevant parts of the letter.

> Your findings seem unequivocal to me clear cut and highly significant—but I do have difficulty seeing their applicability to the economic development problems. This is always the problem with 'model' experiments in which we psychologists attempt to copy real life in the laboratory and draw conclusions from the results of our manipulations there.
>
> Certainly no one could deny that in the pure case (as in your carefully controlled experiment), resource limitation should interact with achievement instructions in the way you found. But look at the limitations you placed on your subjects. You did not let them create resources and you

*Personal communication, May 26, 1967.

> purified the instructions in the n-Ach case so that they could not set up a group achievement goal as suggested by Deutsch. Neither of these conditions is ever, in my experience, so rigidly satisfied in the field situation—we actually found that our n-Ach courses in Kakinada markedly increased cooperation. This might surprise you, but in fact, the men have cooperated much more.
>
> I hope you will think a bit more along these lines before publishing too widely the results of your excellent experiment because they may help contribute to the self-defeating tendency in India's thoughts about how limited her resources are (pp. 1-2).

Later Janak and I (Sinha and Pandey, 1970 a) did conduct a study in which the subjects had the opportunity to create resources. The high n-Ach subjects were also given altruistic or selfish orientations by verbal instructions. The findings only partly supported McClelland. The high n-Ach subjects created more resources, showed better performance, and more effectively manipulated the environment (i.e. hoarded the resources) in order to maximize their achievements. It seemed that they employed "whatever means at their command to maximize their achievement. They were more interested in the final outcome and less in justifiability of means" (p. 216). The altruistically oriented high n-Ach persons hoarded less and used the resources less indiscriminately but were also less efficient. The authors concluded "that probably, altruism puts some constraints on the functioning of the n-Ach, and thus altruism distracts the n-Ach *Ss* from 'minding' their own interest by putting an incongruent set of demands in terms of cooperation, helping the needy, etc. In absence of such a constraint, the n-Ach persons are more facilitated in their achievement maximization attempts" (p. 216).

McClelland did not send any comments this time. But, I am sure, he could have raised similar doubts about the efficacy of our simulation of economic and societal realities. Our first three studies (Rettig and Sinha, 1966; Sinha, 1967; Sinha and Wherry, 1965) did not have any such problems because they were parts of an on going research effort with a widely publicized (with two dozen papers in leading American journals) "running head" which served as the referent point. They did not intend to and hence did not claim to understand as big a chunk of reality as Dr. Pandey and I (Sinha, 1968a; Sinha and Pandey, 1970a) were looking at in our studies. There was no serious flaw in methodology of the five studies (at least none of the editors said so). The real problem was the fact that as we moved from the first set to the second, we kept our commitment to the canons of experimental method, but changed our referent from the familiar, and well researched body of psychological knowledge to something bigger, more relevant, and yet less researched with the social experimental techniques. In other words, the second set involved greater degree of abstraction in the process of simulating the economic and business reality. With the greater distance between the simulated reality and the reality of life, we were open not only to the external criticisms but also to a self-doubt whether our findings have external validity, I kept wondering whether a "pure model" (as McClelland called it) can approximate our complex reality; and if we have to make a choice between the two, should we not opt for the latter rather than the former. The compelling inner voice was : to hell with the rigour of experimental methodology ! Do something which is meaning ful and relevant. This was the beginning of the second shift.

Throughout my dialogue with McClelland, I was also worried over our negative approach. All we were saying was that achievement motivation is an alien construct and its inculcation in India is detrimental to our development. Hence a search for more viable construct for research was latently on. Suddenly one day I realised that the construct was indeed identified long back in 1960 before I actually started my research career. While refuting Dr. Purnima Sinha's (at that time Chowdhary) arguments about what is wrong with Indians, I wrote back in a local English daily that our most serious problem is our excessive dependency. Probably, the same idea tried to crop up into a researchable programme in 1965 (when I was exploring the possibility with Dr. Usha Kumar), but I was probably not ready at that time.

Once disenchanted with the construct of achievement motivation, we launched a vigorous programme on the study of what we called dependence proneness. During the period 1968-1975, we published 14 papers; but only five of them were experimental in nature and only two of 14 (both non-experimental studies) found place in a foreign journal (Sinha, 1968b and c). This was quite a contrast to the fact that earlier mentioned all five studies were experimental and were published in American journals. The present situation was not entirely of our choice. We did decide to stick closer to the social reality, to take up research problems which were of social relevance, to map the domain of dependence proneness with non-experimental studies, and to conduct experimental studies only when the research problems so required. During this period we got some very discouraging feedbacks from the American reviewers; e.g., the variables are not properly operationalized, the concepts are not quite familiar to the American readers, the control groups are not adequate, the checks on experimental manipulations are not appropriate, so on and so forth. However, whenever we stepped out of the frame and followed the American pattern, it was possible to publish experimental (Sinha and Yousuf, 1972) as well as non-experimental (Sinha, 1973) studies in foreign journals. The former study was a revisit to the ethical risk hypothesis. We tried to show how Indian groups also take riskier decisions than the individuals constituting the groups. We further suggested that competence and trust may be the factors for risky shift in the group situation. The second was an invited paper for the special issue of *International Review of Applied Psychology* on psychology and developing countries. The paper reported a survey of the organizational climate of public and private undertakings in India. It highlighted the unique Indian organizational realities and how they can be related to the western ideals of a participative system. While it was a tough entry for us in the foreign journals, the Indian editors were so gullible that we virtually could ram even unpublishable materials down their throat. Probably, this reality of tough-abroad and easy-home combination of publication may also be a factor which led us to the course of investigations that we followed for quite some time and in certain ways are still following.

Through our studies (Sinha, 1970), we did establish that dependence proneness is a viable concept, that it can be reliably measured, that it is fostered and maintained by specific societal forces, that its correlates have direct relevance for the problems of national development, etc., etc. While these studies were meant to prepare a ground for understanding the dynamics of dependence proneness, our main thrust was to understand how it can be changed. We did four experimental studies for the purpose (Sinha and Pandey, 1970b; Sinha and Pandey, 1971a; Sinha and Pandey, 1971b; Saha and Sinha, 1973). We unequivocally established that a person's degree of dependence proneness crucially affects the way he makes decisions. If he is made to believe that he is not really dependent prone, he is likely to make independent decisions, take initiative, etc.; and a training to take initiative on one task is transferred to other tasks implying that dependence proneness can be reduced by suitable intervention programmes. The most revealing finding was that a dependent prone person, if put under a superior who is efficient and takes initiative, works harder and takes more initiative than those who are not dependent prone.

This line of investigation led us to the area of leadership, particularly organizational leadership because of its more structured setting where expectations and demands between superior and subordinates are more legitimised and hence more justifiably manipulable. Soon we realised that there existed in the area a biased and imported view that Indian organizational leaders are authoritarian and that they need to be transformed overnight into participative. We (Sinha, 1980) tried to ascertain the existing patterns of leadership in Indian work organizations, identified three (now five) styles, namely, authoritarian, nurturant-task, and participative, differentiated them in terms of subordinate's perceptions and impacts on organizational effectiveness and employee's satisfaction. We also found that the choice of a style by the leader is contingent on his perception of the subordinates. One of our crucial, though not profound, findings was that the pure types of styles do not exist in reality and that the styles affect organizational climate which in turn determines the levels of organizational effectiveness and subordinate's satisfaction. I call it crucial because it led us to design two experimental studies (Sinha and Sinha, 1977; Sinha and Sinha, 1979) in which the climate factor was controlled and the impacts of leadership styles were examined in three-person groups. We were able to show that the authoritarian style is ineffective, that the participative style when preceded by a phase of nurturant-task leadership is most appropriate for organizational effectiveness, and participative leadership is most conducive to subordinate's satisfaction.

When one of these papers was sent to my friend Dr. Ramadhar Singh, he wrote back,* "In my opinion, the paper has conceptual, methodological, and statistical problems. I simply request that you avoid associating yourself with such papers". I am convinced that Dr. Singh was expressing his sincere and mature evaluation for which I have high regards. He was not alone either. One of the foreign reviewers commented that I was giving "boy-scout definition of leadership" and that "there is no good standardization of the major variable".

I am willing to concede the limitations of my capacity to simulate the real life problems into fool-proof experimental designs, yet I would not like to rule out a possibility that an investigator is likely to be carried away by the raw enthusiasm of hitting upon an idea, the exploration of which may defy proper operationalization, methodological rigour, and statistical sophistication. The optimal solution, as we all know, is to combine the two—the idea and the rigour. But in reality, more often than not, they pose a choice—to handle a fragment of the whole phenomenon at a time with due rigour, or to address oneself to a bigger portion the whole with the risk of sticking one's neck out for all sorts of hits and rebukes.

The choice appears as inevitable particularly in this country where we do not have sufficient number of investigators who can provide research support in terms of standardized tasks and materials, parameters of a phenomenon, or even bench mark data. Furthermore, cultural indifference to team work

*Personal communication, January 11, 1977.

(Sinha and Sinha, 1974) and a related cultural habit to arrange all relationships hierarchically (Sinha Note 1) make most of us a one-man-task-force in pursuit of individually set goals and cherished research ideas.

Time, as a result, becomes a crucial consideration. The rapid inflow of ideas and their slow research processing by a lone investigator (despite multiple authorship) creates a situation where you cannot really eat your cake and have it too. Let me elucidate my point. The constant battering of the reviewers and critics in the recent years, I must confess, has subdued me to the extent that I think I need to pause and examine if I can move a little slowly step by step and tackle complex research problems with due rigour. As a result, some of our ideas are half way while others are still waiting for clearance from conceptual, methodological and statistical desks for about a year. My fear is that they might be displaced by something more recent and interesting or by something which is easy to handle by a factorial design and is familiar to the foreign journal editors. As time passes ideas, like many other things, lose their appeal. An investigator can hardly afford it.

Probably, I am exaggerating. One can still be slow and persistent or can identify a whole set of sequential linkages between the latest western craze and the phenomena that fascinate him. Or, one can go on publishing in prestigious journals without the pangs of being socially relevant or covering any meaningful ground. For, doing experimental social research in which you *control*, *manipulate*, *instruct*, and above all *cause* a phenomenon to appear or disappear may have strong power appeal to which a researcher may inadvertently succumb; unless he counteracts the effect by putting himself at the receiving end of the field forces which follow their own dynamics. I strongly feel that our social psychological research will need to have symbiotic relationship with the social milieu and the demands of the latter will have to be reflected in the former and the findings of the former should influence the latter. I might sound too impatient in my analysis of the process of the inflow of ideas and researches on them; because I see, feel, and smell a milieu which is in a real hurry and wants us to keep pace with it. I gladly subscribe to the guidelines that Dr. Ramadhar Singh* spelled out in his response to my comments on one of his papers, "Research is sometimes very hard and often unrewarding. One has got to believe very strongly in what he is doing and its value. The day to day struggle with subjects, reviewers, editors, and critics is simply unpleasant. The most important thing is to enjoy and value what one does". It so happens that what I enjoy and value are deeply embedded in how I relate myself to the social milieu, and how I search for meaning in this relationship. Research is a part of this process and the experimental social psychological research may even constitute a smaller part of the process.

In summary, I am trying, through this very personalised view of my research activities, to place the following points for further deliberations :

1. Research is a part of an investigator's efforts to relate meaningfully to his milieu.
2. Hence the interactions of the two may have a seemingly evolutionary course with lots of personal involvement and emotional investment. This frame determines what I consider to be researchable.
3. Because not all researchable ideas are amenable to experimental designs, the research activities cannot be confined to the experimental social studies, although one cannot be rigid about the choice of techniques.
4. The problem is accentuated due to the following :

   (a) The absence of a larger number of investigators and, even more important, their unwillingness to provide mutual research support to each other in terms of standardized research materials, procedures, and even bench mark data.
   (b) The absence of a journal in which we can proudly publish.
   (c) The narrowly and rigidly adopted norms for evaluating experimental social studies, and,

*Personal communication, May 7, 1978

(d) The pressure of the inflow of ideas to speed up their research processing.

REFERENCE NOTE

1. J. B. P. Sinha, Power in Indian organizations, unpublished manuscript 1979.

REFERENCES

McClelland, D.C. *The Achieving Society*, New York : Van Nostrand, 1961.

McClelland, D.C. & Writer, D.G. *Motivating Economic Achievement*, New York : Free Press, 1969.

Rettig, S. & Sinha, J.B.P. Bad faith and ethical risk sensitivity, *Journal of Personality*, 1966, **34**, 275-286.

Saha, Sadhana & Sinha, J.B.P. The transfer and model effects on dependence proneness. *Indian Journal of Psychology*, 1973, **48**, 23-29.

Sinha, J.B.P. Ethical risk and censure avoiding behaviour. *Journal of Social Psychology*, 1967, **71**, 267-275.

Sinha, J.B.P. The n-Ach/n-Cooperation under limited/unlimited resource condition. *Journal of Experimental Social Psychology*, 1968b, 233-246.

Sinha, J.B.P. A note on unethical risk hypothesis, *Journal of Social Psychology*, 1968b, **76**, 112-117.

Sinha, J.B.P. The construct of dependence proneness. *Journal of Social Psychology*, **76**, 123-124.

Sinha, J.B.P. *Development Through Behaviour Modification*, Bombay : Allied Publishers, 1970.

Sinha, J.B.P. Organizational climate and problems of management in India. *International Review of Applied Psychology*, 1973; **22**, 56-64.

Sinha, J.B.P. *The Nurturant-Task Leader*. New Delhi : Concept Publishing House, 1980.

Sinha, J.B.P. & Pandey, J. Strategies of high n-Ach persons, *Psychologia*, 1970a, **13**, 210-216.

Sinha, J.B.P. & Pandey, J. Retention of experimentally induced change in dependence proneness as a function of social support. *Indian Journal of Experimental Psychology*, 1970a, **4**, 60-63.

Sinha, J.B.P., & Pandey, J. Dependence prone persons under congruent and incongruent expectations. *Indian Journal of Psychology*, 1971a, **46**, 13-19.

Sinha, J.B.P. & Pandey, J. The process of decision making in dependence prone persons. *Journal of Psychological Research*, 1971b, **16**, 35-37.

Sinha, J.B.P. & Pandey, J. Reinforcement and model's efficiency as factors in decision making of dependence prone persons. *Indian Journal of Psychology*, 1975, **1**, 49-57.

Sinha, J.B.P. & Sinha, Mira. Middle Class values of organizational perspective, *Journal of Social and Economic Studies*, 1974, **1**, 95-114.

Sinha, J.B.P. & Wherry, R.J. Determinants of norm violating behaviour in a simulated industrial setting. *Personnel Psychology*, 1965, **18**, 403-412.

Sinha, J.B.P. & Yousuf, A. Effects of locus of control on choice shift in a crosscultural perspective. *Journal of Social Psychology*, 1972, **88**, 177-183.

Sinha, J.B.P. & Sinha, T.N. Two stage leadership strategy for group effectiveness. *Indian Journal of Industrial Relations*, 1979, **15**, 213-226.

Sinha, T.N. & Sinha, J.B.P. Styles of leadership and their effects on group productivity. *Indian Journal of Industrial Relations*, 1977, **13**, 209-223.

ELEVEN

Amar Kumar Singh

EXPERIMENTAL SOCIAL PSYCHOLOGY IN INDIA
A Note

I WISH to raise a few points about the status of Social Psychology in India, its assumptions, and more important its future direction. These points cover different aspects of the theme and, though, they do not add up to a systematic unfolding of a thesis, they are interlinked, albeit in a loose way. But I do hope that discussions on these would lead to clarification and crystallization of standpoints and perspectives. The objective of this Note is to search the guidelines and arrows directing towards the possible path of future development of Social Psychology in India. Social Psychology in India, experimental and/or non-experimental, has to be Indian, rooted in the Indian soil and oriented to the Indian societal problems. This point, though very simple and of common-place needs to be stressed not as a patriotic sentimental academic slogan but as a sobre, realistic, scientific necessity. Social Psychology is different from Physiological Psychology, and though there cannot be any national Physiological Psychology, Social Psychology, by definition, has to be national, because it is determined by the uniqueness of the cultural, social, historical and economic factors of a nation. Therefore, in a substantive sense, there has to be a Social Psychology which is truly Indian. The first and foremost issue for the present seminar should be a discussion on the progress towards an Indian Social Psychology. Whether it would be experimental and/or non-experimental can only be discussed in relation to the subject matter and content of Indian Social Psychology.

That Indian Social Psychology has to be unique and different from non-Indian or western Social Psychology is realised by the critical Indian researcher at almost every stage and in almost every important area of research. Take, for example, the area of socialization, a crucial bridge which joins several important branches of Psychology : Social, Clinical, Developmental and Personality. The socialization factors which influence an average rural Indian child in the joint family, brought up by grandparents rather than by parents, with strict adherence to the traditional caste rituals, are very different from those in the urban-industrial western societies. Similarly, prejudice is another example which illustrates the basic socio-historical differences between Indian and non-Indian societies. The prejudice between the Hindus and the Muslims is qualitatively different from that between Irish Protestants and Catholics. The prejudice between the upper caste Hindus and the Harijans is different from the prejudice between the Whites and the Blacks. The difference is not only limited to the historical and social factors related to prejudice in the Indian and the non-Indian societies, but it is also evident in the methodology. For example, the tests of measurement of prejudice in White and Black children, based on their physical differences, are not relevant to the measurement of prejudice of Hindu upper caste and lower caste children, or even Hindu and Muslim children. Indian Social Psychology cannot be a parasite. It has to identify, define, and measure its research variables and problems from a purely Indian point of view. Research in Indian Social Psychology has to begin with an original and clear grasp of the Indian Society and the Indian Personality. The discussion on the appropriateness of the methods, experimental or otherwise, must follow the discussion on the content of Indian Social Psychology.

The experimental social psychologists, have a long dismal record of being obsessed with the techniques of research unmindful of its contents. The sophistication of the techniques can never compensate for the triviality of the subject-matter. The content of the research, its subject-matter, the understanding it may offer to the human problems are the essence of socio-psychological research. The methods are only the means and cannot assume greater importance than the goals. At least, the goals do come first, in the sequence of decision, than the roads that may lead to them. Many experimental psychologists have turned into non-thinking robots pursuing non-issues of human existence, intoxicated with the halo of fake science, glorifying the counterfeit and not only missing, but even being unaware of the gold. Adding to the obsession, with techniques of research is the new and growing obsession with statistical analysis. The statistical methods, research design and computer computation can be, and indeed are, important achievements in the progress of human knowledge. But it is also true that the computer may sometimes become a glorified machine in which, as has been cynically said, garbage can go in and refined garbage can come out. One should not forget that the great contributions to the development of psychology, from Freud, Piaget and even Skinner, have come without the aid of complicated and awe-inspiring statistics.

The experimental method is, admittedly, a very important method, but it is not the only method; nor is it the most appropriate method for all Social Psychology research problems, though it certainly may be the best method for some problems. In fact, most researchers realise the necessity of using more than one method even for a single research, when it has various dimensions, and for some dimensions, methods other than experimental are more suitable.

It is indeed amazing to see intelligent persons, turned into experimental psychologists, developing intellectual blinders and blindspots. In their naive admiration and imitation of models of physical sciences, they refuse to see the obvious all-pervasive fact that the subject-matter of psychology, the Man, is much more complex than the subject-matter of physical sciences. Herbert Kelman teases his Harvard students that if they wanted to study a simple and easy subject they should have selected physics, not psychology. Since psychology is more complex than the physical and natural sciences, it needs a different model, suited to its subject-matter. Experimental Social Psychology has entered a blind-alley, and unless it comes out of it and takes the correct direction, it would be lost in the search of a mirage.

There is a story about a traveller who asked a philosopher about the direction of a village he wanted to go. The philosopher told him that if he continued his journey onwards he would never reach his destination or may be he would have to cover the whole wide world. But if he turned back then his village was about half a mile. The experimental social psychologist is like this traveller who is going in the wrong direction, unaware of it, but with self-assured confidence. In the development of Psychology as a science, experimental method has, however, a very important role. In fact, there have been many remarkable contributions based on laboratory studies. The experiments on social conformity, relationship between prejudice and social perception, distortions in communications and rumour are some examples of excellent research. They are first-rate because they have combined experimental rigours with creative imagination.

Finally, I may end my Note by saying that the most important Non-Issue is to examine the role of Experimental Social Psychology in India as a confrontation between experimental and non-experimental methods. The non-issue is Experimental versus Non-experimental; the Issue is : Experimental and Non-Experimental.

TWELVE

EXPERIMENTAL SOCIAL PSYCHOLOGY
Looking Ahead

THE DISCUSSION produced below is from the last session of the workshop. The group of social psychologists, representing different ranges of experiences and areas of professional interests, present in the workshop were asked to verbalize their vision of the future of Experimental Social Psychology in India. We have attempted to present the comments with some minor editing. We have left out circuitous and redundant statements, garbled talk and personal digressions. It is possible that in this process some of the dynamics of the session may have been lost for a content and theme-oriented presentation. However, it is hoped that much of the original flavour and essence of comments made by the participants are retained (the editor).

DURGANAND SINHA (Chairman): We have a brief session which I would like to call as "*looking ahead*". In the last two days we have taken stock of some recent works in the area of experimental social psychology. In this short time, I suggest we concentrate in two directions. The first is related to the content of research and the second is related to the method. The survey research may have its own utility. But, we find that some people are more confident with laboratory experiments, simulations, and field experiments. We have also noted that some of us are committed to social relevance; while some others are committed to methodological refinements. Some of us feel that these two are incompatible. We need to react to this question that whether or not these two are incompatible? Further, I would request you to visualize the future of this discipline. What is going to be the shape of things in social psychology in this country? I will also tag on a question raised by Amar Kumar Singh regarding *Indian Social Psychology*.* I dislike the expression *Indian Psychology*. It has all kinds of connotations. These are some of the questions we have posed in the last two days and if we devote some time responding to them, something may emerge.

JAI B.P. SINHA : As I look to the future, I do not feel that I am a pessimist. I don't foresee that in future we shall have confrontations between one approach and another. As I view the future I find, that we shall have a large number of researches, ranging from highly experimental to highly exploratory with the common goal of discovering new domains and variables which are yet to be covered. There will be meaningful interactions among the researchers of different orientations, at times, sharp ones, sharper than what we have seen this morning or in the last two-three days. But, I do hope that there will be unity of opposites and we shall learn from each other, and we shall serve as catalytic agents to each other rather than try to exclude each other from the domain of scientific social psychology. I would also conjecture that we shall be able to generate data for macro level analysis. We shall have aggregate data at least on a regional basis, to enable us to draw conclusions for policy and planning. We now have a division of *Psychology and National Development* under the *International Association of Applied Psychology* and some of us will be motivated to generate data so that we can play an effective role in plan formulation and its implementation. I do hope that in order to maintain a broad spectrum we shall have an appropriate supportive infrastructure in terms of collaboration, in terms of exchange of reprints and in terms of constructive comments, which we do need. And, eventually,

*In his note circulated earlier in the workshop (a brief version of which is published in this book), Amar Kumar Singh had proposed a case for *Indian Social Psychology*.

we shall have culturally specific social psychology, not necessarily *Indian Social Psychology*, but culturally specific psychology with a profile which will be distinguishable from the psychology elsewhere.

EMMANUEL S.K. GHOSH : So much has been already said that at the risk of repetition I would like to say about things which are pretty mundane and not at all high brow, such as, the distinction between experimental and non-experimental social psychology. I would like to focus on the reality of our situation. Who are the psychologists? For whom are they working? The psychologists in India, I think, are of two kinds. One is the kind of barefoot doctor who has not had opportunity of receiving a foreign training or in depth training in this country and therefore, he finds himself in some way inferior to those specialists who have come from abroad armed with extremely intricate, complicated statistical, experimental, computer simulated models. Given the kind of psychologists that exist in this country we should look ahead to prescribe the best suited future course for us. I think, this is a very important point which is missed when we try to take out debate on higher levels of academic subtleties and nuances. Now, any social science must have a justification to deliver to the society the kinds of goods that it needs. As a discipline, we are supported by our society, and our society, therefore, expects from us something which it can utilize. And in that sense, I think, we are somewhat too far away in continuing traditions which are distinctively western. It happens naturally. It is not putting blame on anybody. When we receive training in a foreign university we get so worked up about their models and theories that there is a natural tendency to come back and continue them in our setting providing either extension or cross-cultural validation of those models. But, we rarely try to look around us and generate the facts from our own social setting first and then test them in the laboratory. And only when those facts become testable facts in the lab., we build our own theory. When we talk about social behaviour of man, we are not only talking about social behaviour which is determined in India by the impact of other people on him, we are also talking about this individual who believes in the stars, in palmistry, in the uncertainty and insecurity of life and so on. Have we ever tried to see how this controls the social behaviour of the individual and his interactions with people?

I do realise that posing problems is considerably easier than offering solutions. However, offering solutions is perhaps considerably riskier than posing problems. In any case, at the risk of being considered naive, I would modestly suggest the following : There should be provision of intensive training in methodology of our discipline to bring our less trained brethren "the bare-foot doctors" at par with the specialists. For in them may lie many original, relevant, unutilized potential ideas for research enquiries. Secondly, an honest appraisal is required by many of us engaged in social research regarding the relevance of the content of their research to the immediate and long term needs of our society. A society which can scarcely support basic needs of its human population, deserves a more substantial return from its rather expensive academics. Thirdly, while not wholly decrying imitative contention of research enquiries (*since science is universal*) a judicious selection of variables can be advocated which would have a closer link to our social reality than scale a tenuous theoretical link to western topics of research. With these few, rather, random ideas, I leave the verdict of the future of experimental social psychology in India for the more distinguished people present here.

RAMADHAR SINGH : I believe more in doing than in saying. I do not have any particular objection to the expressions *Indian Social Psychology* or *Western Social Psychology*. If, Festinger is not hesitant acknowledging Prof. Jamuna Prasad's or Prof. D. Sinha's research, I think, Indians should not be hesitant to acknowledge what Americans are doing. Basically, our goal is to understand behaviour and to give psychology a scientific status. Now, who is doing that should not be a matter of discrimination as long as some one is doing something worthwhile anywhere. We should accept it. For example, when Americans get a publication in *Sankhya* they jump.

When we get a place in *JESP* or *JPSP*, we jump. Not because something has been added to our competence, but because we think that our fellow professionals elsewhere are willing to accept our work. So, if psychology is to make any contribution to this country and society we have to work for the scientific status of psychology.

JANAK PANDEY : I think an effective professional organization for scientific development is a must for any discipline. We all know about violations of standards and norms of professional ethics related to research, doing experiments, publications etc. in this country. The way at some places psychological tests, inventories, and instruments are developed and standardized is well known to us. What I mean is that, the professional organizations which are responsible for enforcing professional ethics, standards, and norms for the professionals, have totally failed in their role. These organizations are not truly committed to and sincerely engaged in developing psychology as a science in this country. Professional organizations have become a body of petty politics for petty gains of a few individuals. The *Indian Psychological Association* which is supposed to provide directions and perspectives in the development of psychology and psychologists, has done little in this connection. I think, *Indian Psychological Association* and the *Indian Journal of Psychology*, need to be activated to build a science responsive to society. The *IPA* needs to take up a role like *APA* to meet the professional needs of psychologists in this country.

SASI MISRA : In my opinion the future of social psychology would not be bright in India unless bright minds are attracted to psychology. If that happens, the future of social psychology is bright. Experimental social psychologists, in India particularly, suffer from the modelling effect. Some of the people with whom they have worked have really dazzled them by the way they work, and by the way they solve certain problems. So, such modelling should be available to the students of those who are accomplished social psychologists. Then only would social psychology advance. In addition, we should develop some programmatic research rather than piecemeal research. For example, it would be good if different people worked in different departments on various aspects of the same problem. This should be supplemented by macro research. The sample size should not be three so that you can say 100 per cent of the subjects agree. If we want to do something about it we have to look around. Look at the journal *Sankhya*, (which Ramadhar mentioned) in Statistics, which is published by Indian Statistical Institute, Calcutta, and has an international reputation. The journals in psychology can also acquire such status in science if we work for it.

SURESH KANEKAR : I would like to respond to some of the things that were said in the morning. Some issues were raised regarding the experimental and the non-experimental approach, the pure science approach and the applied science approach, and so on. Some of the issues are real, some of the issues are pseudo issues, and some of them are semantic issues. I belong to the tribe which believes in the unity of science. We are scientists. We are students of natural phenomena. We believe, that even the behaviour of this exalted animal that we call a human being, is susceptible to scientific analysis just as physical phenomena are susceptible to scientific analysis. I believe in the position of reductionism which cannot be proved empirically just now. I believe that science has a spectrum going all the way from sociology, which is the poor man's science or the beginning of science, through psychology, which has been called the hope of science, all the way to physics, which is the greatest of all the sciences. One can reduce sociological phenomena to psychological phenomena, psychological phenomena to biological phenomena, and biological phenomena to chemical and physical phenomena. There are different levels of approach. One studies different kinds of phenomena and the determinants of these phenomena. Another person may be interested in the cultural aspects of human behaviour. So you have anthropology, which is both a primitive science as well as the science of the primitives, along with sociology which also deals with social behaviour at a very superficial level. All sociological explanations can be reduced to psychological explanations and I also work on the assumption that psychological explanation is reducible to physiological or biological explanation. Thus, we can operate at different levels.

Now experimental social psychology has its own level. It is more superficial than the physiological approach and less superficial than the sociological approach. It has been suggested that we should have an *Indian social psychology*. I think that this is one of the worst things that can happen to social psychology. Then we may also have German social psychology, American social psychology, and so on. I am not saying that cultural variables are not important. They are important, and we have to take into consideration cultural phenomena. In fact, I can say that my interest in non-violence came out of a specific cultural context. If I had been an American, probably I would not have been interested in this problem. Our interests are determined by our cultural environment. Cultural factors are very much there. But like physiological psychology, even social psychology can be studied apart from national and cultural aspects. There are basic social behaviours like pro-social behaviour and antisocial behaviour. There is pro-social behaviour in India, in U.S.A., and in other countries. Reinforcement theory, learning theory, and some of the other basic theories apply irrespective of whether you are an Indian, an American, or an Eskimo. Now, we should not try to convert experimental social psychology into anthropology. Some of us are not interested in the study of some tribes only but are concerned with social behaviour across different nations and cultures.

Social relevance is irrelevant for research. I am putting it rather strongly. I am not saying phenomena like poverty, problems, and so on are not important. What I am trying to say is that in this country hardly any research money is spent on pure research and most of it goes for applied research. There is a bandwagon for applied research on problems like family planning, poverty, slums, etc. A research proposal is expected to justify itself in terms of the application of the research. Benjamin Franklin was once asked about the use of his research and he said, "What is the use of a newborn baby"? So to my mind, while applied research is definitely necessary, it is over emphasized in our country. A case for pure research has to be made to redress the imbalance. Social relevance is not the final value for research. There are certain other values also. There are values like understanding, like explanation, like interest. I think I could be interested in any problem which may not have any direct relevance at all to social welfare. Although, I believe that any contribution to knowledge will be useful in the sense of application sometime or the other. I am not bothered about whether it is useful or not. I am interested in solving a problem, understanding it, and in providing an explanation. While the experimental method is not the only method, some of us believe in it as the best method in social psychology which can be studied as a basic discipline apart from local, national, or cultural constraints. Please leave some room for basic experimental social psychology. Leave some room for the pure researchers. A few of them cannot do much harm to this country.

AMAR KUMAR SINGH : I would start with a clarification. When I mentioned about the necessity of *Indian Social Psychology*, I was not asking for the label. I was advocating for a perspective, for the content and the methodology. The two examples that I had given to illustrate this were : socialization and prejudice. I argued that socialization in India cannot be studied the way it has been studied in western countries. Socialization research in India requires a study of the role of the grandfather but in western country it does not. First, I would emphasize about the model social psychology should follow. Psychology as a science needs a model of man. If you are going to study man, why not study man. Please don't go and study an animal or a machine. If some one wants to know the number of teeth in a man's mouth he should not go looking in a horse's mouth. Now, we want a human model rather than an animal or a machine model. We are not making this suggestion in a romantic way but as a necessity for social psychology. I do subscribe to the view that within the experimental framework and approach, the human behaviour and problems should be studied. But, what I am insisting upon is that the methods and models for the study of human behaviour have to be more innovative than what they have been so far. Therefore, I would advocate for a sort of interlocking research design which would involve both experimental as well as quasi-experimental designs. To sum up, the model of social psychology should be "man" and not animal or machine, the approach should be experimental, and the topic despite Dr. Kanekar's view should be "socially relevant". At a given point in the history of a nation, the social scientists have to combine their search for knowledge with its utility to the society. These two can be combined and such combinations should not be avoided.

RAMA C. TRIPATHI : I am in agreement with Professor A.K. Singh and others on a number of points. But let me say at the outset that there cannot be anything Indian or non-Indian about methods of research, although, some may be more appropriate than others depending upon what is to be studied and what stance one wants to take in studying a particular problem. However, I do believe that forms of social behaviour differ widely from one context to another, and these contexts limit our explanations of social behaviour. In explaining social behaviour, therefore, one will have to inevitably turn to concepts which are rooted in one's socio-cultural context and historical experiences. Social reality cannot be understood in terms of concepts which are borrowed from societies with markedly different historical experiences. Indian social psychologists have rarely made use of concepts rooted in our own social context. I shall give a few examples. Whereas, we borrow a concept like fear of success to explain the behaviour of women in task-achievement situations, it has not occurred to us to explore the explanatory value of concepts like *sankoch* to understand the behaviour of Indian women. Similarly, studies of causal attribution routinely seek attributions in terms of person, entity or situation *à la* Kelley, but ignore concepts rooted in our own experiences, like *karma* and *sanskara* which, I believe, cannot be categorized in any of the above three categories. Research on altruism do not take into account concepts like, *punya*, *pap* and *dan*. I think what we need to do most is to look for these 'particularistic' concepts that may explain social behaviour more adequately and fully in our socio-cultural context. How long can we keep on looking for the lost key under the lamp-post only? If as a result of such an effort a social psychology emerges which comes to be called *Indian Social Psychology*, I would welcome the label. Finally, about social relevance. The social reality in India is too pressing and resources for social research too meagre for any social scientist to say that the issue of 'social relevance' is 'irrelevant'.

KAILASH C. PANDA : I am looking at the future of social psychology from a different point of view. Social psychology should develop in a manner which would contribute to the development of society and individuals. In other words, should pure research be the only academic exercise to enrich the field of social psychology or should it also have some kind of practical relevance. I believe, solutions to the societal problems can come from social psychologists to help the planners and the development agencies. The problems are so complex in our society that I do not think we should have a closed mind of isolating ourselves from pressing social problems and forgetting our role in bringing about social change.

AJIT K. DALAL : I strongly believe that whether social psychology should be experimental or non-experimental is a non-issue. No matter what method we use, understanding social problems should be the primary goal of any research. For this, the social behaviour must be observed, analysed, and interpreted in its proper context. This is possible only when we include in our studies all relevant variables. A cursory glance at the journal articles published in this country or abroad, will reveal that there are hardly any instances where attempts are made to understand social psychological reality in broad perspective. Most of the research reports are based on the study of a few variables only. Any causal statement based on such a small set of variables is bound to be fallible. The moment some more variables are added, the causal relations are moderated and the interaction pattern changes. The question arises, are we methodologically equipped to handle such a complex situation? Based on the present state of art, I would say, 'perhaps not'. It is for this reason that a choice for the researcher lies somewhere between a loosely structured, exploratory type of field study taking a large number of variables, or doing a rigorously controlled, experimental study, taking only three-four variables at a time. In either case social reality escapes our understanding. So we have in front of us a methodological challenge. It is a big challenge, but I am sure experimental social psychology has come of age and is capable of taking up this challenge successfully.

DURGANAND SINHA : To project what is going to be the future shape of social psychological research in India, I think we have to look back and view the problem in the perspective of the kind of research that psychologists in India have been doing for, let us say, the last 30 or 40 years. The first phase looks to me like a replicative or an imitative one. The studies done abroad by some eminent social psychologists were repeated. Repetition of the studies has its own utility. But unfortunately, this was a phase of sporadic efforts and after conducting a stray study or two, the scholars passed on to some other problem. The result was that we could not derive much benefit, theoretical or otherwise, from these isolated studies. The next phase can be called the phase where we were grouping to do studies and draw problems from our own social milieu while keeping the experimental procedure and models the same as used in the West. Thus, we used procedures for studying perceptual conformity, perceptual distortions, leadership in various groups in relation to variables drawn from our own social milieu. That is, while the models and procedures remained those which we had borrowed from abroad, the variables investigated were from the Indian setting. To my mind, this was a more useful and scientifically a more exciting phase because we brought the social psychological research nearer to the Indian social setting. The next phase, which according to me, has not yet crystallized but signs of it are distinctly visible, can be called the phase of re-orientation. It is a phase where we are trying to, if we may put in this manner, outgrow our alien framework and while maintaining whatever we have learned as scientists from western traditions, relate our research more and more to the social milieu of the country and sometimes even suggest and develop models which are distinctive. Now, not only in the west but very much so in our own country there is widespread dissatisfaction with the nature of research in social psychology, both from the point of view of scientific quality and their relevance to our understanding of social life. In fact, many of our colleagues from other disciplines have frequently remarked to us that our research look trivial and probably the only merit in them is that we employ large dose of methodological refinement to give it scientific respectability. I do not think this criticism is fully justified, but there is some truth in it.

In fact, within the last two days we have observed that amongst us even those who are jealous about methodological refinement have never denied the importance of such studies which would help us understand social realities, help us interpret our social world and whose findings may have some action implications. The only stipulation that has been made is, that, if we go ahead with scientific sophistication, socially relevant researches are bound to come in due course. And, if there is constant feedback between the social milieu and our scientific endeavour it would be beneficial to both. It would give us such research which is nearer to social phenomena, and whose results could be applied for solving our social problems. The experiences gained in the field would be brought back to the laboratory which in turn would help us design better and better studies whose implications would be obvious to our understanding of the social processes. I am sure, this would be the characteristic feature of the research efforts of social psychologists in India in years to come.

Now, one more point which I would like to indicate is that during the discussions an impression sometimes got created that methodological refinement and social relevance are incompatible and that they represent bipolar dimensions so that if you have the one you cannot have the other. Nothing could be farther from truth. I am convinced that these two, namely, the methodological refinement and social relevance, are not opposite. The relationship between the two, we can say is orthogonal, so that we can have high degrees of both or low degrees of both, or high of methodological sophistication with low social relevance or vice-versa or combinations of the two in various degrees. In fact, I feel that the quality of social psychological research in future, at least in this country, would be judged in terms of the presence or absence of both these factors. Looking at the condition that prevails in this country and the urgency of social problems that confront us, a research that is low in social relevance has, according to me, no justification taking into account the paucity of resources. Similarly, a research that is low in methodological sophistication can be anything but good science.

Now, what has actually happened, as I have said earlier is, that our social psychologists have escaped into a kind of artificially created scientific world which gives them no problem in manipulation of variables controlling of the relevant factors and producing results which may be scientifically sound. But results of such studies are generally empty because they lack in relevance. What I would like to emphasize is that the social psychologists, particularly in this country, cannot afford to ignore the challenge of complexity. He cannot escape from it. He has to bring in all his inventiveness and scientific resourcefulness to bear on it rather than selecting for his study only such problems for which his existing methods are suitable. Of course, initially we may encounter many difficulties. Our initial endeavours in studying highly complex social phenomena may look somewhat crude from the point of view of strict science. However, if we do not escape from it and if we persist, I am sure our later endeavours are bound to produce not only better scientific refinements but work with higher and higher levels of external validity and social relevance. My feeling is, that a social psychologist, like any other social scientist has to soil his hands with reality. It is only through this encounter that he can understand reality and not by escaping from it. Therefore, only through continuous efforts to increase both of these, i.e., bringing our scientific endeavours nearer to social reality as well as keeping to the rigours of scientific methodology, that our research efforts in social psychology can be meaningful and of some use to society. Therefore, the future direction of social psychological research in India in my opinion, is going to be an increasing effort towards social relevance along with increasing effort to make such research scientifically more and more refined. If we succeed in blending the two, our discipline, namely, social psychology, would find a rightful place in our life. At the end, I would like to add that looking at other social sciences, except probably economics, we are methodologically much more scientific, refined and precise, and if we could combine precision with social relevance, it would really be a great thing, not only for the scientific community but for the society in general.

INDEX